COMMUNITY IN HISTORICAL PERSPECTIVE

COMMUNITY IN HISTORICAL PERSPECTIVE

A translation of selections from
Das deutsche Genossenschaftsrecht
(The German Law of Fellowship)
by
Otto von Gierke

principally from volume 1
Rechtsgeschichte der deutschen Genossenschaft
(The Legal and Moral History of the German Fellowship)

Translated by Mary Fischer

Selected and edited by Antony Black

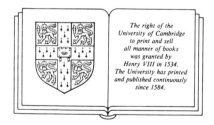

The right of the
University of Cambridge
to print and sell
all manner of books
was granted by
Henry VIII in 1534.
The University has printed
and published continuously
since 1584.

CAMBRIDGE UNIVERSITY PRESS
Cambridge
New York   Port Chester   Melbourne   Sydney

Published by the Press Syndicate of the University of Cambridge
The Pitt Building, Trumpington Street, Cambridge CB2 IRP
40 West 20th Street, New York, NY 10011, USA
10 Stamford Road, Oakleigh, Melbourne 3166, Australia

Originally published in German in 1868 as *Das deutsche Genossenchaftsrecht*, vol. I

First published in English by Cambridge University Press 1990 as *Community in historical perspective*

Printed in Great Britain

British Library cataloguing in publication data

Gierke, Otto 1841–1921
Community in historical perspective: a translation
of selections from Das deutsche Genossenschaftsrecht
(The German law of fellowship) by Otto von Gierke,
principally from volume 1: Rechtsgeschichte der
deutschen Genossenschaft (A legal and moral history
of the German fellowship).
1. Communities
I. Title II. Black, Antony, 1936– II. Deutsche
Genossenschaftsrecht. *English. Selections* 307

Library of Congress cataloguing in publication data

Gierke, Otto Friedrich von, 1841–1921
[Deutsche Genossenschaftsrecht. English. Selections]
Community in historical perspective/translated by Mary Fischer:
selected and edited by Antony Black.
p.   cm.
Includes a translation of the author's Deutsche
Genossenschaftsrecht, vol. 1 plus two chapters of Vol. 2 and
introduction to vol. 3.
ISBN 0 521 33487 X
1. Community–History. 2. Autonomy–History. 3. Associations,
institutions, etc.–Political aspects–Germany–History.
4. Representative government and representation–Germany–History.
5. State, The–History. I. Black, Antony, II. Title.
JC263. G472513 1990
306'.2–dc20   89-31691
                                                                              CIP

ISBN 0 521 33487 X

AL

For Kate and Jane
and
James Maguire

The original work was dedicated to Georg Beseler

CONTENTS

PREFACE

Mary Fischer and I are very grateful to The Nuffield Foundation for a grant of £1,000 to help cover the costs of translation. I would like to thank Dr Joseph Canning of the Department of History, University College of North Wales, Bangor, and Professor Otto Gerhard Oexle of the Max-Planck-Institut für Geschichte, Göttingen, for reading and commenting on a draft introduction; Dr Martyn Thompson for helping search for recent works on Gierke in German; Professor Peter Stein for answering a query about legal terminology; and Professor Hans Reiss for encouraging this project in correspondence some years ago. A special debt of gratitude is owed to Harry Jackson of the German Department at the University of St Andrews (and so indirectly to the *Genossenschaft* of the cricket field) for putting me in touch with Dr Fischer as a translator of Gierke.

I would like to thank Carol McCann and Susan Malloch of the Department of Political Science and Social Policy, University of Dundee, for having started the work of typing, and above all Aileen Pow for having completed it.

A.B.

NOTE ON THE TRANSLATION

The main aim of the translation has been to be as faithful as possible to the spirit of the original while producing an accurate and readable English text. Many of the terms Gierke uses have no direct English equivalent. *Genossenschaft* has regularly been translated as 'fellowship' unless otherwise indicated, though *genossenschaftlich* frequently becomes 'comradely'. It was impossible to keep one English word for *Recht*, which has been rendered as 'Right', 'law', 'rights', 'justice', depending on the context. In other cases, when the original German term has special significance, it has been included in brackets in the text. For further explanation of the meaning and significance of words used problematically or in a specialised way by Gierke, see the glossary; words glossed are indicated by an asterisk the first time they occur in the text.

Only a few examples of Gierke's notes have been included. Italics are Gierke's unless otherwise indicated. The page numbers of the original are indicated in the text, within square brackets. Numbers in square brackets at the end of chapter headings refer to Gierke's chapters. The main chapter headings are the editor's. All sub-headings are Gierke's.

LIFE OF OTTO VON GIERKE

Otto von Gierke was born on 11 January 1841 at Stettin in Prussia (now Szczecyn in Poland). In 1855 both his father, a *Staatssyndikus*, and his mother died of cholera. In 1857 he attended university at Berlin where he was taught by Georg Beseler, to whom *Das deutsche Genossenschaftsrecht* is dedicated. He did active military service in Bismarck's wars of 1866 against Austria and 1870–1 against France, for which he was decorated. From 1872 to 1884 Gierke lectured at Breslau, then at Heidelberg, and from 1887 until his death in Berlin, where he succeeded to Beseler's chair. While at Breslau he married the daughter of a legal historian; they had six children. In 1872 he was vice-president of the Evangelical social congress. He was awarded an honorary doctorate at Harvard in 1909. He donated his library to the commercial high school in Tokyo. He died on 10 October 1921.

THE MAJOR WORKS OF OTTO VON GIERKE

1868 *Das deutsche Genossenschaftsrecht* [*The German Law of Fellowship*], volume 1: *Rechtsgeschichte der deutschen Genossenschaft* [*The Legal and Moral History of the German Fellowship*]† (selections from pp. 1–14 trans. J.D. Lewis, *The Genossenschaft-theory of Otto von Gierke*, University of Wisconsin Studies in Social Sciences and History, 25 (Madison: University of Wisconsin Press), pp. 113–19) (Berlin)

1873 *Das deutsche Genossenschaftsrecht*, volume 2: *Geschichte des deutschen Körperschaftsbegriff* [*The History of the German Concept of Corporation*]† (Berlin)

1874 'Die Grundbegriffe des Staatsrechts und die neuesten Staatsrechts-theorien' ['Basic Principles of Political Justice and Recent Theories of Political Justice'], *Zeitschrift für die gesamte Staatswissenschaft*, 30, 265ff. (trans. J.D. Lewis, Genossenschaft-*theory*, pp. 166–85)

1878 *Johannes Althusius und die Entwicklung der naturrechtlichen Staats-theorien* [*Johannes Althusius and the Development of Natural-Law Political Theories*] (trans. B. Freyd as *The Development of Political Theory*, New York, new edn, 1966) (Breslau) 3rd enlarged edn, 1913

1881 *Das deutsche Genossenschaftsrecht*, volume 3: *Die Staats- und Korporationslehre des Altertums und des Mittelalters und ihre Aufnahme in Deutschland* [*The Ancient and Medieval Doctrine of the State and of Corporations and its Reception in Germany*]† (pp. 8–128 trans. G. Heiman as

---

† All four volumes of *Das deutsche Genossenschaftsrecht* were reprinted by Akademische Druck- u.Verlagsanstalt (Graz, 1954).

xii

Associations and the Law: the Classical and Early Christian Stages, University of Toronto Press, 1977); pp. 501–640 trans. F.W. Maitland as *Political Theories of the Middle Age*, Cambridge University Press, 1900) (Berlin)

1887 *Die genossenschaftliche Theorien und die deutsche Rechtssprechung* [*The Theory of Fellowship and German Legislation*] (Berlin)

1889 'Die soziale Aufgabe des Privatrechts', ed. Erik Wolf, *Quellenbuch zur Geschichte des deutschen Rechtswissenschaft* (Frankfurt-am-Main: Klostermann, 1950)

1895 *Handbuch des deutschen Privatrechts* [*Handbook of German Private Law*], volume 1 (Leipzig)

1902 *Das Wesen der menschlichen Verbände* [*The Nature of Human Groups*] (trans. J.D. Lewis, Genossenschaft-*theory*, pp. 139–57) (inaugural address as rector of Berlin University)

1905 *Handbuch des deutschen Privatrechts*, volume 2 (Leipzig)

1910 'German Constitutional Law in its Relation to the American Constitution', *Harvard Law Review*, 23, 273–90

1913 *Das deutsche Genossenschaftsrecht*, volume 4: *Die Staats- und Korporationslehre der Neuzeit, durchgeführt bis zur Mitte des siebzehnten, für das Natturrecht bis zum Beginn des neunzehnten Jahrhunderts* [*The Theory of the State and of Corporations in Modern Times, Completed up to the Mid-Seventeenth Century, and for Natural Law up to the the Beginning of the Nineteenth Century*][†] (pp. 276–541 trans. Ernest Barker as *Natural Law and the Theory of Society 1500 to 1800*, Cambridge University Press, 1958)

1917 *Handbuch des deutschen Privatrechts*, volume 3 (Leipzig)

1919 *Der germanische Staatsgedanke* (Berlin)

---

† See p. xii, note.

EDITOR'S INTRODUCTION

Otto von Gierke (1841–1921)[1] has been widely misunderstood and for the most part consigned to obscurity. This is perhaps due to the dogmatism and verbosity of his later works. But his first major work – the first volume of *Das deutsche Genossenschaftsrecht* (*The German Law of Fellowship* = *DGR*, 1868), selections of which are here for the first time translated into English – reveals a profoundly original mind wrestling with history and philosophy in an attempt to generate his own (and, he believed, the German people's) answer to the crises of modern society. Gierke's political thought and philosophy of history were a specific response to the challenges posed in the middle third of the nineteenth century to social order and to political idealism. His works, comparable in scope to those of Mill or Marx, worked up elements of the German socio-political tradition and romantic and quasi-Hegelian philosophy. What he proposed was a kind of community or common life (*Gemeinwesen*) expressed by the moral and legal concept of fellowship (*Genossenschaft*).

Gierke is known in jurisprudence and political theory for his concept of fellowship (*Genossenschaft*)[2] and of corporate group personality (*Gesammtpersönlichkeit*)[3] – which, since it reflected the central role of associations in a normal social life and ensured their moral independence from the state, he regarded as the cornerstone of a just constitution and legal system – and also for his notion of an area of 'social law' standing between public and private law. This would include industrial law, laws relating to real estate and tenants' rights – and doubtless, if he were writing today, legislation on the environment and consumers' affairs. In this field Gierke has been regarded as 'prophetic'.[4] Gierke is known among historians for his encyclopaedic analysis of legal, social and political ideas in medieval and early modern Europe in *DGR* volumes 3 and 4 and in his study of Johannes Althusius. Less attention has been paid to *DGR* volume 2, which analyses German ideas about fellowship and corporation.

The *first* volume of *DGR*, translated in selection here, contains the seminal early thought of Gierke as a legal and political philosopher, presenting his analytical and ideological overview of European, and especially German, history from the age of Tacitus to industrial legislation on the very eve of publication (1868). It is important, indeed crucial, for an understanding of Gierke both as philosopher and as historian. We can see how Gierke wished to demonstrate the very considerable extent to which, in his opinion, the real group personality of voluntarily formed associations was implicit in the social forms, legal documents and political evolution actually found throughout German history, for example in the medieval towns and gilds, the Hansa and rural communities. Such bodies, he repeatedly argues, behaved *as if* their members believed they could decide and act as collective unities. With this he contrasted the imposed, artificial unity of groups formed despite or against their members' will, as under feudal lordship and benevolent despotism (*Anstalt, Obrigkeit*). It is obvious that this involved Gierke in reading into historical phenomena the kind of mental attitudes he thought appropriate to the actors, a procedure he discusses in the introduction to volume 2.

Above all, *DGR* volume 1 presents a unique view about the meaning and value of all non-state groups in the social and indeed personal life of human beings; and an original statement about the significance of the different phases of German and European history, and their overall pattern, without which the principal argument of the later volumes (never fully articulated there) cannot fail to be obscure. There are clear parallels with the views of de Tocqueville and J.S. Mill about the central role that voluntary associations could play in modern society.[5]

Volume 1 has been neglected, partly because its historical judgments need revision in the light of later research, partly because of the reputation acquired by his later works, but partly also because of the very mass of the (unindexed) text. But in fact Gierke had presented here a view of associations and the state that was distinctively more liberal than the view he developed from 1871 onwards. Furthermore, the arguments of his later volumes on the history of ideas set out from assumptions which are only clearly articulated in this first volume. There is an analogy here perhaps with the 'early Marx': in Gierke too the starting-points contain some significantly different emphases from those found in later and better-known works.

Even apart from this, volume 1 of *DGR* is a monument of philosophical history on a grand scale, a historical epic of the German people which sweeps us along with literary poise and intellectual force.

The introductions to volumes 2 and 3 have been included, to show how Gierke saw the work as a whole, and the evolution of his plan for it. They provide insight into Gierke's approach to historical research, the introduction to volume 2 especially is an invaluable statement of his methodology. A few short extracts from volume 2 give a glimpse of the argument of that neglected work.[6] Gierke abandoned *DGR* following the publication in 1888 of the new German civil code, which scandalised him by its anti-corporate bias in matters such as tenant's rights. His efforts to justify what he hoped would be a more truly German code of law engendered a second *magnum opus*, his three-volume *Handbuch des deutschen Privatrechts* [*Handbook of German Private Law*, 1895–1917].[7]

Philosophy and history are intimately connected in Gierke's understanding of the world and of law, in his analysis of both the phenomena and the concepts of *Recht*. For, as the Germanist of the historical school, Gierke believed that a correct understanding of authority and association lay embedded in the history and popular consciousness of the Germanic peoples; to reach such an understanding, therefore, one had to delve into the history of institutions and social movements. For the idea of justice (*Recht*) is inherent, not in the cosmos as natural-law theory held, but in humanity; and humanity is not a mere universal, but evolves through specific, historically developing communities with their changing and progressing social forms and ethical ideas. 'Positive' legislation ought to conform to and reflect this evolution, and is invalid if it departs fundamentally from the moral insights thus built up.[8]

Let us consider the scope and merits of *DGR* volume 1, first as an essay in political philosophy, then as a work of historical interpretation. The philosophical point upon which Gierke insisted above all was the existential reality and moral value of groups as persons. Groups really have a personality, a mind and will, and the state and the law ought to recognise this. Gierke meant that individuals really feel themselves to be parts of a group, identify themselves with it, becoming 'inwardly' and 'outwardly' – subjectively and objectively – part of it; so that there actually is a group consciousness that is not a mere sum of individuals' consciousnesses. Gierke used words like *Gemeinwesen* (lit. common being) to indicate not merely shared experience or possessions but a real unity which could on occasion be of greater significance, in people's states of mind and behaviour, than individual personality. Human groups behave as organisms. By combining together, individuals become to some extent different in themselves, in their inner being, so that the groups they form have, from a human point of view, a certain kind of reality, and are not merely accidental. Membership of groups, whether economic, religious, political or purely social and so on, engenders unselfishness and morality. Like Hegel and the German Romantics, Gierke believed that human beings attain their individual potential by belonging to 'a greater whole'.

The opposite view, which Gierke spent his life combating (and which has on the whole been more prevalent in modern Europe) was that groups have a merely *fictional* personality and legal status. This assumes that groups and their actions are reducible to what individuals choose and do, that groups are 'really' nothing but sums of individuals. There is a slight similarity here with methodological individualism versus holism; but it is important not to read history backwards, and in fact Gierke (like Marx) was by no means committed to the view that groups are something *apart from* their members. Rather, he insists that the way people are connected makes a difference to the kind of persons they are as well as to the kind of society they live in. Nor are these connections the results of mere choice; they stem also from the ineradicable circumstances of human existence (economic enterprise groups) and from the intrinsic desires of human beings (cultural and spiritual associations).

Gierke traced the fiction theory (not wholly accurately) back to the jurisprudence of late Rome and the medieval papacy, and he regarded it as an essential part of the ideology of absolutism. If associations have no real being, then they must be the mere creatures of the state, and the state is then justified in deciding according to its own lights when and to which groups associational freedom and corporate status should be permitted, and in revoking such status at will. He seems to have thought that, for freedom of association and corporate status to be acquired and lost by due process of law, one must ascribe real personality to the groups in question. Only then could they enjoy genuine autonomy.[9] Both of these contentions seem unjustified. Whether or not you ascribe real personality to groups need not affect their right to freedom of association and assembly, nor to their recognition as legal persons by due process. But they lay at the root of Gierke's whole understanding of European history; they were what enabled Gierke to give the *German* idea of *fellowship* a star part in the history of liberty and of constitutional government. He firmly believed that the recognition of real group personality, as well as of individual personality, is essential to human liberty, and that the arbitrary treatment of associations is the hallmark of tyranny.

Gierke's view of group personality was made possible because, in the preceding era of Fichte, Hegel and German political thinkers of the romantic school, personality had been conceived as an inner life and consciousness of which sensation and behaviour are but outer manifestations.[10] As Ulrich Stutz said in his precisely formulated obituary, Gierke's thinking was 'to a certain degree influenced by Hegel' but was based above all on 'national romanticism', although compared with Grimm Gierke was 'somewhat abstract and doctrinaire'.[11] Following the thinking of Rousseau and Kant, it could be said that our very experience points towards, is indeed posited upon, the existence of a real inner personal subjectivity. Since (as postulated by the whole romantic way of thinking) there is a direct correlation between the deepest experience of our own feelings and the world outside us, the sense of belonging or togetherness which people from time to time experience in groups, and also the occasions on which a group of persons unanimously agree upon something and, either spontaneously or after deliberation, 'act as one' can only mean – so Gierke thought – that groups possess real personalities. Moral agency is theirs. It was characteristic of Gierke's intellect that, instead of weighing against this the numerous other occasions when persons in groups do not feel, think, will or act as one, he jumped to the conclusion that group personality is the real core which only occasionally manifests itself. (We might, to be sure, say of two people who frequently quarrel that they are 'really' friends, but that is surely because we already regard each of them as having that kind (or, if one prefers, degree) of integrated personality which, in the case of groups, is precisely what is in question.) In giving associations yet greater salience than had de Tocqueville, Gierke relied upon a naive view of social psychology.

According to Gierke, then, group personality can be known both from internal experience and from the external data of cultural history.

> Were we to think away our membership in a particular people and state, a religious community and a church, a professional group, a family . . . we should not recognise ourselves in the miserable remainder . . . We feel that part of the impulse which determines our action comes from the community which permeates us.[12]

One must, therefore, assign personality to groups as well as to individuals. For Gierke the ultimate truth about human society was this 'real personality' of groups. Gierke saw the development of group personality as a moral goal alongside the development of individual personality.

Gierke was a counter-individualist, a communal thinker in the German and romantic manner: for him commonalty itself was a *moral* value. Here he may be compared with Marx: for communism read fellowship. Indeed,

corporatism was extremely popular among German academics throughout the nineteenth century; and the craft-gild system, which had continued
to flourish in parts of Germany as nowhere else before and after the
Napoleonic prohibitions, was a live issue up to the time when Gierke was
writing.[13] Behind even this one may see in the fellowship–lordship
contrast, and in Gierke's warm sympathy for voluntary associations, a
sentiment and conviction that must have come naturally to a Lutheran
Christian.

What distinguishes the *early* Gierke is the liberal element in his corporatist and quasi-collectivist doctrine. First, he believed that fellowship would
resolve the problems of individual and society, and of autonomy and
authority, by generating truly willed and therefore truly free forms of
association. In the groups which people form of their own free will and
with which they identify themselves for part of their lives, there is no clash
between individual and society. Common purposes bind together the
leader or executive committee and the association as a whole, the former
acting as 'organ' of the latter. The modern state itself, being a synthesis of
fellowship and lordship, is somewhat similar: Gierke, following the tradition of Rousseau, envisaged a transformation of 'subjects [*Untertanen*]'
into citizens.

Secondly, the modern association is the immediate outcome of a free
society, which indeed can only be sustained if human beings do in fact
form voluntary associations. Such associations realise human potentiality
in ways the state alone cannot, because they emerge from the immense
variety of actual human concerns, and because their members form them
spontaneously. In modern individualist society, moreover, no one group
can subsume the whole personality of an individual; people normally
belong to several different associations. Thirdly, it follows from both the
real personality of groups and their role in human affairs that groups as
well as individuals possess the capacity for rights and duties (*Rechtssubje*'.-
tivität: 'right-subjectivity'). There are corporate as well as individua
'human rights'.

Fourthly, states being so large, it is only in lesser associations that most
individuals can develop as political beings, only there can the public
virtues of citizenship be acquired. Like J.S. Mill, Gierke saw participation
in public affairs as essential to moral and intellectual development, and
multiple associations make this far more widely available. Associations (as
Hegel said of *der Staat*) lift people out of themselves on to a plane where
they welcome the mutual responsibilities of social life. This was a development of Rousseau along lines already suggested by de Tocqueville: we

realise ourselves as moral beings, concerned with a good other than our own, through a number of 'lesser' associations.

In *DGR* volume I, Gierke was especially concerned to assert fellowship rights against *state* authority which had interfered arbitrarily with, dominated and even suppressed, lesser associations, most of all (in recent German history) under benevolent despotism (*Polizeistaat*). In the modern constitutional state (*Verfassungsstaat*), however, there is achieved a new synthesis between fellowship and sovereignty (*Obrigkeit*, or 'institution': *Anstalt*): here subjects will the existence of the state and consent to its activities. Here, according to Gierke, the state joins the rank of the fellowships.[14] Yet such a state is not generically or morally superior to other human groups; its sovereignty is not absolute but depends upon its role as guardian of laws and representative of common public (national) interests. The state *must*, therefore, recognise, respect and promote associations in their respective spheres.

Much as some might argue that an enhanced sense of individual personality first developed among renaissance Italians, Protestant English or enlightened French, so Gierke – no less spuriously but no more malevolently – believed that this understanding of group personality and fellowship rights had been, and still was being, developed especially by the German people. It was not the Germanic peoples in the broader sense – all the descendants of the original 'Teutonic' migrants in England, Scandinavia and so on – but specifically the Germans who had this heightened perception of fellowship. This was not a racist view. The Germans just led the way, much as English and American historians have commonly believed they did in developing parliamentary government; Gierke frequently cited examples of *Genossenschaft* among other European peoples, and recently in the USA. The rights of fellowship were a benefit which Germany would transmit to other nations, and to humanity at large.

This view of the uniqueness of the German *Genossenschaft* was subjected to careful critique by Rudolph Sohm (1889),[15] who, while generally sceptical, did not dismiss the notion altogether. He found Gierke's theory of fellowship inherently obscure, and thought it misrepresented early Germanic legal concepts, which were in many respects indistinguishable from the 'juristic person' of Roman law, for which Gierke was fond of expressing his contempt. But Sohm thought that some informal groups today do reflect specific features of German fellowship, in the way they combine individual and collective responsibility in ownership and administration. And indeed there may be a case for saying that, more than elsewhere, free-floating associations flourished in Europe from about 1100 to 1450, and again in Europe and North America from about 1750 onwards, achieving a certain dominance in society and political culture. Such a factor ought to enter into discussions of the development of science and of the first industrial revolution. But Gierke claimed more than that; and one would not be justified in saying, as he does, that the Germans – or indeed, outside strictly delimited historical periods, the Europeans – had a special gift for *Genossenschaft*. Something similar might indeed be said about the Greeks regarding philosophy and the city-state, and about the Jews regarding theology.

What Gierke said about *Genossenschaft* as a *general* social and moral phenomenon has much more sense. Here he influenced a generation of English pluralists, including Maitland, Figgis and G.D.H. Cole.[16] The significance of this is once more with us as political scientists have again become aware of the crucial importance of the state–association relationship, with regard to economic, religious and other groups, in the current debate between 'pluralists' and 'corporatists'.[17] It is, I think, especially important when political propaganda has again focussed upon the state–individual relationship – where the individual seems to be winning hands down – to recall that social groups other than families and nations can and do have immeasurable practical and emotional significance for human beings.[18] They too may, for better or worse, become the beneficiaries of 'privatisation'. Yet there is surely an inherent problem in the way Gierke uses an almost self-evident social truth such as this as a basis for claiming, not just the rights of groups *ceteris paribus* to be accorded legal personality, but their status as real persons. That apart, Gierke's theory of fellowship rights is at least one way of expressing the *irreducibly* social character of human persons, upon which accumulating evidence from both the human and the biological sciences seems to be shedding ever clearer light.[19]

One reason why *DGR* volume I retains special importance today is that, in his later writings, Gierke tacitly abandoned the more liberal – and pluralist - democratic – elements in his theory of fellowship. This followed what he described as an almost religious experience:

There are hours in which the community spirit manifests itself with primitive force in almost tangible form and so fills and dominates our inner being that we are scarcely conscious of our single existence as such. Such a sacred hour I experienced here in Berlin's *Unter den Linden* on 15 July 1870.[20]

From then on the supreme fellowship for Gierke was the German nation-state, or its Second Empire. He yielded to a *Zeitgeist*. And from that moment the creativity of his mind seemed to ebb, its edge dulled by an infection of mystical nationalism, whose existential basis it was not easy to conceive or validate except in ever more convoluted language and obscure mental idiom. Gierke's later works decline into tortuous abstraction and vapid prose, even though the impetus of his creative youth still carried him into extensive original historical research. The irritating thing about the later Gierke is that one feels there is something there but he never quite gets it out; that something does come out tolerably clearly in volume 1. There we have the fiery scholarship of youthful toil; the rest is pale and sickly by comparison.

Nothing illustrates this flaccid evolution of Gierke's mind better than his later views on the relationship between the state and associations. In *DGR* volume 1, Gierke graphically portrayed the historic autonomy of associations in the European past. With ironic zest he belaboured the early-modern regimes of central Europe for their despotic monolithic policies of centralisation: by the seventeenth century nothing was left between the 'atomised individual' and the 'authoritarian mentality' but privileged corporations locked in self-interest. Like de Tocqueville, he welcomed the spontaneous blooming of independent associations in his own century. But after 1868 he made hardly any noteworthy contribution to the question of how state and association are related.[21] Perhaps he was caught in the historicist's dilemma: some of the most dynamic associations in modern Germany were the Social Democratic Party and labour unions, with which Gierke was out of sympathy. It was idiosyncratic to compare the constitution of Wilhelmine Germany with that of the USA.[22]

Compare again his treatment of economic fellowships in DGR volume 1 (1868) and in *Handbuch des deutschen Privatrechts* (= *Deutsches Privatrecht*) volume 1 (1895). The former ends with a lengthy and original analysis of all kinds of potentially fellowship-like groups in modern economic life, in Britain, France and Germany, for example, building societies, friendly societies, labour unions. This culminates in an original discussion of joint-stock companies and finally – as the fullest embodiment of the fellowship principle in the modern economy – of producers' co-operatives of all kinds. In *Deutsches Privatrecht*, under 'economic fellowships', 'fellowships of persons' merit only six lines about insurance companies.[23] One must, therefore, turn to *DGR* volume 1 if one is to appreciate Gierke's contribution to pluralist and corporatist thought in its full vigour. Directly aimed at contemporary legal and constitutional questions, this work is remarkably radical, not least in its derisive treatment of the *Polizeistaat* of which, after all, eighteenth-century Prussia had been the leading exemplar.

Gierke's earlier pluralist ideals were often more vigorously championed by liberals and socialists: one has only to think of municipal and gild socialism, and the Paris Commune of 1870-1, to perceive the irony in Gierke's position. Gierke himself contributed patriotic pamphlets to the war effort of 1914-1918. He continued to walk in to work when street-fighting broke out in Berlin in 1918-19. Reflecting on the defeat of 1918, he hoped that the national idea would find deeper roots in the German people, and in 1920, just before his death, he joined the conservative German National Party.[24] It is true that Gierke's works were more widely read after 1933, and one may find parallels between Gierke's belief in a distinctive German political culture - and the lessons mankind could learn from the German fellowship system - and elements in National-Socialist ideology. But it would be naive to suppose that such an ideology was implicit in Gierke's way of thinking or indeed (in my opinion) in the national political culture and social philosophy upon which Gierke drew. The National Socialists, rather, hi-jacked such notions and used them in a deeply perverted form. Gierke's teaching on the self-substantive nature of associations could hardly have been more at variance with National-Socialist thought or practice.[25] Certainly, Hitler too preached that individuals should submit themselves to 'a greater whole',[26] but it would be fair to say that what he meant by this was quite different from what Gierke had meant. Gierke's last work, *Der germanische Staatsgedanke* (1919), was an appeal for a 'national state', an 'organically constructed community', that would follow 'Germanic political thought' in being a constitutional and socially-oriented state (*Rechtsstaat . . . sozialer Staat*).[27] Gierke's ideal polity was a unique synthesis.

Gierke's work on the *history* of legal and political ideas was monumental in scope and a mine of original interpretations. His bold image of past, present and future enabled him to delve unflinchingly into an unparalleled prolixity of sources, to juxtapose whole chunks of historical evidence customarily studied only in detail and in isolation. This could lead to unwarranted speculation, but it could also illuminate. It enabled both Gierke and succeeding generations of scholars to order otherwise unmanageable material, and to formulate questions about the nature of medieval and early modern European history which, because they appeared to have pressing contemporary significance, impelled energetic study. Gierke's contribution was ambivalent, since the actual historical interpretations he proposed were frequently dictated by *a priori* assumptions designed to give scientific support to the moral ideal of fellowship, and were, as historical propositions, false or tendentious; yet they have in some cases remained influential. The first volume of *DGR* is crucial here because in it Gierke laid down the foundations for the conceptual scheme and interpretative pattern of the subsequent (and better-known) volumes 3 and 4 which are to this day widely read and occasionally cited by scholars; admittedly, in language-starved Britain, this is mainly confined to sections translated into English, but these do occasionally feature on undergraduate reading-lists. The name of Gierke still commands respect, if only because people are a little ashamed of how little of him they have actually read. Yet without volume I it is often impossible to see what Gierke was driving at.

    DGR volume I is also a virtually untapped mine of information about the kinds of things a post-Hegelian philosophical historian could get up to. For Gierke, history consisted of the progressive, dialectical development of institutions and ideas. German history was characterised by the dialectical interaction, and conflict between, fellowship (*Genossenschaft*) and lordship (*Herrschaft*). The contribution the Germans were destined to make to world history and human civilisation was the idea and practice of fellowship in a multiplicity of human groups; and also the synthesis of fellowship and lordship in the modern constitutional state. Gierke maps out German and European history in five epochs, distinguished by specific relationships between fellowship and lordship. In the first period, up to AD 800 (the coronation of Charlemagne), primitive German society was shot through with fellowship; then gradually, with the emergence of the feudal system, lordship gained ground (*DGR* vol. I, pp. 12–152). In the second period (800–1200), the feudal epoch *par excellence*, lordship dominated; but already fellowship had made a comeback in gilds and towns (pp. 153–295). The third period (1200–1525, ending with the abortive Peasants' Revolt in Germany) saw the fullest flowering yet of fellowship – in gilds, towns, confederations, estates. But this 'union movement' did not embrace the peasantry; the failure of the Peasants' Revolt signalled a resurgence of lordship (pp. 296–637). During the fourth period (from 1525 to 1806, the year when the last Holy Roman Emperor of the German Nation resigned, periods 4 and 5 being treated together: pp. 638–1111), the sovereign state emerged to become the paternalist or interventionist state of enlightened despotism, while gilds, towns and estates declined into mere self-interested corporations. The fifth period, however (1806 onwards), is witnessing the final triumphant revival of fellowship in the 'association-movement'. This combines enhanced individualism with a greater capacity for forming self-managing associations for all aspects of human activity. The legal or constitutional state (*Rechtsstaat, Verfassungsstaat*) combines fellowship and lordship in a sovereign but consensual order. The volume concludes with a detailed analysis of economic associations, and especially of joint-stock companies and producers' co-operatives; Gierke saw the latter as the fullest embodiment of fellowship today.

Gierke's influence upon the study of medieval jurisprudence and political thought, at least among English-speaking historians, has been decisive and is still noticeable. He was, it is true, only one of numerous historians – but perhaps the most magisterial – who lent academic respectability to the Tacitean image of early Germanic society as comparatively egalitarian and democratic. But he more than anyone creates the myth of a democratic–egalitarian 'comradely [*genossenschaftlich*]' ethos persisting throughout the Middle Ages at a popular level, for which there seems to be no reliable evidence.[28] He contrasted this with the 'authoritarian' (*obrigkeitlich*) mentality supposedly prevalent in ruling circles, among the church hierarchy, canon and civil jurists, and courtier-literati of renaissance tendencies. It was Gierke (not Ullmann) who presented the history of political ideas as a recurring clash between the fellowship, with its consensual and mainly democratic contours, and lordship which gave rise to modern *étatisme*, culminating in the *Polizeistaat* of the territorial princes. Walter Ullmann (as we shall see) derived his principal tools of analysis – the 'ascending' and 'descending' 'themes of government' (*Gedanke*) – from a not-too-subtle adaptation of Gierke. In Acton's copy of *DGR*,[29] the tell-tale pencil marks and slips of paper, still undisturbed, show with what interest Acton read the work; it might indeed have been a parallel to his own projected history of liberty. Tönnies owed much to Gierke for his famous distinction between affective community (*Gemeinschaft*) and rational–instrumental association (*Gesellschaft*).[30]

Gierke's 'reception' in Britain was primarily due to Maitland's perceptiveness. In his homeland, Gierke's interpretation of Germany history was rapidly undermined by Georg von Below who argued that the state and its 'constitutional history', not fellowships, were the dominant feature of German social and political history, linking the Middle Ages to the present. There was a contemporary political edge to this debate: Below was a conservative monarchist who found Gierke a little too 'republican' (both, incidentally, were Prussians).[31]

Gierke's reading of history clearly had a millenarist aspect, similar to what we find in Hegel and Marx: today is witnessing the consummation of historical development, and all the promise of the past ages is going to be fulfilled in the not too distant future. What brings Gierke especially close to Marx is that he finds producers' co-operatives, rather than joint-stock companies, to be the truest bearers of fellowship, and believes therefore that they are the pattern of the future. Economic groups in which property (capital) rather than personality (labour) dominates are really lordship groups; Gierke savagely attacked the tendency to deny 'labour' – labouring people – their rights. He conceived German history, moreover, as characterised by abrupt dialectical swings between the ascendancy of fellowship and of lordship. But for Gierke (unlike Marx) the modern association movement required no revolution to extend it to the working-class. Rather, national harmony remained an overriding optimum for Gierke; the prospect of class conflict made him uneasy. His solution lay in the development of fellowships within the working-class itself. Socialism and communism, for example the French national workshops of 1848 and Lassalle's programme for Germany, represent lordship, since they seek to reintroduce the state control of the *Polizeistaat*, reducing individuals to an inert mass.

In some respects, none the less, Gierke's analysis of the relation between capital and labour is identical to that of Marx (below, pp. 211–14). Yet it seems probable that Gierke arrived at some of the same conclusions as Marx (whom he never mentions) because both shared a common moral and intellectual heritage, namely the romantic movement in Germany, and Hegel. Eduard Gans, for example, Professor of Law at Berlin University in the 1830s, who 'strongly influenced' Marx and 'many of [whose] ideas were to reappear in Marx's writings', advocated the free corporation as the remedy to capitalist domination.[32] If Gierke actually was unaware of the content of Marx's writings, a whole new vista for the contextual under-standings of Marx would seem to be opened up, revealing that Marx owed far more than has been thought to this common tradition.

While Gierke's concept of historical pattern is woven around ethical ideas, his method of interpreting history was not strictly speaking idealist. He insists that the relation between ideas and actual 'forms of life' is one of 'two-sided causality' or 'reciprocal action' (*DGR* vol. 2, pp. 3–4: below, pp. 237–8). He speaks of institutions as embodying ideas. The nearest he comes to a general historical *explanans* is the German people, in whose national life and consciousness (*Volksbewusstsein*) fellowship and lordship ebb and flow. But even here he does not, I think, imply that people develop institutions because they have a mind to: that would be a necessary but not a sufficient condition, for he clearly thinks that circumstances have to be appropriate. Gierke makes some tantalisingly brief remarks about the relation between deductive reasoning and empirical research in the study of ideological history (below, p. 236–7). It may be that behind Gierke's historical approach lay Kantian providence, which could work as well through material as through spiritual factors.[33] What Gierke did was to highlight shifts in ideological and philosophical patterns and to claim previously unsuspected connections between sets of ideas. His achievements in this field make him one of the first major students of *mentalités*.

In particular, he may be credited with having developed and applied in detail Beseler's distinction between learned and popular consciousness.[34] This he emphasised time and again. It forms the basis for his argument that a true understanding of fellowship and of the accompanying notion of group (or joint) personality was latently grasped by ordinary people in the Middle Ages but betrayed by jurists and philosophers, who opted rather for the 'Roman' notion of merely fictional collective personality (according to which corporate status was the gift of the state). Gierke contrasted the idea of organic community existing in popular Germanic thought (*Körperschaftsbegriff*) – which is examined in *DGR* volume 2 – with the doctrine about human groups enunciated by jurisprudents in a technical manner with a view to legal application (*Korporationslehre*) – dealt with in *DGR* volumes 3 and 4. His point here was that technical jurisprudence, though it was influenced by German as well as Roman ideas and sought to come to terms with existing social realities, never gave satisfactory legal formulation to the German *Körperschaftsbegriff*, as this was unreflectingly held in everyday life. This was due to the split between people (*Volk*) and learning (*Wissenschaft*), and to the domination of the latter by late-Roman, and hence authoritarian, ideas. It left open the way for the replacement of such genuinely corporative and associative ideas as had been sporadically germinated in the high and later Middle Ages, by 'foreign' (that is, Roman, Latin) ideas and the all-inclusive sovereignty of the state. Today, therefore, when the association-movement is in full swing and new forms of fellowship are developing, it is essential for the German jurisprudent to formulate satisfactorily that concept of group personality, based upon fellowship, which eluded his predecessors. This Gierke saw as his own task.

Such intellectual events, then, enabled lordship gradually to oust fellowship from the fifteenth century onwards. This does indeed suggest one way in which Gierke used ideas to explain historical change: namely, in an enabling role, as legitimators or facilitators of a process, or again by blocking off an otherwise possible alternative. It is probably true that he placed more emphasis than would most historians, especially today, on the causal significance of such an intellectual factor. But I question whether this places him in a different historiographical category from those who, like most of us, regard ideas, including the widespread cultural attitudes of *Volksbewusstsein*, as, precisely, capable of facilitating or legitimating social and institutional change.[35]

Gierke's theory of history was not only about how one ought to study the past, but about the actual content, in main outline at least, of that past. And here his theory was not intended to be at all hypothetical but a definitive, substantive statement about the main trends of European history. Gierke amassed a very impressive amount of empirical evidence in support of what he said. Some of his specific interpretations were shared by others, others were developed largely by himself; sometimes he cited the most recent specialist literature, but often, and increasingly in later parts of volume 1 and throughout volumes 3 and 4, he went to the sources himself. But he must be criticised for his underlying assumption – which comes across in the tone of his writing – that his substantive propositions were already so strongly supported by the evidence as to be indisputable. Let us consider just a few specific points.

In accordance with his belief that the essence of a specifically Germanic concept of justice lay embedded in the history of the German people, their institutions and folk consciousness, Gierke fully endorsed the Tacitean view of early Teutonic society as distinctively free and quasi-democratic, a view much contested in his own day and since. Historical research has shown that we know virtually nothing about this society prior to its entry into and mingling with Roman society; Gierke was just one of the fabricators of a 'Germanic' myth, but in the long term one of the most influential.[36]

As for his view that medieval society, especially in Germanic and northern areas, was distinctively rich in lesser associations, a corporate ethos and sense of community, there is impressive evidence for this in the milieux of the craft gilds, towns and to a lesser degree villages; and it may be true that European society at this period was distinctive in this respect. Gierke's mistake was to maintain that there was something morally elevated in such phenomena. Gilds and towns brought people together in relatively small numbers out of economic and military need, and in order to promote collective economic interests, often to the detriment of outsiders (for example, rural workers), and often thereby impeding economic progress. Over time, commerce and industry gravitated towards non-gild towns and country areas.[37]

Gierke's interpretation of the medieval jurists played a central role in the argument of volume 3 and much of his reputation as a historian rests on this.[38] As we have seen, he argued that the canon and civil jurists, instead of developing a German notion of corporate personality, introduced a false Roman one, which legitimated and legalised the domination of associations by neo-feudal and autocratic rulers. It has been very clearly demonstrated that Gierke failed to grasp what the medieval texts were saying concerning corporate persons.[39] The construction of a popular-Germanic and a learned-Roman view about group persons, and the contrast between them, were largely the work of Gierke's own imagination. Again, Gierke interpreted texts written by city fathers, chroniclers and the gilds themselves (or their notaries), which invoke unity, brotherhood and so on, as evidence for a prevailing popular Germanic ideology of fellowship. It can often be shown that this is quite misleading, for it neglects precisely the ideological purpose behind those very texts.[40] We find Gierke misinterpreting the sources and reading into them things that were never there. The prolixity of Gierke's footnotes is legendary, but scholars have increasingly found that the sources often do not mean what he makes them mean. He could be a master of selective quotation.

Gierke's approach to and interpretation of medieval history, especially the history of legal and political thought, received, albeit in a slightly adapted form, a tremendous boost from the work of Walter Ullmann. Ullmann had a profound respect for Gierke, although I question whether (as often happens in such cases) he quite recognised the extent of his debt. For, like Gierke, Ullmann interpreted vast swathes of history as the gradual unfolding of a single master-idea, as in his account of 'The Growth of Papal Government in the Middle Ages'.[41] Indeed he was inclined to be more idealist than Gierke, perhaps sometimes rather naively so.[42] He too often interpreted texts according to his own preconceived notions without due regard for the context. Ullmann too saw European ideological history as a series of conflicts between what he eventually termed the 'ascending' and 'descending' 'themes of government'.[43] Like Gierke's 'fellowship', Ullmann's 'ascending theme' is allegedly found in primitive Teutonic society, and among the medieval gilds, towns, sects and the like; and, like Gierke's 'lordship', Ullmann's 'descending theme' is found in ecclesiastical notions of hierarchy and kingship, and in the papacy. There the parallels end, however, for Ullmann put feudalism in the ascending compartment, whereas for Gierke it embodied *Herrschaft*; and Ullmann saw the Renaissance as the harbinger not of late-Roman absolutism but of individualism and ultimately democracy. It is all the more unfortunate that Ullmann's views have attained the status, particularly among non-medievalists, of received wisdom.[44]

Gierke's theory of history, boldly set before us in volume 1, steadily fell apart as the evidence proved impossible to fit into the conceptual framework. Gierke never substantially modified his theory, which is perhaps why later volumes became so prolix in explanation, so pleonastic in style; and, perhaps, why the work was never finished.

Gierke furnishes a splendid example of the kind of thinking against which the empirical sociologist Max Weber and the legal positivist Hans Kelsen reacted. For Gierke, both history and law were essentially moral; he was the type case of what Weber called 'the professor (carrying) the marshal's baton of the statesman or reformer in his knapsack'.[45] None the less, some of his historical interpretations are useful even today, provided we treat them only as hypotheses.[46] And he gave associations their proper and neglected place in moral political theory. If we ignore his metaphysics, Gierke's idea of the self-substantive rights of associations and communities – *Genossenschaftsrecht* – is as true and as serviceable today as it was in 1868.

GLOSSARY

The first occurrence in the text of a word which appears in the glossary and its notes is indicated by an asterisk.

Anstalt: Institution. Gierke means by this a form of organisation imposed upon a group from outside.

Association: See note 1 (p. xxxiii)

Einung: See note 1 (p. xxxiii)

Gemeinde: Local community, commune

Gemeinschaft: Community

Gemeinwesen: Common life

It is essential to be aware of the distinction which exists in German usage between these three terms; this is not fully expressed by the English term 'community'. Originally both *Gemeinde* and *Gemeinschaft* referred to the common land of the community. *Gemeinde* has retained this sense of a distinct territorial area and can refer to 'neighbourhood' and 'the commons' as well as 'community'. It is further used to refer to the inhabitants and area of a self-governing community, or to a unit of local government (cf. the French *commune*, Italian *comune*) within a state, whether its relationship to central government be subordinate, federal or confederal. *Gemeinschaft* denotes a closer, integrated, organic community. *Gemeinwesen* refers to the common structures within the (local) community. See also René Koenig, *The Community*, trans. E. Fitzgerald (London: Routledge and Kegan Paul, 1968), pp. 14–21.

Genossenschaft: Fellowship, comradeship, association. Conventionally, this may mean an (economic) co-operative society (which in modern Germany embraces a wider category of commercial companies than in the UK), a (historical) brotherhood such as a gild, or (religious) solidarity. It can refer to the abstract quality of 'fellowship' or 'comradeship' as well as to particular groups possessing this. Gierke used it specifically to mean a group in which members are voluntarily combined yet form a really cohesive unit able to 'think and act as one', which he believed to be peculiar to Germanic culture. Cf. chapter XVII, n.1 (p. 260).

Gesammtperson: Collective or group person.

xxxi

Gesammtpersönlichkeit: Collective or group personality. Gierke used these as both general and legal terms, to indicate (i) a state of personal and inter-personal consciousness in which several persons belonging to the same group (usually some kind of *Genossenschaft*) think and act as one, and (ii) the more formal recognition of this by law and the outside world, as when a group acquires corporate legal personality. Cf. Maitland's introd. to his translation of *DGR* vol. 3 at pp. xxvi and liii.

Gesellig: Social, i.e. relating to interpersonal transactions of a non-functional, non-instrumental nature, e.g. someone's 'social life'.

Gesellschaft: Society at large; society in the sense of club; mercantile company.

Gilde: See note 2 (p. xxxiii).

Innung: See note 2 (p. xxxiii).

Körperschaft: A corporate body in Gierke's 'German-law' sense, i.e. with legal personality more or less automatically following from members' awareness of their collective personality.

Korporation: Corporation (Latin, *universitas*) in Gierke's 'Roman-law' sense, i.e. with legal personality withheld, or conceded, by the state authority regardless of whether members have a collective consciousness or not.

Land: Territory; countryside. Where possible, *Land* has been kept untranslated to convey both the physical and the political aspects of the concept.

Landschaft: Territorial estates; 'the assembled *Land*'. In pre-Enlightenment Germany, used to denote the collectivity of the estates of people subject to a territorial lord.

Mark: The common lands on which a rural community is based.

Obrigkeit: Sovereignty; authority. Gierke used this to indicate absolute authority, especially as held under the *ancien régime* (or *Polizeistaat*), i.e. unrelated to the subjects' consent, imposed from without, not legally constrained, and commonly used in an 'authoritarian' way.

Organ: 'Organ' or agent of a social collectivity; it may be an individual (such as a town mayor) or a group (such as an executive committee, or the executive board of a trading company). Gierke used this term with the implication that a specifically organic relation existed between group and agent, the agent being empowered to act on behalf of the group so long as he or it actually represented the group's will.

Polizei: Police; policy. In Gierke, this seldom meant 'police' in our sense; rather, it referred to authoritative supervision or control, usually by a state, especially of social and economic activities (compare 'social policy' today). He used it especially in connection with the cameralist state or benevolent despotism, with its interventionist (and commonly mercantilist) approach, organising and dispensing national assets for the benefit of the state *qua* land and people, without consent.

Polizeistaat: An interventionist, supervisory and usually authoritarian state, but not a 'police state' in the twentieth-century sense. See chapter XI, n.3 (p. 257-8).

Recht: Right, justice, law, rights; sometimes rendered 'Right' so as to signal the special combination of moral and legal overtones in the German word.

Rechtlich: This has usually been translated 'legal and moral' (see *Recht*).

Rechtssubjektivität: Legal personality enabling an individual or group to sue and

be sued; applied by Gierke with special emphasis to groups and implying that
the group in question also has a moral unity or *Gesammtpersönlichkeit* (q.v.).
Verband: See note 1 below.
Verbindung: See note 1 below.
Verein: See note 1 below.
Vereinigung: See note 1 below.
Zunft: See note 2 below.

NOTES

1. German is notoriously rich, and English notoriously poor, in words signifying group or association, and Gierke used a wide range of these. *Verband* is the most general ('group'). *Verbindung* emphasises the common bond in the group, and may be rendered 'combination'. *Vereinigung*, while also a general term, suggests the drawing-together of persons into a unity. *Einung* (lit. union) is used by Gierke to signify a specifically medieval type of voluntary association, namely a deliberately willed union which tended to embrace the whole person in all aspects of his or her social transactions. The gild would be a type-case. *Association* is mainly used to signify what Gierke saw as the specifically nineteenth-century type of voluntary association, namely a freely formed group for relatively specific purposes, not embracing the whole person, leaving him or her free to join other groups for other purposes. *Verein* is used sometimes as a general term ('group', 'association'), sometimes synonymously with *Association*.

2. Gierke used the wide variety of German words available to mean some form of gild. Among these, *Gilde* is the most general, signifying any kind of brotherhood, for specific or general purposes. *Zunft* means a craft gild with some official status, commonly in English called a 'craft'. *Innung* emphasises the official status still more, and may be rendered 'corporation'.

3. *Deutsch* (translated 'German') refers, in Gierke as elsewhere, to that which pertains to the Germans specifically, whereas *germanisch* (translated 'Germanic') refers to that which pertains to Germans and also to kindred peoples with languages (e.g. English, Flemish, etc.) and, in Gierke's view, customs that are closely related to those of the Germans.

THE GERMAN LAW OF FELLOWSHIP

VOLUME I: THE LEGAL AND MORAL HISTORY OF THE GERMAN FELLOWSHIP

Preface to volume 1

Gierke emphasised the interdependence of volumes 1 and 2, which at this time were to comprise the whole work. Volume 1 would be a historical account, volume 2 a juristic analysis, of the German *Genossenschaft*.* He remarked that 'there is an enormous, almost oppressive amount of source material; even to plan to work through it exhaustively would be the height of folly' (p. ix): 'if [the present work] were to be finished to perfection, [it] would probably require the labour of a lifetime' (p. x). Concluding, he wrote:

If the author might cherish the further hope of contributing to an understanding of the connection between current movements aimed at unification and the most primordial and fundamental possessions of the Germanic peoples, and of promoting an awareness that one of the German people's most secure guarantees for the future lies in today's reborn system of fellowship, then the work might also be of direct practical use. *Berlin, July 1868*

Introduction: the meaning of association; scope and plan of the work

[1] Man owes what he is to union with his fellow man. The possibility of forming associations [*Associationen**], which not only increase the power of those alive at the time, but also – and most importantly, because the existence of the association outspans that of the individual personality – unite past generations with those to come, gave us the possibility of evolution, of history.

As the progress of world history unfolds inexorably, there rises the unending arch of the noble edifice of those organic associations which, in ever greater and increasingly broad spheres, lend external form and efficacy to the coherence of all human existence and to unity in all its varied complexity. From marriage, the highest of those associations which do not outlast the life of the individual, come families, extended families [*Geschlechter*], tribes and nations, local communities [*Gemeinden**], states and confederations in rich gradations; and there is no conceivable limit to this development, other than that at some time in the remote future all men unite in a single organised common life and give visible expression to the fact that they are simply elements of one great whole.

But this development from apparently insurmountable complexity to unity presents only one facet of social progress. All the life of the intellect, all human excellence would atrophy and be lost if the idea of unity were to triumph alone to the exclusion of all others. The opposing principle forges its path with equal power and necessity; the idea of the plurality that persists within every all-embracing unity, the particular within the general, the principle of the rights and independence of all the lesser unities which go to make up the greater whole, down to the single individual – the idea of *freedom*.

[2] The struggle of these two great principles determines one of the most powerful motive forces in history. Their reconciliation, in a form suited to

2

the age, nationality, culture and all other existing circumstances, represents the good fortune of a people; one-sided dominance of one or other, or unequal or unsuitable division of their domain, is its misfortune. And as up to the present all those splendid world empires which neglected freedom for the sake of unity have collapsed, so no people which was incapable of limiting the independence of its constituent parts in favour of a higher unity has been able to withstand the tempests of history.

At nearly all times and in all lands we perceive a condition which is far removed from pleasant harmony – not just from the ideal which is by its nature unattainable, but even from that which is possible and attainable. Perfectly understandable! For humanity does not fulfil its destiny in steady peaceful progress! All history, like all life, is a battle; and the initial successes in battle seldom lead to harmony, more often to the oppression of the defeated and the tyranny of the victor. This is not only the case in battles between individuals and peoples, but also in the battle of ideas. When an idea enters the arena of history it grows with youthful vigour; all hostility on the part of the ageing ideas, which had dominated the world until this time and suspect the child to be their mortal enemy, only serves to invigorate it and give it training in warfare. It extends itself and makes violent inroads into the foreign territory. There comes an open breach; both ideas experience defeats and victories. Finally the idea to which the future belongs gains the decisive victory: and then it rules over society, often with merciless tyranny, until one day new-born ideas, perhaps the children of the ideas it had previously defeated, deliver it to the same fate. In the same way, a newly developing unity, more extensive in range and content than its predecessor, usually comes into sharp opposition with those entities subordinate to it, and attempts to suppress completely organisations which it would be wiser simply to confine. Conversely, a newly won freedom often denies to the generality what it must necessarily sacrifice if it is not to lead to individualism. If an approximate balance cannot be achieved, then a long-held freedom often founders on a new unity, or a new freedom annuls a long-established unity; until gradually, if the possibility of development still exists on both sides, the principle which has been overwhelmed is imbued with new substance, and a new struggle flares up.

But the more advanced the age, the more a new factor comes into play, increasing the prospect of finally attaining the longed-for harmony: the growing intelligence and consciousness of the peoples. Nations awake to self-knowledge later than the individual. But when it does happen, then more and more what had once been the result of a vague impulse becomes the consequence of a considered act, and movements find form and goal through [3] a more exact knowledge of the opposing elements, through the increased patience which necessarily results from this and from the growing sense of community (*Gemeinsinn*).

Of all the peoples mentioned in history, none has been so deeply or powerfully gripped by the opposing forces depicted above, none is more suited by its innermost temperament to the realisation of both principles and therefore to their final reconciliation, than the Germanic* people. It seems almost as if this people alone had been called to create states which are at once united and free, as if the Latin peoples only had a share in this in so far as they had received a fraction of Germanic characteristics with the fraction of Germanic blood flowing in their veins, or had borrowed them from institutions created by the Germanic spirit.

Second to none in the march to universality and in their ability to organise states, surpassing most in their love of freedom, the Germanic people have a gift other peoples lack, by means of which they have given the idea of freedom a special substance and the idea of unity a more secure foundation – they have the gift of forming fellowships [*Genossenschaften*]. The people of antiquity recognised, as do the non-Germanic peoples of today, the existence, between the highest generality and the individual, of many gradations of natural and arbitrary associations. But their love of the corporate life, their sense of family, community and nation, their ability and enthusiasm for free association, cannot even remotely be compared with that inexhaustible Germanic spirit of association, which alone is able to guarantee an independent existence to all the lesser conformations within the state, while maintaining sufficient power to create from the still uncommitted energy within the people a vast profusion of lively, active fellowships, inspired not from above but from within, for the most general as well as the most isolated purposes of human existence.

These more restricted communities [*Gemeinwesen**] and fellowships, which appear to the generality as particular cases, but which for their members are themselves the universality, alone offer the opportunity to combine a large and all-encompassing unitary state with active civic freedom and with self-administration. The lack of them is the main reason which prevents so many Latin people from attaining civic freedom, their presence the most secure guarantee of English and American freedom. Although, or perhaps because, our German* nation developed, more thoroughly than its sister nations, these basic Germanic attitudes which press forward to universality as well as to individual freedom and reconcile both in the spirit of fellowship, it has suffered longer and more deeply than they under the opposing principles. A short time ago it was still possible to say that where unity was lacking the independence of the separate elements celebrated a dismal triumph,[1] while in single states the freedom of communities and organisations had sunk to a miserable sham in the face of exaggerated unity. But the mighty [4] progress of our day has shown that the German people is aware of its aim in both directions, and gives cause to hope that the latest of the European confederations will be the most perfect. And that strength which has characterised the Germanic people since the beginning of history and which always rose victorious above all the vicissitudes of fate – the creative power of association – lives on and is at work, more than in any other people, in the German people of today.

If then the system of association in its totality is of the greatest importance for German life in the present and future, it is certainly worthwhile to submit even a relatively small part of this subject to a more detailed examination. This will be the task of *The German Law* [*Recht**] *of Fellowship* in the following investigations. The area which will come under scrutiny will be isolated from the concept of association in general by the following boundaries.

Only the juridical aspects of the German law of fellowship will be discussed. The concept of German association is endangered by foreign influence in the sphere of law more than in any other and even today the Germanic concept of Right is engaged in persistent struggles to regain many positions which have been wrested from it. For even today national law has been dispossessed, by the majority of jurists, of any characteristic perception of those associations which have developed to independent unity; even today the German system of fellowship is confined in both theory and practice in the strait-jacket of the Latin corporation – not, of course, that of the ancient Romans, but that which was debased to a shadow of its former independence under the Byzantine empire.[2] It is true that eminent Germanists have made a significant start in reconstructing the German law of fellowship from first principles.[3] However, there is still lacking a more comprehensive survey, which on the one hand would follow the moral and legal idea [*Rechtsgedanke*] of the German fellowship and its transformation through history, and on the other give equal consideration to public and private law – two areas equally caught up in and transformed by this concept. Alongside the legal and moral [*recht-lich**] aspect of fellowship, its cultural-historical, economic, social and ethical aspects should of course not be neglected; but these will only be considered either in so far as they are necessary for understanding the formation of law, or in order to demonstrate the insoluble link which exists between matters of Right and cultural life as a whole.

The law of the German fellowship *per se* excludes both related legal structures outside Germany and those associations which have grown up within Germany from foreign roots (in particular the church with its rich corporate life), or simple imitations of Latin institutions. It will none the less be necessary to include from time to time similar legal structures [5] in kindred nations for purposes of comparison, and a detailed examination of the influence of foreign – and especially canon-law and Latin – concepts upon the formation of German fellowship, will also be indispensable in order to attain the main aim of the present work, which is: to reassert this attribute of the German spirit, impoverished by jurisprudence itself in precisely this area, by means of an independent conceptual structure, and thereby to demonstrate one of the most significant bases of the German state and legal system of German freedom and German autonomy.

The subject to be discussed is the law of the German fellowship, not the German law of association in general. The term 'fellowship' will be understood in its narrowest technical sense as every body subject to German law and based on the free association of its members – that is, an organisation with an independent legal personality. This is how it is used in the work of Beseler,[4] who first used the word as a technical term. In a wider sense, the local communities and the state itself come under this notion of fellowship; but they also have a wider significance and are therefore to some extent beyond the scope of our subject. In Germany, however, state and local community, while they arose partly from a heightening of the concept of fellowship, arose also partly from a heightening of its opposite. Consequently (according to the tendency of the age), they have retained and developed elements of the concept of fellowship to a very varied degree; the history of previous centuries, for example, is characterised by its almost total extinction, the transformation of the present by its re-awakening. And so state and local communities come within the range of our discussion in two respects: with regard to their origins and with regard to their inner structure. On the other hand those organisations or moral and legal associations which have not been able to assert an independent dominant group identity over their members are completely excluded.

The subject matter is to be the German law of fellowship, not of individual fellowships. As in all branches of history, so in moral and legal or again constitutional history only the developing principle is truly lasting and fundamental, while the factual and material world can merely offer symptoms and a source by which the principle can be recognised. The actual subject matter of the investigation will therefore be the development and the present form of the legal and moral idea of the German fellowship. As far as is possible, however, this idea will be pursued in all its ramifications and everywhere the general sought out from among the particular.

The German law of fellowship will within the above limitations be treated in its entirety and therefore both as a developing and as a developed unity [*als ein werdendes wie als gewordenes*]. The present state of the law can only be grasped completely through a comprehensive historical explanation; conversely it is only possible to approach an understanding of the history of German fellowship when the current movement, [6] as its most recent and familiar manifestation, is taken into consideration. Therefore for practical reasons the material as a whole is not separated into 'history' and 'current law', but instead a different division will be chosen, according to historical and juridical methods. To this end Part I will deal with 'the history of the law of German fellowship' and Part II with 'the nature of the law of German fellowship'. In the first part exposition will predominate, in the second investigation. In Part I the present condition appears as the last phase of a great historical process of development; in Part II the historical process appears as the cradle of concepts of law valid today. In Part I, detailed questions regarding juristic constructs will not be subject to close scrutiny but rather, in so far as it is imperative that they be discussed, the reader will be referred to the results of Part II, so that an overall picture of the German fellowship movement can emerge, unbroken by any wide-ranging debate. Conversely, in Part II, so that the juridical debate is not crushed beneath factual and material considerations, the foundation laid in Part I is taken for granted. Part I takes as its point of departure a general view of an age and, by arranging the study according to periods of time, attempts to present the internal and external fate of the system of fellowship according to its sources. Part II starts from and culminates in one cardinal question: the ideology appropriate for an independent legal entity present within a pluralistic structure – or, expressed differently, the issue of the nature of the ideal legal personality of an association (constitutional personality and legal person). Because it is precisely the presence of such a personality which makes the association a 'corporation [*Körperschaft**]' and distinguishes the corporation from other associations, so the investigation of the concept of corporation devolves on Part II. . .

[7] Part I has the dual purpose of, first, furnishing, at least in outline, an

independent legal history of German fellowship and its influence on the formation of the German state and law as a whole, as a basis for autonomy; and, second, of providing a foundation for the specific discussion of Part II.

Chapter I

The five periods of European history [1]

[8] True history is a current which flows ceaselessly and admits of no division. With ours more than with any other people, local and temporal variations have determined the variety of activity in the sphere of Right, often producing entirely divergent developments or, at the very least, often displacing the boundaries of old and new by centuries. In Germany, to a greater extent than elsewhere, the products of older philosophies have persisted in full vigour alongside the products of what is by and large the dominant idea of the epoch, while at the same time the seeds of the principle destined to dominate the future have already been developing in profusion. None the less, if one examines the development of German law in its entirety with regard to the form of human association which predominates in it, periods naturally suggest themselves, which, despite their arbitrariness and imperfection, are indispensable (if artificial) tools of historical study and indicate the main turning-points of the German system of fellowship. And so periods emerge, each of which was dominated by its own characteristic constitutional principle and therefore developed its own peculiar social structure which became the characteristic one of the age in specific spheres of activity, as well as in more general ones up to and including the state.

There are five such periods. The first of these extends from the earliest history until the imperial coronation of Charles the Great (800). Although the circumstances at the beginning and end of this millennium have little in common, it can be summed up as the time when the Germanic concept of Right came to reside in a predominantly *patriarchal* perception of all human associations. At the end of the period the principle of the basic *freedom of the people* is still, at least in theory, the foundation of public life, although the opposing principle of *lordship and service* has of course already become the sole source of creative [9] development. And so

9

throughout this whole period the basic form of all society [*Verbindung**]
is that which corresponds to the patriarchal concept of the freedom of the
people – the *free fellowship of the old law*; which, since it rests on a union
for upholding peace and law based on *natural* affinity, transfers all right
to the collectivity. But, from the beginning, it is confronted by the opposite
form of human community, in which one individual is the bond of all –
the *lordship group* in its patriarchal, personal form; and the irresistible
development of this principle increasingly pushes the other back. The
conflict between lordship and fellowship intersects with the conflict
between the old idea of personality and the new idea of the material
character [*Dinglichkeit*] of all groups: the fellowships become property-
based communities, the lordship groups become territorial lordships and
at the end of this period the patriarchal concept of the constitution is on
the point of yielding to the patrimonial concept of law and the state.

In the second period, which extends until 1200, comes the definitive
victory of lordship over fellowship and material over personal conceptions. The *patrimonial and feudal* principle of organisation dominates the
life of the nation. A powerful edifice of lords and servants towers up within
the church and Empire, extending up to heaven itself, but each relationship between lord and servant has become real [sc. material: *dinglich*] and
therefore patrimonial. The old free fellowship only survives to any great
extent in a subordinate position and in those areas which are cut off from
the main movement of the age. Yet the corporate idea [*korperativer
Gedanke*] is so deeply seated in the German spirit that it penetrates the
lordship groups themselves, first restructuring them and then dissolving
them. And so a new form of association arises, which is characteristic of
this second period: the *dependent or lordship-based fellowship*. This
develops its own collective Right around and beneath the lords, who
represent the original unity of the group. But towards the end of the period
a newer and more powerful principle is already emerging, the principle
which finally reduces the feudal state to ruins. This is the principle of free
association [*Vereinigung**] – union [*Einung**]. In place of the old fellowships which were based on purely natural association, it produces voluntary
[*gewillkürte*] fellowships, but in the towns it combines the freely chosen
union with the natural base and so simultaneously produces the first local
community and the first state on German soil.

In the third period (which ends with the close of the Middle Ages), while
the feudal state and hierarchical structure collapse irretrievably, the principle of *union* creates the most magnificent organisations from below by
means of *freely chosen* [gekorenen] *fellowships*. Fellowships, and com-

munities [*Gemeinwesen*] based on them, unite in *confederations* to encompass even greater areas; they prepare the way for the emancipation of
personality from its base in the land, without conversely invalidating the
independence [10] of the law of property which had been achieved. They
lead to the separation of public and private law, give birth to the concept
of the ideal personality of the group [*ideale Gesammtpersönlichkeit**] as
state, local community and corporation: and, by means of free association
from below, they *almost* succeed in creating a German state. But not quite!
For the system of fellowship in this period does not have the strength to
complete its task. Incapable of breaking through the barriers of the system
of estates which it has, on the contrary, made more rigid, and above all
incapable of drawing the peasantry into the movement, it finally begins to
atrophy in its established forms and is unable to resist a new force which
is working towards the levelling of the estates, the fusing of town and
country, and a greater and more focussed unity within the state. This force
is territorial independence [*Landeshoheit*], and it succeeds in transforming
lordship over land into the territorial state and in making itself sole
representative of the modern concept of state.

The fourth period – until 1806 – sees the definitive victory of territorial
independence, and with it of the principle of *sovereignty* [*Obrigkeit**],
which it had developed by taking over Roman law. The sovereign-state
idea develops, and with it the supervisory and tutelary state [*Polizei-* und*
Bevormundungstaat]. The fellowship structure is toppled and replaced by
a system of privileged corporations which establish themselves exclusively
on a basis of private law and thereby give up any further participation in
public Right. In the face of these corporations, which no longer perceive
themselves as part of the generality but as privileged exceptions, yet are
unwilling to undertake the duties corresponding to their privileges, the
power of a unified state which can bend or break them is a necessity. To
begin with, this naturally meant the destruction of the earlier freedom and
autonomy. The state moves away from and above the people; whatever
wishes to be recognised in public law can only continue to exist as a
function of the state, while the *dependent corporations based on private law*
– the characteristic type of association in this period – cannot revive their
extinguished public significance. Absolute state and absolute individuality
become the emblems of the age. However, with the dissolution of all the
old associations, territorial independence also destroys the privileges and
inequalities of public Right and brings the idea of the equality of all before
the law and – for the first time in history – the idea of individual freedom
for all within the grasp of its subjects. Although it has little at first to do

with civic freedom, although a German's rights to political freedom were mercilessly destroyed, the transitional period is indispensable in order to prepare the ground for the civic freedom of *all* men, which in our century replaces the freedom of the estates.

We are now at the beginning of the fifth period, from which we expect the reconciliation of the age-old opposites in the ideas of general state citizenship and the representative state. Despite the short duration [11] of this period up to now, we can say that the real creative principle is, and will be, the *free association* in its modern form. In this epoch German fellowship, reawoken after a death-like sleep to more vigorous life, has reached fulfilment. No longer bound by the chains of the estates, not limited by exclusiveness, infinitely flexible and divisible in its form, equally suitable for the noblest and humblest ends, for the most comprehensive and most isolated purposes, enriched by many of the merits of the Roman concepts of Right, but long since ridiculing the narrow Roman mould itself (into which theory and practice still attempt to force it) – this is the ancient German idea of fellowship newborn, bringing forth an incalculable wealth of new forms of community and giving new substance to the old. It is taking part in the transformation of the German *community* [*Gemeinde*] and state, which have only achieved progress in the past and will only advance in the future by means of a return to the root of fellowship. This alone is creator of a free form of association, becoming involved in and transforming all areas of public and private life; and, although it has already achieved great things, it will achieve even more in the near and distant future.

Chapter II

Up to AD 800; the feudal system, 800–1200 [2, 19]

[12] When they first entered history, the Germanic peoples had already long ago developed beyond those earliest beginnings of communal life which we can still observe today among primitive peoples. The family connections, which among our people too at one time were undoubtedly the only organised associations conscious of their common bond, had extended to form bigger communities, in which individuals are held together by a bond other than blood relationship.

Regarding their social structure, in all these groups the two great opposing principles which cleft the whole development of the German polity were already making an impact: the opposing principles of *fellowship* and *lordship*. Both opposites were visible as prototypes in the family. For since time immemorial the family had divided itself into two spheres, the domestic community and the wider family circle or extended family [*Geschlecht*]. The former was organised on the lordship pattern and the latter as a fellowship. From the extension and imitation of these associations, there developed on the one hand lordships and on the other hand fellowships of a higher order. The domestic protective lordship was extended to include client relationships with dependants, but beyond that it had attained a truly public dimension in that both free men and the nobility were retained within the companies [*Gefolgschaften*]. None the less, real political organisation was still based on the expanded family groups, in the fellowships of free men in tribes and inter-tribal groups. The dynastic constitution prevailed in the associations. But they were by no means simply extended or artificial families. In place of the idea of the blood brotherhood there was, rather, the idea of tribal and folk friendship; this characteristic personal legal relationship constituted the cement of the associations. But, if the tribal and racial communities did not take the idea of family association from the dynasties, they did take over something that

13

was applicable to them: the idea of *personal* [13] *fellowship*. Therefore fellowship became a generic concept which included groupings based on lineage, tribe and race.

As to the nature of the old Germanic fellowship, . . . its general characteristic emerges in a personal community where membership is hereditary and gives rise to a specific type of *peace*[1] and of Right. Membership of this fellowship means *freedom*. This freedom expresses itself either passively – in the new enjoyment of the peace, justice and protection offered by the collective or by a specific member; or else actively – in bearing full responsibility for the collective peace, justice and joint administration of internal and external affairs. The former is the freedom of *dependent members* [*Schutzgenossen*], the latter the freedom of *full members* [*Vollgenossen*]. Full members consist only of men born to full membership and capable of bearing arms. But in so far as they are members, they are completely equal. The totality of these full members is the fellowship. Hence it is the source, keeper and protector of the fellowship's peace and justice. If these are infringed, it exercises revenge or accepts atonement, opposing the infringement externally as an army and internally as a court of law. It elects the members to whom it will entrust a part of its authority or Right; it protects both the person and possessions of every member. Therefore the peace, Right and wealth to which the fellowship is entitled as a legal and moral entity belongs to the collectivity [*Gesammtheit*]. Each member of the collective has the same rights and responsibilities within it; it can be controlled by no one but the assembly of all, which manifests the unity scattered among all members. Finally, the old fellowship is not, as has been thought, simply an association guaranteeing peace and Right; rather, it commands the whole person, surrounds him with the same might in all aspects of life and thereby forms a religious, social, moral and economic association.

Fellowship and lordship combine in the course of time; within the fellowship a lord emerges as leader, while in the lordship a fellowship of subordinates emerges. Yet there is no inner reconciliation of the two principles. Instead, first one and then the other comes to the fore. The millennium with which we must first deal contains a period of uninterrupted progress of the lordship against the fellowship principle, which by the end of the period only exists in a pure form in limited and lesser spheres of existence. These conflicts intersect with another, and their results have equal influence on the formation of the German system of association.

Next, we have the conflict of those more recent but no less radical opposites: the rights of persons and the rights of property. The Germanic peoples, at the time of their first entrance on to the historical stage, had already developed beyond the primitive economic conditions in which animal husbandry, hunting and [14] war are the sole sources of gain. They were no longer nomads but had secured habitable areas . . . [and] a fairly well developed system of agriculture . . . In this way a completely new unifying factor emerged alongside the personal tie . . .: the relationship of the groups and their members to the *Land*.* In the beginning the significance of stock-farming and hunting outweighed that of agriculture and therefore there was a preponderance of personal elements in the polity. As this relationship came to be reversed, the basis of law came to be the piece of land or area to which it related; it became property based. The inevitable result of this was that neighbourly existence, common life in agriculture, and the distribution of pieces of land, which had initially simply been the consequences of personal connections, became the basis and conditioned and determined these connections. Yet this transformation was an extremely slow one. It began in the inmost circles of the community and extended only very gradually to the leadership of the people. In spite of its thousand-year duration, this whole period is an ever-fluid one, in which either the personal or the spatial and material factor predominates to a different degree according to whether we consider its beginning or its end. But at all times the two opposing principles are only superficially mixed, not internally fused . . .

[Gierke proceeds to discuss (a) 'the free Fellowship of the old Law', (i) 'as a Personal group' (chapters 3–6): including 'the Fellowship of the People' (chapter 4), lineages [*Stämme*] and kingship (chapter 6); and (ii) in the context of 'the involvement of free Fellowship with the land' (chapters 7–10), notably in the community of the *Mark** [*Markgemeinde*:² chapters 8–9]. He then discusses (b) 'the Lordship group', (i) as a Personal group and (ii) in the context of its 'involvement with the land' (chapters 11–13). Having discussed the 'foreign influences' of Rome and the church, and then Charlemagne (chapters 16–18), he proceeds to the second period].

The second period: 800–1200
The character of the feudal system

From [153] the time when the monarchy of Charles the Great was rushing headlong into disintegration . . . and the German Empire, as the only one of its component parts in which the essence of the German character emerged victorious, followed its own course, the development of those legal and constitutional principles which were in conflict with the ancient Germanic freedom of the people, and which had momentarily been checked, progressed unabated.

Two movements – one, acting from above, suppressing national freedom by means of lordship and servitude, the other, acting from below, vesting all legal rights in the land and making them dependent on land ownership – came to maturity and combined in one single current. When this had taken place the feudal state in its final form emerged; for its distinctive characteristic is the fusion of lordship and property.

Lordship and servitude became the motive force and formative principle not only for the law but for the entire inner and external life of the nation. In the religion, poetry, customs and morality of the time all relationships – of man to God, man to man, even of a man to his lady – are brought under the heading of servitude and decked out in a form reproducing the ancient fidelity of servant to lord. The substance of such relationships was always selfless devotion and a ready willingness to serve: obedience and loyalty on the one side, and the guarantee of protection or privilege on the other.

As for politics, fealty became the bond which held together the entire state. But everyone was not bound directly to the head of the Empire by equal obligations of servitude. Instead, the relationships of lordship and service were formed very differently according to the status of each particular lord and servant [154] and the content of their duties and obligations; each lord was in turn the vassal of a higher lord, while the servant could be lord of an inferior vassal. This resulted in a graduated system of many groups of dependants, of which each, through its own chief, was a member of a larger group; in the highly complex relationships of indirect lordship and indirect subordination; and in the conception of all public authority as an obligation conferred by a higher lord, which had come from God to the emperor, from the latter to the imperial vassals, from these to their men and subjects, and so down to each individual holder of the least significant public office. Alongside and deeply intertwined with this worldly hierarchy of service existed a rival, dangerous precisely because of the degree of internal interconnection: the similarly organised hierarchy of the church.

Second, in an Empire organised in this way, with the passing of the transitional period of the ninth and early tenth centuries, the dependence of all Right on land increased to the most extreme degree.[3] It came not far short of personifying the pieces of land themselves and elevating *them* to be the holders of all rights and duties, while reducing the people to the status of their mere representatives. In this way all lordship and all servitude became the appurtenance of a piece of land, or, if separated from it, counted as an independent property right. The inevitable consequence of this was that all public law was conceived of in terms of property law and of the system of patrimonial powers. Seen from above as a duty of service and from below as a right of lordship, every duty and all executive power became hereditary, alienable, and qualitatively as well as quantitatively divisible. All law took on the character of private law; the contract was everything and the law nothing; there were now only legal relationships [*Rechtsverhältnisse*] between one individual and another. At the apex of this structure was the feudal system which had developed out of the fusion of vassaldom and the benefice system. The lordship of land, along with seignorial law and immunity, formed its basis; and both rested equally on the same principle . . .

The real subject of discussion for this period is constituted by precisely those structures which existed in opposition to the principle dominating law and the constitution; we will not deal with the nature of the feudal system but with those points in which it was *not* fully realised. For the lordship groups themselves [155] do not contain any elements of fellowship and, where fellowship existed elsewhere, such groups worked to its disadvantage; but in spite of this predominant constitutional principle, the German form of fellowship remained significant in three areas even during this period. First, the old fellowship remained, although much constrained and changed, in many lesser areas of life; second, dependent fellowships were formed on the same pattern within the lordship groups, albeit in a subservient position; finally, the beginnings of a quite new form of association were in evidence throughout the period – that of *free union*, which was destined to be the means of bringing the German system of fellowship to a resplendent rebirth, and of breaking up the feudal system.

[Gierke discusses (pp. 155–219) 'the lordly fellowship' of the feudal household (chapters 20–3), and such 'free associations of the old law' as the village and *Mark* communities (chapters 24–5).]

Chapter III

Free union: gilds and craft gilds [26, 27]

[220] Even in its heyday the feudal system was never implemented in its pure form. It was only true in theory that all power and law came from above, from God, the pope and the emperor, and was passed on by them through a series of other holders; in reality to a great extent a man's own authority was always recognised alongside delegated power; there was always the law they chose alongside the law which was handed down. Lordship and service were never the only relationships under public law; the reciprocal and equal relationship of fellows who derived their rights from the collectivity continued to exist or was in the course of being rebuilt. And finally, the dependence of personal rights and obligations on ownership of land and connection to the land was never so total that there was not still room for independent connections based on individual people. But both the fellowships based on the seignorial Right – of exacting service and of investiture – and the ancient ones based on the Right of the people (which served as models for the former) only occupied a subordinate position within the feudal system and had no part in the concept of the *state* being formed by the consciousness of the age. In this [221] development, fellowship had to be rejuvenated by being receptive to a new idea, an idea which was more powerful than the grand concept of feudal monarchy and universal hierarchy.

The idea was found. It was the idea of *free union*. That a fellowship did not – or did not solely – owe its existence to natural affinity or to an external unity imposed by a lord, but had the basis of its solidarity in the free will of its members – this was the new idea which built up a branching structure of popular associations *from below* during the last three centuries of the Middle Ages,[1] while the old ways of life broke down for lack of support. But long before it was raised to its real significance for transforming and dominating the whole life of the nation, this idea had been active

18

in lesser spheres and from modest beginnings had produced ever-expanding legal structures. These grew constantly and broke through the barriers of the feudal system as the harbingers of a new age.

The idea of union had already demonstrated its power in two ways: by new creation and by transformation. It brought arbitrary [sc. voluntary: *gewillkürte*] fellowships into being, and changed the nature of the natural or given associations [*gegebene Verbände**] by merging them with the older principle. The two groups of associations differ sharply in their subsequent development. In one of them free will alone produces the association and is its basis. In the other, the existence or non-existence of the association is independent of the free will of the associates, and is determined instead by something beyond it, whether natural necessity or a higher will; its specific legal [*rechtlich*] form, however, and therefore the possibility of legal existence, is derived from free will. These·two forms of fellowship must be regarded as the prototype and nursery for two groups of associations. For the simple form of the arbitrary fellowship the prototype was the old Germanic gild system. But the combination of the natural or given base with the freely willed, conscious organisation was first achieved in the towns of the eleventh and twelfth centuries by means of the fusion of the old principle of the market community with the new principle of free union. These became the oldest German community [*Gemeinwesen*] and therefore simultaneously the embryo of the German state and the German commune [sc. local community: *Gemeinde*] . . .

[222] The origins and significance of the earliest Germanic gilds have so far not been fully explained, and perhaps never will be. The consequences of the first free association, produced by a people which had formerly regarded all communities as simply the products of nature, are immeasurable. Alongside those associations which had simply developed, the first created association was no less important in the life of a people than the first conscious act of an individual. But, as in the life of an individual the maturing of self-confidence is hidden from an observer, so it is to an even greater degree with the origin and growth of a new idea in the consciousness of a people. Since we cannot see the inner process but only the outward symptoms, such progress always retains something of the miraculous. The new idea is there, complete, and we do not know whence it has come.

Opinions about the origins of the gild system diverge greatly. Some see connections with pagan sacrificial feasts and ceremonial gatherings of the people, others with Christian and ecclesiastical institutions. Wilda suggests that the gild system arises from a fusion of ancient pagan customs of sacrifice and feasting with the Christian idea of fraternal love. Sybel finds in the gild the ruins of ancient dynastic systems. Münter and Winzer regard them as an extension of the close bonds of friendship and vengeance among the Scandinavian warriors. Finally, Hartwig dispenses with attempting to find the derivation of the gild system in a single root and considers the earliest free associations of the Middle Ages to be the groups established for charitable purposes and mutual support, to which the political gild corporations were joined in the eighth and ninth centuries as a guarantee of freedom and property.[2]

While we must agree in general with the essentially negative results of the careful enquiries of the above-mentioned scholar, too little prominence appears to have been given by him to the uniform, homogeneous nature of these associations, despite their various forms. The particular purpose of the particular fellowship appears to have been stressed too greatly and he seems to have been misled into treating them in isolation; above all, the actual Germanic gild system appears to have been too little differentiated from older institutions, with which it did perhaps have external links. If we attempt to reconcile the superficial facts available in the sources [223] with contemporary history, something approaching the following result emerges.[3]

Originally all those objects which we see pursued by deliberately formed fellowships were achieved by fellowships which had grown up naturally. The community of the family, neighbourhood, *Mark*, district and nation each satisfied in the same way the political, legal, religious, moral and social needs of the participants. There was therefore no reason for forming particular associations. But in time, as we have seen, some of these fellowships, like the family associations, were disbanded and others at the very least shaken to their foundations. Among and above them arose the lordship groups, founded on an extension of the domestic households, and these produced, to an even greater extent than the old fellowships, a community which embraced all of life, just as a household by its very nature had always been more close-knit than an extended family. There was more opportunity for participation in political life through the bond of service than the freeman had found among his fellows: the legal protection afforded by the lord was more secure and more comprehensive; the religious community which bound one to temporal or spiritual overlords was more intimate; the bond of loyalty was stronger and morally deeper than that of the fellowship which was its members' birthright; social intercourse at the lord's court was freer and more relaxed. Because men's lords were freely chosen, to relinquish the old freedom appeared to mean relinquishing natural bonds in favour of a freely chosen personal liaison. And so everywhere the lordship associations were winning the ground which the fellowships were losing. While the extended family, the association of the *Mark* and even membership of a province, were no longer able sufficiently to protect freedom and property, to bind their members solemnly and firmly enough, or adequately to satisfy their need for self-denial and bonds of alliance, all of this was fulfilled by the free choice of a lord. However, not all were willing to sacrifice their total freedom; the great number of exhortations to do so brought forth a reaction born of the people's innate sense of independence and equality. If one could freely choose a lord, it was only a short step to the idea of choosing fellows, friends, brothers and to bind oneself by means of an oath, in the same way as servant and lord and formerly even dynasty and people were bound. Even in the old dynastic fellowships the admission of a stranger who had bound himself to the fellowship by oath had not been unknown; even local communities could make non-members into members of the fellowship. Correspondingly, among a group of men who had first been brought together closely and frequently by common bonds of worship, interest, conviviality or charitable works, it was even easier for there to emerge the idea of binding themselves reciprocally by oath or vow, and for them to unite themselves closely and enduringly as fellows. When this had happened once, then naturally the analogy with organisations governed by popular law was available for the new relationship. A fellowship, like that [224] of the extended family, community, or nation, had been constituted. The differences inherent in the nature of these associations were superseded by what they all had in common. The fellowship's peace and Right, its collective rights and duties, self-regulation and self-management, the election of a principal, the equality of the members among themselves – the basic characteristics of a German fellowship – all these were recognised here as before. However, this fellowship had come to be at a precise moment: mutual oath-taking and a solemn declaration of intent had brought it into being. Therefore, instead of an involuntary link, the *free will of the associates* had to be recognised as the sole bond; and from now on, once the possibility had been established, similar fellowships could be founded after methodical consideration and a freely taken decision. The stage of the conscious constitutive act and of voluntary associations had been reached . . .

We do not have reliable reports of true unions clearly founded on Germanic lines, until the year 779 in the Kingdom of the Franks. Before this time of course, we have reports of gilds, but they indicate only transient assemblies and unorganised societies for the purposes of conviviality and worship. [225] In the former Roman provinces, colleges and societies of a Roman kind continued to exist in a state of gradual decay, while some limited associations might be formed on the basis of Roman law among the Christian clergy and laymen connected with them. These had as their aim mutual support, charity or religious welfare. The only type of structure which could not be found among all these associations was a truly gild-like organisation which assumes the existence of its own jurisdiction, its gild-peace[4] and gild-justice. There are, finally, both before and after this period, frequent reports of 'conspiracies' among clerics and laymen, directed against their superiors or for the execution of a special purpose; but it is impossible to tell whether these constituted permanent groups[5] . . .

[226] The internal reason for the formation of the free associations of German law was to be found not in the existence of various organisations which lent themselves to being transformed into gilds, but in the *self-help of the people*. When the natural fellowships, which had existed since time immemorial, partly began to dissolve, and partly were no longer adequate for all their purposes, this gave a new expression in freely created forms to the idea of fellowship which had lived on in the consciousness of the people.

Therefore, despite all the variety of external appearances, the nature of all sworn unions rested on one fact: the transference of the fellowship of German popular law [*Volksrecht*] to voluntary associations. But where, as is particularly the case in the church, foreign institutions continued to exist formally, these too were quickly transformed to correspond to German moral and legal thought [*Rechtsgedanke*].

All gilds were, therefore, like the old fellowships, associations of men each of whom was equal to all others, united by a bond of personal affinity. For they were fellowships and their members fellows and *pares* [peers: lit. equals]. Yet the bond was an extremely close one, comparable only with the most close-knit of similar institutions which had existed under popular law. Hence they were called brotherhoods, for brothers were the first and closest fellows. This most significant name was the only one which remained common to all forms of voluntary unions. It takes us one step further towards a recognition of their nature. Brothers are not bonded for one specific purpose: their relationship contains the whole person and extends to *all* aspects of life. That was how it was, as we have seen, in all the fellowships of the earliest law, and that was how it was too (with only insignificant modifications) in the voluntary unions throughout almost the entire Middle Ages.

Today we are used to thinking of the free association in contrast to state and local community as an association for specific purposes only: nothing is more foreign to the youth of a nation than such a concept. Our present system of association, which resembles a great number of infinitely intersecting circles, rests on the possibility of belonging with one part, one aspect of one's [227] individuality, perhaps with only one closely defined part of one's range of ability, to one organisation, and with others to others. This presupposes a freeing of the individual, which only occurs in later phases of the development of a people. The medieval fellowship demanded the whole person; and therefore originally its members could belong to no other association (unless it contained the fellowship as the part contains the whole). Gradually of course exceptions were allowed. However, by and large this principle was maintained; it is a characteristic which differentiates the medieval association from our own.

Therefore, despite the great variety of corporations contained within it, the Empire remained the sum total of these circles, of which one might encircle the other (or several others) without intersecting them. It would not tally with the facts if, as most have assumed . . . , the gild system in its earliest form had recognised fellowships which were limited to single precisely formulated purposes . . .

[228] [rather] each Germanic gild simultaneously had religious, social, moral and political goals, and aims relating to private law. Even when they later separated out into specific types, when religious and secular types – and among the latter protective and trade gilds – became more sharply differentiated, only their *main* purpose belonged to different categories; while for a long time the bond remained effective in other respects as well.

As a religious and cultic community . . . each gild had a saint as a patron, from whom it normally took its name, and by whom members swore their oath; it had a special altar which it maintained. The endowment of charitable institutions . . . , perpetual masses and the like, gifts to the church, alms and support for pilgrimages, provision of the requisite candles for divine service and other pious acts – these were all the affair and purpose of the association. Responsibility for the burial of a deceased fellow and thereafter his salvation fell to the collectivity. Finally, regular meetings were the rule in every gild; these preserved its religious character, partly as a relic of pagan sacrificial and funeral feasts, and partly as a Christian celebration of love.[6] At the same time, they represented the *social* [*gesellige**] side of the community, which frequently became so [229] dominant that the gilds even came to be called *convivia*, and legislation was directed against the extension of feasting and banquets, even to the point where the statutes of many gilds were almost exclusively concerned with stipulations about the arrangements of the feasts and the order of ceremonies. However, at the feasts and social gatherings of the brotherhoods, gilds and corporations, specially designated days, masses, devotional practices or other customs always reminded them of the religious origin.

But it was not religious and social issues alone that bound the gild closely together: the fellows were to offer each other mutual support in all the vicissitudes of life. The collective [*Gesammtheit*] had to care for its sick, poor or needy brother, often having to give a subvention for travel. Out of this, specific regulations emerged in many gilds concerning the nature and means of such support and the extent to which it ought to be granted for specific incidents affecting a person or his property. It was often agreed that the collective should afford a precise sum to a fellow who had been injured by ship-wreck, flood, fire, theft or robbery. To this end regular contributions were demanded [230] from individuals, and since it seemed necessary to regulate this matter more exactly, aspects of their work relating to the law of property came to predominate in such associations. None the less, these gilds were never purely insurance associations based on private law like our insurance companies.

The gilds did not limit themselves to religion, fraternal love and self-taxation as a means of facing the perils of soul and body; they also took a stand in public law as corporations [*Körperschaften*] for resisting injustice. Having come into existence at a time when the safety of person and possessions were equally at risk, when officials, instead of preventing the suppression of freedom and the extortion of fines and forced conveyance of land, took an active part in it, each association was forced to assume the character of a *protective gild*, which attempted, by means of self-help, to provide legal protection [*Rechtsschutz*] which was no longer given by the state.[7] Thus the London peace gilds were not merely intent on making pecuniary recompense to fellows who had been robbed; they also made the prosecution of the thief a common concern and the duty of each individual too, used gild funds to put a price on the thief's head, and called on the help of courts in other shires into which the thief had fled . . . They not only took part in sentencing and executing the sentences, [231] but even shared the confiscated estate of the criminal with the king or the territorial lord . . . As with property, the gild also protected the person, life and, above all, the widely threatened freedom of each fellow. It afforded him assistance in court by making it the duty of all fellows to stand by him as witnesses and character referees, and to help him in all just causes. Even in a case of murder committed by a fellow, if it was not entirely unpardon-able, the gild would pay the fine for him out of the gild's coffers.

If the gild was similar to the old system of fellowship in the comprehen-siveness of its aims, it was even more similar in respect of its *internal organisation*. But for all that, because the basis of the association was different, this similarity went hand in hand with an internal transfor-mation in points of details. The gild too was based on common law and obligations, which, in contrast to the rights and obligations of the in-dividual, was vested in the totality of all fellows.

As with the community and nation, this totality became apparent at the assembly of all full members. This might take place at regular intervals or at special convocations. Alongside the full members was a circle of fellows who only enjoyed passive rights; among these we must include women and children, and later journeymen and apprentices . . . As in the national community the real power in matters of the fellowship was vested in the assembly of the gild. This was the representative of a [232] specific gild-peace which encompassed all fellows and which was therefore present in a higher form in the assembly of the gild; it was the assembly's duty to establish, maintain and secure this peace. Therefore the fines imposed for a breach of the peace fell to this assembly; where a fine was not imposed or seemed inadmissible, it expelled a member from the gild. The contents of the regulations, formulated at its discretion, together with these prac-tices accepted by it as hallowed by custom and convention, made up the gild Right; while each member had a share in this, only the collective was empowered to extend or limit it. As far as the gild Right ran, the assembly also had jurisdiction over infringements and law-enforcement. It was responsible for the highest levels of administration of all gild business, for decision-making and the choice of a leader [*Vorstand*].

The head of the gild resembled an elected judge of a national com-munity. It was his duty to summon and direct the assembly and the court, to enforce exclusions from the peace of the gild; he therefore also had a say in breaches of the peace, he had to put into effect judgments and decisions, and to represent the gild to the outside world. He was also responsible for the collection and administration of fines and contri-butions; these went into a special gild fund. Such moneys, together with entrance fees due from new members, formed a joint disposable asset to be used for the good of all. They were used both for the specific purposes of the corporation (for example pious donations, support of individuals, damages, etc.) and for common requirements, such as banquets and drinking festivals. They might even be distributed among members. The gild also normally had a meeting house and other immovable joint assets.

The ultimate basis for all these collective rights and corresponding collective duties imposed upon individuals was [233] (as for associations in general) the free will of all fellows, manifested and made binding by a sworn declaration or other statements. Therefore the whole relationship was regarded as a freely entered agreement, contract or bargain. The internal discipline and law of the gild had the nature of self-imposed discipline and self-willed law. The court of the gild was like a court of arbitration where adjudicators settled disputes. The powers conferred by the election of an official were plenary in appearance only. Finally, the principle of self-taxation, unknown to the old system of fellowship, was introduced. Originally, it meant no more than the consolidation of separate assets to enable them to be used as common property; and it was also connected with the entrance fee levied from new members who would naturally want a share in the existing common property. In the gilds, therefore, the old concept of fellowship was continued but also enriched and extended.

Having thus found expression in a viable form, the new principle of free union was bound to penetrate increasingly wide spheres. The secular and ecclesiastical authorities could not treat it with indifference. They had either to proscribe and delimit this new free association, which was making inroads into all aspects of private and public law, or to absorb it into their system. The former happened in the Frankish kingdom, the latter in England and the North: in the one case, then, we find a complete victory for the feudal system, and in the other a compromise between freedom and lordship.

In England, the statutes of the London peace gilds, composed under King Athelstan (925–40), testify to a thoroughgoing 'reception' of the union movement into the body of the state; these statutes are approved by the king's sheriff and the bishop. The power of the state, therefore, expressly approved their far-reaching political activity. It was the same [234] with gilds of other English towns. But it went even further: the principle of union was applied to the structure of the kingdom itself by constituting gild-like associations as the bottom link in the constitution and also by introducing isolated norms from the gild movement into higher fellowships. This happened in approximately the following manner. When the kinship groups began to dissolve, it was demanded of the lesser freemen who were not represented and vouchsafed for by a lord with responsibility for them, that they either join an association of lords (this was demanded unconditionally of the landless) or put forward other freemen as guarantors of their good conduct and, if necessary, of their appearance in court. This gave rise to an idiosyncratic theory of legal guarantees under constitutional law, according to which no one should be without guarantors. The older gilds, although their ties were not as close as those of the extended family, but none the less closer than those of the community of the mark and hundred, were suited to providing such guarantees and, where they existed, they undertook them . . . These gradually developed into the much-debated Tens or *frithborgas*, which in the Norman period united ten neighbouring men under a leader who was vested with judicial powers in minor affairs.

[235] These associations for guaranteeing the peace were, therefore, fellowships enforced by the state; analogously with the gilds, they bound a community (or part of it) by a close legal association, to some extent replacing the links of the old lineages. But even the larger fellowships based on popular law – hundreds and shires – were correspondingly conceived of as gild-like groups, as peace-gilds created by free association yet necessary and compulsory. Perhaps [236] this facilitated the retention, in the county constitution, of autonomy and especially of elements of fellowship, and helped produce a course of development so at variance with the destinies of the continental hundreds and administrative regions. The whole English state, finally, has been likened to a huge protective gild, with free men as sworn members of the gild, bound and unified under the supreme overlordship of the king for the maintenance of peace and justice. In this comparison more than anywhere else, the continued existence of the concept of fellowship and its compromise with the principle of lordship, which characterises English constitutional history, became apparent.

In England, the system of union had from its inception been brought into an organic relationship with the state by virtue of the fact that free union was acknowledged by the legislative power but simultaneously made dependent upon it. In the structure of the state itself, furthermore, the administrative and policy divisions emanating from above were amalgamated with the gild element in a way quite characteristic of this state; and finally, something of the nature of union was taken over into the concept of the whole community. The gilds were similarly ratified in Denmark. But in the Frankish kingdom, and, initially, in the German Empire, state and church took a resolute stand against them. Oft-repeated royal ordinances attempted either to suppress the gilds or to confine them to single purposes within private law: but above all they attempted to prevent the fellows binding themselves by oath.[8] Canon [237] law and conciliar decisions set their face equally often against the brotherhoods, directing their prohibitions in particular at the moral dangers of drinking festivals. Yet, consciously or unconsciously, these secular and ecclesiastical prohibitions were not simply based on a policy opposed to single aspects of the gild system, but on fear of free association as a whole. For both the representatives of the ecclesiastical hierarchy and the representatives of the system developing in the Empire, in which lordship came from above and each individual was bound to another by duty, were well aware of the distant but certain danger with which freely willed union threatened them. But no legislation can defy the idea of the age. Even legislation against the system of association was incapable of preventing free union from expanding and developing in a number of established institutions, and from penetrating into the most varied areas of life. They only intensified the contradictions and led to an even more violent conflict.

[Having first discussed spiritual brotherhoods and protection-gilds, Gierke proceeds to vocational gilds (*Berufsgilden*).]

[242] As city constitutions developed, the gilds' role of affording legal protection to a large degree receded. Both old and new gilds now developed largely as fellowships of collective interest, and these interests, determined by the diversity of urban trades, became more and more the basis of corporational structure. The purposes of the gilds still embraced the whole of life; they remained fraternal associations for mutual support, religious and social intercourse, the exercise of political rights, [243] the protection of each individual against injustice and violence . . . But more than all these the *professional interest* of the members now became the decisive factor in determining the form and scope of their association.

Thus among those former burgesses [*Vollbürger*] who had become Elders [*Altbürger*] the traditional or newly formed gilds took on the character of fellowships for the exercise and upholding of *political privilege* and generally for guaranteeing the rights of those of patrician rank. But the great majority of the citizens who made their living from the urban trades which were flourishing and becoming independent, adopted the common trade interest as the main issue in the existing or newly founded brotherhoods. The ever-increasing numbers of gilds which were appearing now unified only those citizens who practised the same trade. Since this now by and large determined the content and policy of the association, they became true trade gilds and consequently economic fellowships.

Among the trade gilds [*Gewerbsgilden*], the merchant gilds or hansas were by far the oldest. Ever since fully free Germans had lived in towns, they had begun to combine wholesale trade with possession of urban land, the latter remaining then as before the basis of their rights. Thus, among the members of the civic protection gilds, merchants were always a majority and they began at an early stage to insert regulations for the furtherance of trade into their statutes, using the fellowship's wealth in the interests of merchants and to obtain trading privileges as corporate rights (for example, the right of staple, customs immunity, protection of goods, and market rights). With the increase in trade and in the number of free members of the population engaged in it, either the old protection gilds turned into pure trade corporations, and as such became the basis of the civic constitution; or, alternatively, new merchant gilds arose alongside the protection gilds (which were increasingly changing into corporations of Elders), and, to the same extent as the latter withdrew from commercial enterprises, these new gilds saw the true purpose of the association as the safeguarding of mutual [244] trade interests.

In Cologne as early as the eleventh and twelfth centuries, alongside the *Richerzeche* there appears to have existed a great *fraternitas mercatorum* (also called *fraternitas vini*), which later split into several mercantile societies.[9] In those cities which were originally founded as trading posts (such as Freiburg and Lübeck), the gilds of the burgesses had the character of trade corporations from the beginning. Lastly, members of the merchant class emerging from serfdom had either to try to join existing hansas, or to try to form their own.

From early on, gilds which pursued both trading interests and legal protection were added to these corporations of urban merchants; as trade increased, merchants from the same town or area or who spoke the same language were in the habit of joining them when they were abroad. But, if the origins of the German hansas in London, Bruges, Wisby and elsewhere reach back to the twelfth and even eleventh centuries, their characteristic development, like that of the merchant gilds, does not come until the subsequent period.

The same was true to an even greater extent of the *trade gilds of the artisans*, the free 'craft gilds' [*Zünfte**][10] [245]. The oldest document pertaining to a craft gild which we possess is a deed from Cologne dating to 1149, in which the judges, lay assessors and worthy citizens, with the agreement of the community, ratify the existence of a brotherhood set up by the blanket-weavers. The condition, according to which all those who intended to pursue the trade in the town were obliged to join it and comply with its regulations, demonstrates that this brotherhood was a craft gild. It was not the only trade gild in Cologne at that time, because the deed established that an area where linen-weavers sold their goods should be the common property of their craft gild and that of the blanket-weavers.[11] It too had existed before 1149, having previously used gild funds (*a communi bono eiusdem fraternitatis*) to drain the site. But this document gives some information not only about the age, but also about the origins, of these craft gilds. For it clearly indicates the two separate factors which combined to bring about the formation of the system of craft gilds [*Zunftwesen*]: the *free union* of the fellows and the bestowal of the craft on the fellowship as its *official function* [*Amt*].

The basis of the corporate organisation of the artisans had always been freely willed association. In the deed of 1149 this is already clearly indicated as the legal basis both for the fellowship's existence and for its constitution . . .

[246] The trade gilds did not have their origins in dependency but in freedom, not in seignorial law but in opposition to it; they were modelled not on the official functions exercised under seignorial law [*Hofrecht*: feudal law], but on the gilds and brotherhoods of free men, in particular those of the merchants[12] . . . Artisan fellowships were only formed when, and to the extent to which, freemen (albeit from among the humbler ranks) joined with artisans who had been freed from seignorial law . . . to create a free group of artisans. In all probability, the earliest of these arose completely free from the influence of seignorial law, by means of voluntary association among the earliest freemen and the better-off tradesmen (weavers, gold-smiths and so on) . . .

Once free craft gilds existed, those artisans who were not yet fully free of seignorial law were compelled to form similar corporate unions. Sometimes they succeeded in transforming the office (*Amt*) incumbent on them under feudal law into a craft gild . . . In all probability, however, the precise origin of a free voluntary fellowship was more often an explicit constitutive act undertaken in defiance [247] of the lord. A sworn union was formed, not only among members of the feudal office but also by artisans outside this system – indeed a brotherhood [*Bruderbund*]. Its purposes were mutual aid, piety, conviviality and advancement of the trade; but also the protection of already acquired rights to freedom and the acquisition of further such rights. When repeated prohibitions and reprimands failed to suppress the unions, the lord usually tolerated them at first and finally recognised them . . .

In the long term, therefore, it was as impossible to deny artisans recognition of their corporations as it was to doubt their freedom, in which, according to Germanic notions, the Right of union was always present. For the trade gilds, on the other hand, it was always important to achieve explicit recognition of their rights of fellowship. Hence, for the sake of ratification by the city fathers, they complied with many limitations on their autonomy . . . But, if ratification on the part of the lord or civic authority was useful for the exercise of corporate rights, viewed differently it was essential for the actual commercial side of these corporations; this should be seen as a second factor which had a part in the formation of the craft gilds.

In the system of feudal and seignorial law (*Recht*), each trade and each craft was an act of service which was carried out for a lord; [248] the performance of this act of service together with its associated privileges constituted a public office or *officium* under the lordship system. With the liberation of the artisans, this idea was not abandoned but underwent a change in application. In the course of his work the artisan no longer served a lord but his fellow citizens, or rather the collectivity of citizens in an organised form – the community [*Gemeinwesen*]. The exercise of a particular craft was, therefore, now a *public or civic office* instead of one which . . . pertained to the lordship system; yet it remained a duty. Whether the civic authorities alone represented the town in conferring the office of tradesman, or whether the royal official or lord of the town conferred it, it was established that under any circumstances the rights and obligations of a trade were a public office which had to be bestowed on its holder. If the craft gilds wanted to practise their trade they had to have the office, which was soon called 'gild', 'corporation' [etc.] . . .

From this followed a series of consequences which could not have arisen from the principle of union alone. [249] The dependence of the craft gilds in matters of trade (and even to an extent of fellowship) . . . [and also] the rights of town lord or town in appointing their overseers, in admitting members and establishing their statutes and the tasks and duties of the trade – all these in the main stemmed from rights comparable to those of a lord paramount over the craft, handed down in the manner of a feudal office. But the notion that craft work was a public office is linked above all with the origin of *obligatory membership* of a craft gild . . .

Since the fellowship was more or less free to control admission and under certain circumstances could refuse it or at least make it very difficult, occasionally the corporations brought about a true monopoly, independent even of the town, by means of which they possessed the craft office to the exclusion of all non-members. Finally, as was the fate of all medieval public offices, the office of craftsman came to be more and more regarded as a property right; this resulted in the total membership of the craft gild becoming fixed, positions within it becoming heritable, saleable and even divisible, and all possible conditions being laid down for the exclusion of strangers – in short the corruption of the system of craft gilds.

Chapter IV

The medieval cities, 1200–1525 [28, 33, 34, 35]

The emergence of the City commonwealth [städtische Gemeinwesen] *out of the Adoption of the principle of union within the fellowship of the local community* [Gemeindegenossenschaft]

[249] The idea of union had already, even at the time when the idea of service was flourishing most vigorously, created a wealth of voluntary associations. In the final two centuries of this period [sc. 1000–1200] it brought forth a new form of association in the *city commonwealth*, by transforming individual communal fellowship into free citizenship. [250] This has incalculable importance for legal and constitutional development.

The origins of medieval civic freedom have not yet been fully clarified.[1] However, in spite of doubts remaining on individual points, it is possible to describe the basic elements from which it developed. Its basis was the old Germanic free fellowship; this became a civic community by assimilating the notion of free union and amalgamating it with the principle of the community of the mark . . .

[Gierke outlines two alternative theories about the origins of medieval German towns, based on continuity with the Roman *municipium* and an extension of communities founded on seignorial lines: he rejects both. Rather,] [252] the content of the development of our cities was not a development of seignorial law but the squeezing-out of seignorial law by the expanded and enriched popular law of the old free fellowship, as it was first revealed in the episcopal cities . . .

[Gierke proceeds to discuss 'the development of city freedom in the old episcopal towns' (chapter 29), 'cities growing out of court communities or manorial lordships' (chapter 30) and finally 'the church and fellowship' (chapter 31).]

The Third Period, 1200–1525

[Gierke chooses, for reasons that become clear, the Peasants' War of 1525 as the end-point of this epoch, which is characterised by 'the system of union as its ruling principle'. This is distinct from the later 'system of incorporation', and also from the modern fellowship-system characterised by 'free association' [chapter 32).]

The towns as fellowships: the significance and role of the German civic system [Städtewesen]

[300] The rise of the German towns in the thirteenth and fourteenth centuries is almost miraculous, surpassed perhaps only by the colonisation of the ancient Greeks and the growth of the American towns in our own day. Still less often in history has external growth gone hand in hand with a steady and radical internal transformation of all conditions and philosophies [*Anschauungen*], as happened in the German cities of the Middle Ages. In almost every respect the towns were the intermediaries between the old age and the new. They were the birthplace of new ideas which still exercise us today . . .

It was the areas of Law and of the constitution that were most affected by the transformation which first took place within the city walls. Our entire present conception of law and the state has developed from medieval ideas mediated by the towns. It was in the towns that public and private law and rights [*Recht*] were first distinguished, and the unity and inalienability inherent in public law first recognised. The idea of a unitary power and administration, a law which bound all equally – in short a state in its characteristic German form – was produced in the cities and transferred thence to princely territories, the military, administrative [*Polizei*] and fiscal policies of which were also modelled on civic institutions. Civic self-administration and the grand concept of the correspondence between civic duties and rights – which today we are attempting to realise [301] in the state and to restore in the local community–were recognised in the medieval cities as guiding principles within their lesser sphere, and were often fully implemented.

Although the individual German towns cannot bear comparison in external splendour, the magnificence of their inner development in political power, or again in revolutionary or reactionary violence, with the cities of the Netherlands and Italy, which prospered earlier and more extensively than the German ones, nothing could be more one-sided than to declare their constitutional history to be relatively insignificant, or their internal development to be an incidental part of the moral and legal history of the Fatherland. Since, in all aspects of the development of legal justice [*Recht*], more weight is given to the internal progress of concepts and institutions than to the external extent of their application, . . . it could all the more easily be maintained that the capacity of the German citizenry – operating in silence – for the development of law and justice contributed more to the enduring advancement of the legal system and the constitution than did the history of Right in the much-admired city-republics of Italy, which consumed one social and legal constitution after another in the chaos of the most ferocious factional conflicts, and came to an end in the mortal sleep of tyranny! . . .

Not only did existing [German] cities expand rapidly in wealth, population, political and military power by virtue of expanding commerce and the vigour of their tradesmen; the number of towns too was progressively increased by a host of newly founded towns . . . Not only Germany but bordering foreign territory was strewn with German cities, and as far as Russia, Scandinavia, Hungary and Poland, German communities with municipal constitutions prospered, as had the colonies of the Greeks before. It was [302] primarily these which made a lasting conquest of all the eastern part of present-day Germany for the Fatherland's way of life[2] . . .

The constitution of the towns as an unfolding [Fortbildung] *of fellowship*

[310] We have already indicated above that the system of law and constitution in the towns developed wholly on the basis of the old Germanic fellowship after the latter had been modified and enriched by the assimilation of the principle of voluntary union. But one of the most important consequences of this fusion was only referred to in passing. This was the unification of the idea of the property basis [*Dinglichkeit*] of all law (which had gained almost exclusive overlordship within the community) with the personal nature of law, which held sway throughout the gild system, so as to form a higher unity.

We know that, according to the older view, persons and real property existed largely independently, in opposition to one another [sc. in the towns], so that the person alone did not predominate, as in the most ancient fellowships, nor conversely did personal rights become rooted in the land, as in the feudal and seignorial systems. Thus the system of personal rights and personal associations directly confronted the system whereby all rights were attached to specific pieces of land, and all human associations [311] to specific spatial units. It was in the towns first of all that unity was more and more sought and found, that internal links increasingly developed between the rights of the city [*Stadtrecht*] and the rights of the citizens [*Bürgerrecht*], between the civic territory [*Stadtgebiet*] and the citizenry [*Bürgerschaft*] . . . The expression of this new unity was the elevation of the ideal concept of the town into a single legal entity [*Rechtseinheit*].

In current idiom we might say that the town became a 'juristic person', were this expression not associated with a concept related to Roman ideas, thus making us think primarily in terms of private law about a phenomenon which relates equally to all aspects of law and justice.

With the emergence of this inner unity, the inner development of the constitution of the towns had reached a conclusion. This is not to say that development had come to an end here: on the contrary it was only just properly starting. It was now a matter of giving the inner unity an outer form, of establishing the rights of the plurality within this unity, and of the individual within the plurality. But it represented, if I may put it in this way, a certain basic form which all towns had to achieve before they could really be counted as towns, and which, once achieved, remained the framework for all future developments.

In fact among all the almost incalculable variety thrown up by the constitutions of individual towns during the rich and sublime vitality of the thirteenth and fourteenth centuries, it is impossible to miss a certain basic form which is common to them all. It is beyond dispute that none of the upheavals which the bigger cities experienced destroyed this basic form; rather, they extended it. This basic form can be briefly described as follows.

Objectively speaking, the town in its essence was a sphere of peace and Right, outwardly and inwardly sundered . . . from the *Land*, and from its Right. With this sphere were associated a series of privileges of a political and commercial kind; more or less complete freedom, as to person and property, of its territory and inhabitants; a distinct municipal jurisdiction; self-administration and autonomy; and lastly common property in both movable goods and real estate. The shifting boundary of this sphere of right bordered on the opposing rights of the emperor and of unfree towns, and beyond this on the sovereign rights and revenue prerogatives of a lord or his official.

[312] The following subjective conditions pertained to this sphere of rights:

(1) Its real subject was the town, conceived as a group personality [*Gesammtpersönlichkeit*].

(2) The entire population of the town, including visitors and non-resident citizens, had a passive share, as a large protective association, in the Right. But a claim for protection was contingent upon the fulfilment of civic duty.

(3) Those actively entitled, the actual bearers of the municipal Right, were a more limited circle, the fellowship of full citizens [*Vollbürger*].

(4) These rights were not exercised by the collectivity but by its agency [*Organ**], and ultimately this agency of the community was always a council, with the office of mayor at its head . . .

Regarding (1), it remained above all an uncontested principle that the town, standing above all classes [*Stände*], factions and authorities as a higher unity, was the actual subject of all power and all rights based on the community. Thus all citizens saw the profit, honour and advantage of the town – the advancement of the community life – as the motivating principle behind each statute and each change in the law. By taking an oath to the town, the council recognised that it was exercising not its own Right and power but those of a third party – that it was an organ, not a lord, of the town.

All the public and private Right common to all citizens was focussed in the concept of the town. The town was therefore the subject of all sovereign rights both externally and internally; it was the town which sealed alliances and treaties through its envoys, waged war through its citizens and mercenaries, protected and represented each of its members, even abroad; the town laid down the laws, ruled and judged internally through its authorities, and made claims on the individual for the common good by means of taxation and military service. And because the town was a unity, all the branches of the administration had to become more and more focused externally too. Here there could not be a series of independent titles to hold office, like the offices which still existed under the system of lordship: instead, all those active in the service of the community, from the mayor to the watchman on the tower, served only one master – the town. The revenues, indirect and direct taxes (here emerging for the first time) were raised for the city and not, as in the feudal state, for the occupant of the office; the monies were kept and spent in its name and for its ends. The town was the territorial lord of its entire area and the possessor in private Right of the public streets, [313] squares and buildings as well as the common land. The town was debtor for the public debt, creditor for public claims, it brought actions in court and had actions brought against it. It concluded legal affairs with third parties, just as with citizens. As the external sign of its unity it had a special seal and bore a standard and coat of arms. The more that factional currents arose in the community, the more precisely this whole idea revealed itself, and the more clearly it was expressed; for in the midst of all change the city's unity was unshakable and enduring.

Further, the notion that a collegiate administration with a unitary leadership – which everywhere gradually became mayor and council – represented the town as its agency [*Organ*] both internally and externally, remained inviolate. There was no attempt anywhere to replace it with a solitary overlord or the overlordship of the collectivity. In other respects, there were of course fundamental differences on many points.

To begin with, the collectivity [*Gesammtheit*] of burgesses never *completely* transferred the exercise of power to the council. Instead, it acted to a modest degree in the capacity of assistant and supervisor. Generally speaking, however, its jurisdiction in due course decreased and its meetings became less frequent. It was originally the highest court and legislative assembly because it preserved the existence of the true assembly [*Ding*] of the popular law. For the same reason, its participation was frequently demanded at a later stage in the drawing-up of new statutes, the sealing of alliances and the decision to undertake military campaigns, in the imposition of new taxes or contracting of a civic debt, in the renewal of the civic peace, or in other [314] exceptional matters. Lastly, in cases where the council did not fill its own vacant seats, it conducted elections.[3]

In all these respects, however, the council tended to make itself increasingly independent of the collective of burghers. Hence it frequently came into some degree of conflict with them, especially when it filled its own vacancies, thereby permanently excluding a section of the citizenry. Thus disputes arose which then led to the imposition of further limitations on the collectivity's jurisdiction, to a different composition of the council or frequently . . . to the emergence of a second communal committee distinct from the council. This led to the creation of a narrower and a broader council.[4] These were in fact simply two parts of the civic agency and so they only represented the town itself when they came together as the 'common council [*Rath gemeiniglich*]', in which case the first was regarded as the authority [*Obrigkeit*] and the second more as a representative body. In one sense such a creation was not new, for (as we have seen) the first council in those towns which were originally governed by a board of lay assessors owed its emergence to a similar process . . . A true outer [sc. broader] council was formed, for example, by the twenty-four new jurors [*conjurati*] elected by the community of citizens in Freiburg in 1248 after a successful uprising against the twenty-four old *conjurati*, who were said to have governed the town arbitrarily and without consulting the citizens. The old twenty-four were not supposed to take any administrative measures without consulting the new twenty-four. On the other hand, jurisdiction remained with the old twenty-four; but, when one of the new board criticised a judgment, the community itself was to act as a tribunal . . . In a similar way the council in [315] Zürich and other cities added to its numbers for important business by means of a committee of citizens which it chose . . . In most cities, however, the broader council resulted from an extension of the full-citizen community to include craftsmen [*Handwerker*]: a specific board of craftsmen was set up which the council had to consult on certain matters, as at Basel, Worms and elsewhere. Alternatively, the council might for more important matters add to its number the members of the outgoing council or its predecessor, so that the whole council consisted of two or three colleges (as at Speier and Lübeck). Richest in this respect, as in all others, was the history of the constitution at Cologne, where not only did a dynastic, narrowly based council exist alongside a broader council consisting of representatives of the fellowship of citizens – that is the wider community – but, in addition, all those who had sat in one of the councils during the last ten years would be called for in specific cases; so that [316] the agency of the town was sometimes formed by the narrowly based council alone, sometimes by the narrowly based one with the broader one, sometimes by the narrowly based one with its former members, sometimes by the resultant narrow council with the broad one, and sometimes by all councils (i.e. the narrowly based, the broad and the former members of both); while for the imposition of completely new taxes all burgesses had to be consulted in addition to these.

Most of the bigger towns had a similar division of the council into several colleges. In a sense, some of the constitutions which emerged in this way can be regarded as representing the transition to our present system of the separation of the council and the city representatives,[5] except that the authoritative character of one board and the representative nature of the other did not emerge as distinctly as today. Rather, even in the cases of the clearest division, each of the councils was both authority and representative of the community (although also of various ranks and classes amongst them). Further, the assembly of all citizens might be preserved even alongside an extended council as the highest authority, even if it was only called on in supremely important cases which affected the rights and interests of each individual.

But, even if we disregard these duplications, there was often an extremely large number of municipal authorities and officials in addition to the council and its leaders. These became increasingly numerous as the towns acquired more offices of lordship (or made such offices dependent on it), and as the mechanism of administration became more complicated. Courts, judges and special boards of lay assessors emerged alongside the council. Special authorities or offices came into being for all branches of administration, for policy [*Polizei*] relating to the market, trade, security and aliens, for the municipal economy, for the chancellery and ambassadors, for legal representation, for municipal buildings and other civic work, for the lands belonging to the town and for military [317] affairs and fortifications. Instead of being exercised by enfeoffed tenure, the revenue prerogatives acquired by the town were now exercised by municipal officials, customs officers, coiners and the like. Indeed, with increasing centralisation, both the leaders of once quasi-independent neighbouring communities and officials of individual gilds and corporations, sank to the level of civil servants. But all these new offices, whether now run by conciliar committees or delegated to individuals, became increasingly dependent on the council, and were in its gift and managed under its supervision. None of them represented an independent and all-embracing agency of the civic community; all had power of attorney for specific purposes only, and in a sense were offices of the council first and only indirectly offices of the town. Only the office of mayor, with time, attained a more independent status, by elevating itself to the position of being a true communal agency with independent rights to govern alongside the council. It thereby incorporated the idea of unity more clearly than the council; thus it was no longer the council alone but the mayor and council combined, that were necessary for the full representation of the town . . . The nature of the composition of the civic agency was the main battlefield on which were brought about the constitutional changes sought by factions and it was here that the individual peculiarities of each town could find expression.

Here we encounter a truly inexhaustible variety of combinations. The number of mayors and of councillors and the lengths of their terms of office were different everywhere. The only proviso was that the council must consist of several members, while the office of mayor could also be held by one individual. Periodic (usually annual) change of offices was regarded as the norm, whether all offices were changed simultaneously or not. At the same time one could also find councillors and mayors appointed for life . . .

[319] In cases of elections by the citizens, there arose the further question of who could participate in the election and to what extent; whether candidates should be taken from among the citizens as individuals or from the civic corporations (parishes or trade gilds) . . . It was often prescribed that a specific number of those elected should be taken from different classes or corporations. Finally the mayors often had to belong to special classes and were elected in the most diverse ways.

But, despite the frequent alterations made in these areas as a result of factional tendencies, the existence of the council as the real agency of the town was never in dispute, and there was never an attempt to transfer the centre of power back to the general assembly of citizens, or to elevate one individual. This is a not insignificant difference between the constitutional struggles in our German towns and those of antiquity and of medieval Italy.

The division of the population of the town into full citizens and citizens with protective rights only[6] was also never in dispute. It could not be disputed because monasteries, religious orders, Jewish communities, [320] visitors, citizens of other towns, journeymen, servants, dependants etc., always formed a circle of denizens who did not take an active part in the government of the town. But the subject of the most violent conflicts of all was how far the rights of full citizenship should extend.

In time the existing community of full citizens became more or less aristocratic in character. Where it was formed from among the ranks of the knights and burgesses (as in the ancient episcopal and royal towns), the chivalric element [*das ritterliche Element*] either melted into the more numerous and powerful burgesses or, after a long struggle, had to take leave of town life. But the newly emerging community of burgesses was not purely bourgeois, even on the basis of their occupation and patterns of ownership. Rather it formed a partial intermediary between the old and the new epoch, by being active in municipal trade and business (in so far as these were not seen as crafts – they could be called merchant trading and wholesale manufacture). At the same time the chivalric element also possessed extensive real estate inside and outside the town, and always invested their profit in real estate, thus maintaining free and genuine possession of land as a necessary prerequisite for full citizenship within the town constitution. And, even where neither an estate of knights nor an old-established citizenry existed such as in those towns constructed from the start as trading centres (e.g. Lübeck, Freiburg, Hamburg), a quite similar community of full citizens grew up in time from among the land-owning merchants.[7]

To the same extent, therefore, to which a purely mercantile estate blossomed forth from the emancipation of [321] movable capital from real estate, and a free estate of artisans from the emancipation of manual craft proper from serfdom, alongside that community of full citizens the majority of the population excluded therefrom were bound to perceive themselves as *part of the citizenry*, and the lordship of the full citizens as an aristocracy. In the patrician community [*Altbürgergemeinde*], the earlier consciousness of being the bearers of civic development changed into the class consciousness [*Standesbewusstsein*] of a privileged group [*Klasse*]. They no longer felt themselves to be, or called themselves, simply citizens, but lords of the town. The earlier power to assimilate others into their full freedom was transformed into exclusivity, which revealed itself all the more brusquely and nervously, the more their exclusive overlordship became an internal injustice and was therefore disputed. In short, the oldest citizens became patricians unnoticed and created a new hereditary estate and even described themselves, in accordance with this newest characteristic, as dynasts [*Geschlechter*].

The community of patricians chose, as an external means of guaranteeing their privileges, the form which dominated the entire era: union. Where they had been united in protection gilds since time immemorial, they simply closed ranks against new elements which were pressing forward; they were the first to become a pure aristocracy. This was the case at Cologne when, as early as the twelfth century, the *Richerzeche* and the fraternity of lay assessors merged as strictly aristocratic corporations controlling the town government. But in other cities too, sooner or later, one or several patrician gilds emerged, in all probability in opposition to the trade gilds; and the patricians attempted to assert their lordship and class privilege through them.

But the classes excluded from full citizenship were no less conscious of the power which lay in association. After they had been released from the bonds of serfdom, they too attempted to achieve prosperity, political and economic independence, and finally lordship, by means of union. Everywhere they were grouped in closed associations as gilds and corporations, whose rise the patricians tried in vain to prevent. The gilds were in violent and hostile [322] opposition to the patricians, only slightly moderated by the frequent presence of intermediate classes from the ranks of the merchants or higher tradesmen, of whom some but not all were entitled to the rights of full citizenship.

The first thing that the craft gilds had to win was their corporate independence, the abolition of the tutelage which for all practical purposes the dynasts had imposed on them, and the dissolution of the conditions of direct dependence which the lordship association threatened to introduce into the civic fellowship, particularly in the form of widespread client status. Their efforts were largely successful in all these respects.

But the artisans could not leave it at this. The more the idea of a civic community – the concept of the state in miniature – permeated all classes, the more the notion, unknown till then, of the correspondence between the rights and duties of a citizen was bound to be aroused. The artisans were obliged to serve the city with their money and their blood in the same way as the full citizens; from this they deduced the right to question, as did [323] the burgesses, what should be meant by 'the profit, honour and gain of the town', and the right to work, like the burgesses, for the common good – that is to govern. Above all they could demand participation in ensuring that the taxes to which they contributed were used in the interests of the generality and not of individuals, that the rights afforded by the town were shared equally by all, and that the possessions of the town were used for the good of all[8] . . .

A conflict, therefore, could not fail to break out in all the larger and more ancient cities, a conflict which was conducted on occasion in the most bloody and violent [324] manner, and sometimes ran its course in silence. Conflict was only altogether absent in cities founded quite recently, where from the outset the artisans were members of the citizenry. The premature stirrings of the thirteenth or even twelfth centuries ran their course largely without success, chiefly because the artisans were at that time unable to rely upon their own strength, but either were used by town lords quarrelling with the civic community as tools for their own ends, or else took advantage of partisan factionalism within the community of full burgesses. But in most towns in the fourteenth century the artisans gained victory by unifying their own forces, which, in harmony with the spirit of the age, took the extreme form of a confederacy of all craft gilds.[9]

Almost everywhere [325], either at one go or in various stages, they achieved constitutional changes favourable to themselves. These took very diverse and often changing forms: sixteen different constitutions, for example, have survived from Strasbourg for the period 1334–1482. Sometimes the craft gilds at first achieved participation only in less important offices; sometimes they never achieved even this. But generally they won participation in the council itself, either by being entitled to participate actively and passively in council elections (so that craft-gild members entered the old council); or alternatively through committees of their own trade gild – sometimes consisting only of master craftsmen or their deputies – emerging as a particular bench in the council or as a separate board alongside the old council. The craft gilds also usually won influence in making appointments to the office of mayor. [326] In many towns, this resulted in a veritable gild constitution [*Zunftverfassung*], each citizen being required to join a craft gild with the old patrician gilds being reduced to the same level. At this point, the town was no longer divisible into citizens but rather represented a union of unions, a confederation of fellowships. In the process, the trade gilds themselves were of course bound to change in their nature and became purely political institutions, their trade functions being carried on by other associations, now called corporations [*Innungen**].

The gild movement was victorious almost everywhere. Even if there were towns in which it was unable to break down the aristocratic method of government, or was obliged to allow old-established families to retain significant political privileges, [327] there was one unalterable result: the creation of a uniform *burgher class* [*Bürgerstand*] throughout Germany, no longer based on landownership, and of *unitary burgher-fellowships* in each town. If there were still grades of political rights, if the hereditary citizens or those from old lineages, or again members of certain corporations, still enjoyed certain privileges, the artisans had won entry for ever into the community of full burghers to which the city's legal claims belonged. Class segmentation had given way to equal status [*Standesgleichheit*] within the new free bourgeois class [*Bürgerstand*]. If former knights and patricians were unwilling to recognise the expansion of the burgher community . . . , they were obliged to turn their back altogether on town life and take refuge in the country, where the continued existence of class differences afforded them the privilege of nobility.

With the craft-gild movement, the development of the town on the basis of fellowship and the perfection of the new concepts of law and justice were complete. A large fellowship of citizens, bound by the same law and the same duty, both a community and a sworn union based on the free agreement of all members, thus reproducing in rejuvenated form the most ancient Germanic ideas, had taken possession of the town. What had only been dimly recognised in the oldest fellowship – unity in plurality, *the common life* living in all yet standing above all – here achieved full consciousness [*klares Bewusstsein*].

More and more was this thought realised in individual instances. But above all it had to bring about a totally changed concept of the relation of individual to collectivity, a changed basis for the rights and duties of fellowship. The highest expression which it achieved in this respect was the correspondence, or rather unity, of Right and duty. [328] Civil Right [*Bürgerrecht*] was no longer one-sidedly hereditary or based on particular claims; it was the consequence of duty fulfilled in the interest of the common life. Conversely this was no one-sided obligation derived from servitude . . . , but the living expression of belonging to a greater whole. Since equal rights [*Recht*] derived from equal duties, equal rights should entail equal duties; there should no longer be any exemptions for privileged ranks [*Stände*] of society.

Community life made demands on the individual principally in two ways: in respect of his person and of his property. With his person the citizen was obliged to serve his town on demand as an official; in the towns the *obligation* to accept office became a rule. Above all, in times of emergency the citizen was obliged to participate in the military levy, and even in peacetime to carry out guard-duty and keep weapons at the ready. The existence and maintenance of weapons was subject to inspection. In this way the oldest principle of the German popular fellowship – universal conscription – reasserted itself once again; as the people and the army had once been identical concepts, so now the citizenry entered battle under the town banner as the civic army, organised at first by neighbourhoods, later by trade gilds. Once again the collectivity of fellows was at the same time the army . . .

The citizen was no less obliged to serve the town with his property. For the sake of the common utility of the town . . . , he was obliged like all the others to bear the common burdens of the citizens . . . . Those who, like the knights of Basel, [329] were unwilling to submit to the common system of taxation, forfeited their civil rights and had to leave the town . . .

[330] However much the community of full burgesses might expand and constitute itself as a fellowship with equal rights and obligations, it was always a narrower concept than the community of the city [*Stadt-gemeinde*]. The vast majority of inhabitants took only a passive, not an active, part in the protection and rights of the city fellowship; either because they lacked independence (such as women, minors, journeymen, apprentices, servants etc., who were fellows only by virtue of the burgess who represented them), or because only part of their legal sphere belonged to the citizens' circle (such as strangers who were only temporarily residing in the town, visitors passing through, all kinds of citizens away from home, subjects of the city, Jewish communities, monastic and chivalric orders and the numerous religious and clerics). All these quite dissimilar classes of inhabitant, or associates, are united at one point: they enjoy the civic protection and – at least in particular respects – civil Rights, and they are

protected fellows of the burgher community. It was natural that, as the notion of the correspondence between Right and duty developed, the city should demand the same of them too. Participation in the civic protective association must correspond to a participation in civic burdens. For helpers, [331] confederates, servants and mercenaries, the provision of protection and the act of service performed for it were both already connected by way of a contract. The individual citizen fulfilled . . . civic duties on behalf of the dependants he represented. For example, each one had to pay duty on his wife's or children's estate . . . [as their guardian]. Visitors who wanted to settle permanently were frequently required to acquire citizenship. After towns acquired rights to tax Jews, Jewish communities were taxed in proportion to the degree of protection afforded to them. But violent conflicts usually flared up over the tax liability of monasteries and clergy . . . The history of nearly all towns is full of disputes and compromises with bishops and clergy over [such matters], during which the cities always clung to the principle that a share in the city's rights must always correspond to a share in civic burdens . . . For their intention was [332] that there should be but one set of rights [*Recht*] and one set of duties [*Pflicht*] in town territory, the rights and duties of the comradely [*genossenschaftlich*] common life of the city . . .

The organisation of the citizenry into separate communities

While the town in its overall institutions was in increasingly pure form perfecting the principle of a truly political common life, within its citizenry it permitted extremely rich and independent comradely activity. This represented the main point of difference between the community of a German town and the Greek *polis* or the Roman *civitas* . . . However important the limitations imposed on the smaller associations through the concentration of governmental power, their inherent central vitality was little affected . . . Just as cities did not absorb the personality of the individual citizens, so they also left an independent individual sphere of rights to the narrower fellowship. If the civic corporations proper were sections of the citizenry and essential members of the city's constitution, they also had a specific small common life whose basis of existence lay not in the will of the state but in the circle of associates . . .

[Gierke here discusses urban neighbourhoods [*quartieri*], Jewish communities and other groups. He then looks at aristocratic gilds (chapter 36) and merchant gilds (chapter 37), before turning to the golden age of the craft gilds.]

Chapter V

The golden age of the craft gilds [38]

The fellowships of the artisans: the system of the free craft gilds

[358] Although the artisans, the great mass of whom only slowly rose from serfdom to freedom, were the last to be affected by the idea of union, it was with them that the might of the new principle revealed itself most magnificently. Prosperity and prestige, education and inner strength, bourgeois virtues and finally lordship in the towns – all these were won by means of free comradely unification, by the organisation of the craft gilds. In the course of the centuries the craft gilds, while still maintaining their external forms, changed in their essence more than any other institution. Mention of their name today conjures up mainly their pitiful remnants in the present, their degradation and decline in the seventeenth and eighteenth centuries when they, like almost all corporations [359] left over from a greater past, served only a hidebound desire for privilege, the meanest spirit of monopoly and the most ossified self-seeking. Yet this must not make us forget that those craft gilds which were flourishing at the time of medieval civic freedom differed from this later caricature in almost everything but form and name. They produced a magnificent collective organisation for industrial labour, such as the world has never seen before or since, which brought recognition for the first time in history to *the rights and honour of labour*.

The basis of this organisation was freedom. The free labour of this time was of course not the arbitrary employment brought by free competition in its unrestrained form. Where earlier the rule of overlords, and later monopoly, had had a limiting effect, the only limits now were the self-imposed constitution of the fellowship and the interests of the collective body. The system of free craft gilds is therefore in its very essence distinct from the two phases of labour between which it stands in history: the

46

unfree economy of compulsory labour with its seignorial functions (which only began, through its court corporations, to pave the way for the transition to artisan independence), and the privileged labour of the exclusive private-law corporations (which treated the right to trade as a well-established property right). Echoes of seignorial law reach down beyond the end of the Middle Ages; traces of its incipient transformation along the lines of the later understanding of labour extend back into the fourteenth century. Only in its basic characteristics can the craft-gild system of the thirteenth to the early sixteenth century be presented as a collective phenomenon diametrically opposed both to its predecessors and to later developments.

In terms of their basic nature, the free craft gilds were unions or gilds of tradesmen related by their common profession – not just the skilled craftsmen and manual labourers themselves but also shopkeepers and vendors who did not count as merchants . . .

Therefore the craft gild was an association based on a union which was entered into freely, a freely chosen fellowship which, like other gilds, encompassed the whole person as today only family and state do, and united all its members as brothers. It was, and called itself, a brotherhood (*fraternitas, confraternitas*), a fellowship or society (*consortium, societas, solidatum, convivium*), a sworn union (*unio, conjuratio*) or corporation (*Gilde, Zeche, Gaffel, Zunft*):[1] names which all point to the *free will of the associates* [360] as the basis of their existence. While in the corporations under seignorial law the will of the lord, and in the privileged craft gilds the common monopoly, was the ultimate basis of the institution, in the free craft gilds the idea of union was, and always remained, the basis of the fellowship. It was confidently proclaimed that for the individual fellow his own will was the reason for his submission to the law of the craft gild and its court. Desire to be part of the union was not motivated by the specific aims of the company but by the community itself, so that the craft gild did not exist either exclusively or chiefly for the purposes of trade. However, although the craft gild was of the most direct political, military, social, religious and moral significance, and of significance for the legal concept of fellowship, it saw the trades of its members, which were normally similar, as one of the main objects of its attention. Yet this remained one of many consequences of the unification of the comrades; the union of comrades was not, as it later became, the result of the common right to ply a trade. The right to ply a trade was still a means to an end for the craft gild; the gild was not the means of acquiring the right to ply a trade.[2]

Another important aspect of the craft-gild system was that usually, though not necessarily, the practice of a particular craft or trade was incumbent on such voluntary unions as their collective duty and was available to them as their collective right. But this collective right did not originally have any of the characteristics we attribute to *private law*, but rather related to *public law*. It was and was called a *public office* [*Amt*]. The fellowship itself was called . . . an 'office' (*ammet, officium, hantwerk* or *gewerk, opus*), and also a fief, since the conferment of the office was often seen as a feudal transaction. [361] At the time of civic freedom, this office, in which the concept of *duty* came *before that of rights*, was a duty to the community, a civic duty, public in nature: in this way it differed from the patrimonial service of the court artisan as much as from the later private-law trade monopoly. The office as such had no assets in the civic community. What the gild member acquired through his craft were the fruits of his labour, not the fruits of an exclusive right. Very important consequences followed from this.

Above all, *compulsory gild membership* [*Zunftzwang*], which necessarily followed from the concept of an 'office', was bound to have quite a different meaning from the one it had later. Its content was originally only that the trade gilds were granted the right to compel everyone who acquired the relevant craft 'office' (or trade right) to enter the fellowship; the actual enforcement of this compulsion remained in part with the civic authorities and fell in part to the trade 'offices' themselves. Later, since the decision whether or not to admit someone fell to the gild, compulsory gild membership was greatly extended so that with it the conferment of the office itself came to be within the authority of the gild, or at least of the gild in co-operation with the city lord or council. [362] But the original conception was still not altered. The craft gild only demanded the right of compulsory membership because *the honour of the craft and overall excellence* could only be guaranteed, and the supervision of work and the trade and the control of discipline could only be carried out, when the fellowship contained all the craftsmen belonging to an office. Therefore the aim of this endeavour was not the exclusion of outsiders from the profits of the trade, but the subjection of the entire trade to the craft gild. If a selfish motive crept in, it was certainly not self-interest and fear of competition, but rather ambition for power. The aim was still to elevate the *fellowship* rather than the *fellows* . . .

The craft gild as a component [Glied] of the city

[371] The position of the gilds as voluntary associations, whose duty it was to practise a trade as an official office within the civic communities, resulted in an ambivalent relationship with the town or its overlord. On the one hand they were part of, and agencies of, the town; on the other they were independent fellowships with a self-contained sphere of rights in private and public law . . .

[372] As an agency and member of the state, the gild was subordinated to the collectivity above all in matters of trade . . . It did not exercise the supervisory [*polizeilich*] and judicial powers associated with its office in its own name, but in the name of the town. Beyond this it was usually an elective body within the town; its leaders or deputies were not simply representatives of their corporation on the municipal boards, but helped to represent the entire citizenry. Even where there was no gild constitution, it also had to fulfil political functions. It played an important part in the fiscal constitution of the town. The gilds formed their own divisions in the citizen army. These were assembled and led by their masters, fought under the banner of the gild and in peacetime kept in readiness weapons which were checked by the elders under the overall supervision of the council. Thus in every respect the gild officials were also officials of the town . . . [373] In places where a true gild constitution had been introduced, the political and military importance of the gilds increased to such an extent that the town appeared almost as a federation of separate communities [*Gemeinwesen*], and the gilds as local communes within the commune.

On the other hand the gild was a body existing in its own right; although its sphere of rights and influence was limited by the opposing rights of the civic overlord and the town, it was none the less independent. As a free fellowship it had all the rights in corporate matters which were appropriate to a fellowship under German law . . .

In relation to the civic overlord and his officials, or alternatively to the town and its representative council (or its committees and bodies concerned with trade), the ambivalent position of the gilds resulted in a mixture of freedom and dependence. The extent of its independence . . . was affected partly by the more or less free status of the town itself, partly by the status of tradesmen within the citizenry. While the gild movement produced extensive corporate independence for its members almost everywhere, any continued existence of an aristocratic mode of government militated against it in the most extreme manner. In spite of this diversity, the restrictions on corporate rights . . . [under] the free gilds, can be characterised as emerging from one principle, as different from the notion on which earlier restrictions were based as from the principle of later law, which was also hostile to corporations.

At the time of seignorial law, the restrictions on the autonomy of corporations [374] were derived from the real or personal rights of lordship . . . From the end of the Middle Ages, when, with the infiltration of the idea of sovereignty [*Obrigkeit*] and the Roman theory of corporations, corporate independence was once more reduced or breached and often suppressed . . . the basis of the new restrictions was the spirit of sovereignty and paternalistic [*polizeilich*] concern. In the intervening period of free craft gilds, the restrictions . . . were based on the quite different idea of mediation between the independent rights of the craft gild as a free fellowship and the higher rights of the unitary common life of the town. There was no attempt either to transform the gilds into municipal institutions or to isolate them completely, but rather to strike a balance between self-administration and the right of supervision – between corporate freedom and civic unity.

Let us look at this in detail. With regard to the establishment of individual gilds, the principle was maintained that the voluntary union of the members was sufficient to bring about a fellowship group [*Genossenverband*]. According to German notions, freedom and the right to association had always gone together. But, in order that the union should not remain a self-willed association but should rather be a craft gild with the commercial and administrative powers due to it under the civic constitution, the authorisation of the council or . . . civic overlord had also to be forthcoming . . . [375] On the whole, the principle that the union itself was a matter of free will, and that only the conferment of specific corporate trade rights was a matter for the authorities, was upheld. This was still far removed from regarding the will of the town as the actual basis of the existence of a free gild. That idea only began to prevail with the help of Roman law from the sixteenth century onwards, when the council became sovereign [*Obrigkeit*] and the citizens subjects [*Untertanen*].

The question of legal authority for abolishing a gild can be answered in the same way. We can be sure that such an event presupposed a legal proceeding in front of the competent court, and proof of a misuse of official privileges or some other misdemeanour. However, in extraordinary cases, such as after unrest and reaction, all a town's gilds were often abolished by *dictat* of the emperor, prince or city council [376] without any actual sentence being passed, and in this event the gild seal, symbol of corporate independence, would be broken and the gild charters destroyed.

When complete freedom did not exist, the gilds had patricians or functionaries imposed on them from outside as overseers . . . In Cologne patrician superintendents remained alongside the masters of the trade chosen by the gilds until the end of the fourteenth century. They were imposed on the gilds by the *Richerzeche* as a kind of official guardian. But gradually it came to be an established right everywhere that the leadership of the gild was chosen from among its members. The power to nominate or at least authorise the elders or masters still remained, none the less, frequently with the council or city overlord. On the other hand, [377] where gild freedom had developed to its fullest extent the gild had an uncontested right to choose its leadership from its own members and to determine its own organisation in all matters.

A similar procedure obtained with the gilds' right to free assembly. During periods of full gild freedom this was usually recognised without any restrictions, but where the gilds had come to form the government, as for example in the Hansa towns and the territorial towns in the north, it was linked to the approval of the council . . . [378] In political and military affairs the gilds were of course subordinate to the general supervision of the council and the civic authorities in all respects. Significant limitations on corporate independence in matters of trade were not only the consequence of the fact that communities of citizens had, early on, acquired jurisdiction in matters of business and trade, but also of the nature of trade as a public service . . . The gilds were also inhibited by trade legislation, which at an early stage imposed general regulations in opposition to gild practices; and, finally, by the regulations controlling trade and markets which exerted their influence at an early stage by the imposition of fixed prices, the supervision of trade, regulations concerning labour and guarantees against counterfeiting and deception. In all these matters, it was active co-operation, the balancing and complementing of the activities of the [town] authority and the corporations, that enabled the Middle Ages to avoid the rigidity of later times, and to provide equally for the interests of producers and consumers . . .

[380] The relationship between corporate [*genossenschaftlichen*] autonomy and the legislative power of the city authority, between the law imposed on the gild and the law chosen by the gild [*gegebenen . . . gekorenen Recht*] had to be regulated by the same principles. Since free gilds had replaced corporations based on seignorial Law, corporate custom and statute was recognised within certain limitations as the source of law. In matters of trade in particular, on the other hand, the authority of the [city] council unilaterally to issue regulations which interfered with

corporate Right in important respects, was undisputed. The total *Recht* of a gild in all its respects was thus a combination of the *Recht* it formulated itself and that which was imposed on it; it was developed as much by custom and arbitrary decree as by laws and statutes. The craft statutes as a whole had to be confirmed by city council or overlord, not least because their validity was not [381] restricted to the sphere of the fellowship but affected the public and private Right of the whole citizenry. But the true source, even of gild law which was approved by the authorities, was *voluntary corporate agreement*, even where the ruler's Right was particularly strong (as for example in Lübeck) . . . Even where the council was granted the power to alter or abolish statutes at will, the sovereign ordinances of the council were nevertheless basically restricted to sanctioning the Right created by the fellowship. But, according to the point of view determining this form of co-operation between town and fellowship, the respective benefits of trade and town should be jointly pursued and balanced against each other, the interests of fellow-craftsmen and of the community being equally represented.

Since the gild was an independent fellowship, possessing not only its own capital but also its own independent system of public law, and since, as was manifest in the bearing of a special gild seal, it formed a self-contained legal entity, it could will and act as an entity – or, in modern usage, as a juristic person; it could enter into contracts and arrangements of all kinds both with individuals and with other gilds. It could also bring actions against them; indeed it could bring action against the town itself, or agree terms with it, in spite of being a constituent part of the town . . . Although the town safeguarded the interests of all its members externally and could therefore act in the name of one of the individual gilds, the gilds too were empowered to enter into associations and agreements in matters of trade with similar gilds of other towns . . .

The craft gild was an independent entity with regard to its own members as well as the outside world, and had rights and obligations *vis-à-vis* individual members. This can be seen primarily by the diversity of its aims. For, since it united its members for all purposes that human groups have in common, it was for them a community [*Gemeinwesen*] in miniature. The honour, influence and reputation of the fellowship could be equally potent motivating forces for the individual as the honour, power and standing of the town were to the citizen.

[384] In its political and military aspects, the craft gild was for its members first of all a scaled-down representation of the town. Through the gild, they were enabled to take part in the government of the town and

in municipal duties and obligations. Any of the public affairs of the town, as well as those of the trade, might be discussed at the craft-gild assemblies. Taxes and dues were paid through the gild; a close brotherhood in arms united the fellows. Despite all the constitutional wrangles and disputes in the town, we hear little of discord within the gild; the gilds entered the lists almost as one man.

This aspect of the gild's role became most significant where an actual gild constitution was introduced. But it was where this happened that the political and trade aspects of the gild frequently became separate, as in the course of time the community of profession and trade disappeared . . . Because membership of a gild was the sole guarantee of a role in the town government, and even the corporations of those who were not engaged in trade were made into gilds, those who were not craftsmen joined gilds, and craftsmen belonging to another trade joined the gilds which had originally only had members who plied the same trade. As trades multiplied and new branches of an art or manual craft emerged, these gilds were not then modified, so they often united different types of profession which had little in common. On the other hand, a need existed, as it always had, for a closer union among craftsmen of the same type . . . Thus trade corporations gradually emerged, which were no longer or incompletely identical with the political and military craft gilds . . . Some [fellowships] tended to pursue the public aspect of the old gild system, while others, since they were exclusively oriented towards trade, increasingly took on the character of private corporations . . .

[386] Closely connected with the importance the gild had in religion was its social [*gesellige*] significance. Wine and beer played an important part in both entrance fees and fines; the provision of a meal for the gild was a necessary condition of gaining full rights of membership; the order of ceremonies, social decorum and good manners at the festive gathering of the fellows and their wives, were the subject of gild statutes. A series of prescribed customs was set up, clothing both daily life in the gild workshops and inns, and the individual ceremonies of the fellowship, in appropriate forms; only later did these degenerate into formal, compulsory ceremonies. Even the social-artistic school of the Mastersingers, which in many respects extended gild organisation into the art of poetry, emerged out of an extension of a community of the craft brothers.

[387] The gild was also a moral [*sittlich*] association: it was able to imbue the moral significance it derived from its position mid-way between the family and the state with a legal form. It did this especially in two ways: it made practical fraternal love the duty of its fellows in relation to one

another, and it exercised control over the members' conduct. In the first respect, brother office-bearers were enjoined to bear love and sorrow with one another. They were to be united by close friendship, so that each new master had to put aside all disputes with any fellow before entering the gild. They were to support each other at all times of need, and after the death of a brother to pay his body their last respects. They were to give financial support to impoverished or sick brothers from the gild coffers, and provide the dead with an honourable burial and care for his soul. Thus gild funds were also insurance funds for the sick, poor and deceased . . . For journeymen and apprentices, idleness, absences from their master's house overnight, drinking, gaming and debauchery were forbidden on pain of punishment. [388] As *economic fellowships* the gilds transferred the principle of a moral fellowship into the sphere of commerce. They presented themselves as producers' co-operatives [*Produktivgenossenschaften*][3] in which, in contrast to today's forms of collective production, gain was only the means to the end, but the end in itself was personality. This led to moral endeavour in order to fulfil the office incumbent on the gild as loyally and as dutifully as possible; and, on the other hand, to a ban on free competition, and the application of the opposing principles of fraternity and equality among fellows. This protected the rights of personality rather than those of ownership – in economic terms, the rights of labour as against the rights of capital.

With regard to the first of these points, the organisation of the craft gild was based on concordance between what was *best for the collectivity* and *the honour of trade*. By caring for the interests of the consumers by means of internal controls on standards, control of morals and self-restraint, they at the same time promoted both the common good and the honour of their own work, and so brought about a felicitous harmony between the opposing interests. This was of course possible only as long as the sense of community prevailed over egotism, and love of honour over desire for profit . . .

[390] Respecting the relations of fellows to each other, gild organisation was based on the perception that the duties and rights of labour belonged to the fellowship: each fellow as a member of this community was, by virtue of his personality, equally committed to the work and equally entitled to a share in the fruits of labour. The notion of *duty* was always in the foreground. The office was incumbent on the collectivity as a personal duty, each member being obliged to undertake his share of the work and do it *in person*. An attempt was made to keep the honour of

labour, as an economic manifestation of personality, free from all taint. On one hand, where the danger existed that labour might degenerate into dependent wage-labour, this tendency was curbed by prohibitions on processing of material from outwith the gild. On the other hand, in gilds where there was a danger that individuals might accumulate disproportionately powerful amounts of capital, the evaluation of capital over labour [391] was prevented by restrictions on production exceeding the capacity of personal enterprise. Hence personal labour remained the decisive factor in production; and the essential capital – whether it was possessed by individuals, or (in the case of communal workshops, market-halls and tools) collectively – was at the service of labour.[4] From this it followed that, in the distribution of benefits and matters of individual Right, the exclusive consideration was personality and hence the unconditional equality of all fellows, which the gild saw as its main task to achieve, both in law and in fact. Working together on this basis presupposed the most rigorous implementation of the moral relationships of the fellows to each other, that is of brotherliness applied to matters of trade.

The inevitable outcome of this was a prohibition of free competition between fellows and in its stead severe limitations on the individual in favour of the collectivity in the field of production and distribution. The bonds which this imposed on the individual were first felt as such when the sentiment of the age, and circumstances, changed. At the height of the gild system, the community took the place of the individual: what he lost in the scope of his freedom as an individual – greater than average profits which would have enabled him to lead a pleasant and prosperous life – was not yet perceived as a need; while the age's lively sense of community [*Gemeinsinn*] still prevented the stronger brother from regarding the impossibility of oppressing the weaker as a hindrance. Of course, total production suffered under this system; but the individual product gained. The individual was prevented from developing that economic basis of power which today often makes him the equal of kings; but a comfortable prosperity for all raised the status of tradesmen as a whole to one of respectability, enlightenment and power. The refinement of craft into art [*des Handwerks zur Kunst*] which we so marvel at in the Middle Ages, the unrepeated heyday of the craftsmen's estate in the cities – these would have been inconceivable without the comradely organisation of labour and labour's social and material equality with the rights of ownership. In juristic terms, the particular limitations placed on individual enterprise [392] by the collectivity can be summed up in the notion that although each fellow had an equal share in the trading function to which the fellowship as a whole was entitled, he participated not in his own right but only as a member of the brotherhood . . .

[396] If, in economic terms, the gild was a labour fellowship which regarded its common trade as a public office and practised it according to principles of equality and fraternity, equally in terms of property rights it was not a society of capital (in which specific quotas of the common property would be allocated to individuals), but one in which movable and immovable collective assets belonged to the fellowship as such. The gild assets (consisting of the gildhall, gild inn, seal, banner and the common areas, workshops, tools and capital . . .) served therefore not only for genuinely communal purposes (such as business jurisdiction, cult, charity, poor relief, burial, expenses incurred in administration, payment of wages etc.), but were also used for the individual economic and ethical aims of the fellows. However, individuals held no private rights but were only authorised to use and profit from such assets as gild members . . . Each had an equal right to use the gild rooms for purposes of recreation, especially for family celebrations; the common trade establishments and tools were equally at the disposal of all; finally, the fellows had equal claims on the capital assets of the gild, from which not only financial assistance but also advances and loans to needy fellows were given. Thus the gild was not only constituted as an asylum for the poor, sick and widows, but was also a mutual credit society.

If, as we have seen, the gild was a political, military, religious and social, moral, economic and financial entity, the link which connected and gave a common character to all these diverse threads lay in the fact that it was an entity with its own peace and law, a *fellowship in Right* [*Rechtsgenossenschaft*]. It was the embodiment of a sphere of rights which encompassed all members and in certain respects even non-fellows. By means of custom and autonomy, precedent and voluntary contract [397] it built up the Right of the fellowship; this Right, confirmed and supplemented from above, was the totality of ordinances valid for the gild. It enjoyed a specific peace, the management, safeguarding and maintenance of which was its own responsibility. It protected its Right and its peace both internally and externally by means of the *gild court*, which was formed according to the principles of fellowship and invested with the authority of the fellowship. All disputes among fellows had to be brought before this gild court before they went to the ordinary judge; all decisions on matters relating to their trade – especially any breach of the peace of the fellowship, misdemeanours against the traditions and statutes relating to the craft office, and sometimes even minor cases of debt – belonged to the gild court. Finally, this was the agency by which the gild controlled morals and trade; it was therefore the court of first instance in many matters, even for outsiders. The most severe punishment which the gild [398] could impose . . . was total or temporary expulsion from the gild, which entailed loss of the craft office . . .

This fellowship, constituted both internally and externally as a single entity, was structured and organised in the same way as the other Germanic gilds. The real *representative* [*Trägerin*] of the entire Right of the fellowship, source of all peace and power, was the assembly of full members – those master craftsmen who were entitled to practise their trade independently. A man could only become a master craftsman by application and acceptance into membership of the fellowship . . . Conversely, by leaving or being expelled from the fellowship, he lost the right to call himself a master craftsman. The meetings of master craftsmen . . . were modelled on the . . . *Things* of the free community; like these they held supreme power, could enact laws and enter into voluntary contracts, had executive power [399] in matters pertaining to the craft office, could pass sentence in more important cases, and chose the leadership and the committees.

The *agency* [*Organ*] of the collectivity was the master craftsmen or elders . . . These gradually united the functions of a Germanic judge with those of a true agent of the gild, at once ruler and representative. It was their duty to convoke the assembly, at which they were chairmen and guaranteed the peace. They collected fines and dues. Either alone, with fellow officials or with a committee of their fellows, they judged civil and criminal cases. They had the duty and authority to ensure that the laws of the craft office were upheld . . . They administered gild capital, [400] carried out the control of morals and trade practices appropriate to the gild, in particular inspection and supervision. They presided over social gatherings, led the gild in war and were usually its representatives on the [town] council and other civic boards. In treaties and disputes they represented the corporation externally and to other fellows. In a word, they were the sworn and responsible government of the gild . . . As recompense for their efforts and the many honorary duties associated therewith, they enjoyed special pecuniary or business advantages and frequently drew a proportion of the fines and entrance fees.

Alongside the elders, in larger gilds there were committees or assessors;

their function was partly to be a board of jurors and partly to represent the collectivity over against the leaders and to keep a check on them.[5] . . .

[401] As with every German fellowship, in addition to the fellows with full rights a circle of fellows with rights to protection only belonged to the union; these only participated *passively* in the peace and Right of the corporation. First, there were the wives and children of the fellows. They naturally had no independent rights in the gild, but it is often expressly stated that they were its members, and this stands to reason in an association which stood mid-way between family and community. The protection of the gild extended to them too, just as they in turn were subject to the control and jurisdiction of the fellowship. They took part in religious services and festivities, and, although (apart from the head of the family) they had no independent rights to the trade, they were none the less closer than others by virtue of birth or marriage, with the result that the continuation of a trade by a widow and preferential treatment of sons and sons-in-law in learning the trade [402], and admission to full membership, appeared as only the natural consequence of the close community which embraced the whole household of all fellows. Indeed, the wife of a master craftsmen was regarded as such an important link in the fellowship that it was also demended of her that she should be worthy of holding office; a master craftsman who did not choose as his wife a women of stainless character and of legitimate German parentage was threatened with the loss of his rights in the fellowship. Occasionally, too, women, girls and girl apprentices with independent rights in the trade could be found among the master craftsmen, lads and apprentices; or even in special women's gilds under the leadership of elected mistresses . . .

[405] Finally, the fellowship, divided into full members and protected members and organised under the terms of its constitution, was both internally and externally in both public and private law a *collective personality* [*Gesammtpersönlichkeit*]. Just as, in the town, the community as such stood above inhabitants, with citizens and council as the supreme legal personality, so too the invisible entity living within the collectivity of the gild fellows – the craft gild as such – was elevated to the status of the actual subject of rights for which the visible [406] collectivity was merely the body and the gild officials merely the organs.

As has already been noted, in contrast to later attempts to keep corporations separate, the dominant impulse at work in all medieval fellowships was to unite themselves with similar groups to form a greater whole. This impulse brought towns together into city-leagues and city-leagues into unions with the associations [*Gesellschaften**] of other estates. It created larger joint hansas from the isolated merchant gilds and finally brought

about the basis for a universal German Hansa. The fellowships of craftsmen also endeavoured to create *bands of corporations* [*Innungsvereine*]
above the individual craft gilds. The different gilds of the same town were
united, sometimes temporarily and sometimes on a permanent basis, in a
more or less organised group. The object of this was to give weight to the
common commercial or political interests of the craftsman class. Beyond
this there were occasionally *local associations* of all the gilds in one area
or *Land*. More common were associations among similar craft gilds in a
number of neighbouring towns, or in towns with commercial links. Very
diverse in form and content, some were only contracts or arrangements
concerning single points (in particular similar treatment and disciplining
of journeymen), others were formal unions or alliances, others joint gilds
in the full sense. But such associations always [407] contained the first
beginnings of the establishment of universal trade regulations, which later
came exclusively from the sovereign.

The craft gilds' links with one another, based on tradition and established by custom, went even further than explicit treaties and formal
organisation. In particular, the custom (which later became the rule) that
journeymen should be *itinerant* produced a connection between all trade
fellowships of the same type, and in a sense between all members of trades,
encompassing the entire Empire. Just as the whole knightly estate perceived itself as one great body, just as the merchants of the Holy Roman
Empire regarded themselves as a joint gild, so too the craftsmen also liked
to think that each art and each branch of manufacture formed but a single
great fellowship throughout the entire German Empire; and, further, that
the fellowships of the individual trades were allied to each other . . . By
virtue of this idea, common practices were formed in the individual trades,
and in manual craft generally, throughout the whole of Germany. A
common German craft law developed. If, then, the German tradesman
found protection and acceptance in his gild . . . , had precisely defined
rights and duties with respect to it, and was already familiar with its
customs and habits, the significance of this national link for the maintenance and invigoration of German national consciousness should by no
means be underestimated. The real embodiments of this community were
of course much less the masters than the itinerant journeymen, and, after
separate gilds of journeymen came into existence alongside those of the
master craftsmen, it was these especially which entered into lively contact
with one another, producing an association of journeymen right across the
Empire, a common law for all journeymen, and similar attitudes and
customs . . .

[408] In one trade in particular, the coming together of the single gilds

found *formal* expression, even local fraternities taking second place to the joint fellowship: the stone-masons. They, like others, at first came together in fellowships in single towns and areas; but, from the beginning, the idea that all these fellowships in the whole German Empire formed but one great brotherhood was particularly active among their ranks. By means of an unwritten law, passed on by tradition and traced back in legend to the saints, this association gradually took on a definite form.

Its acknowledged head was the Strasbourg corporation; this was both the focal point of their assemblies and the source of their regulations. In the later Middle Ages, what had long existed as custom was written down; ten years after the completion of the tower on the Strasbourg Minster (1452), the formal and complete organisation of the joint association was established and codified by a collective decision at Strasbourg. All stone-masonries were divided into four chief corporations: Strasbourg, Cologne, Vienna and Zürich. The office of Grand Master of the entire fraternity devolved on whoever was Master of Works at the Strasbourg Minster . . . Under the Grand Lodge came the main lodges, and below these the circle and district lodges, and the executives of independent regional and circle associations; these had special courts and assemblies, and enacted their own specific regulations. The most close-knit independent fellowships however were formed by the individual corporations, which were established by the meeting of sworn German stone-masons [409] wherever a master stone-mason was in charge of a building . . . These had their own Right and each fraternity its own assets. Although all members of the fraternity were equal to one another, one could only be first admitted to the fraternity after one had duly learned the trade, completed the period of itinerant work, and undergone initiation with ceremonial rites into the secrets of building, and finally sworn an oath, backed by guarantors, to perform one's fraternal duties. Before this the pupil was only a member of the trade (stone-masonry), not of the brotherhood. Since the joint association regarded itself as the possessor of the art and of its technical rules, and only passed these on to brothers under an obligation to keep them secret, the significance of this great association of German stone-masons for the blossoming of German architecture in the Middle Ages was immense . . . It is more than probable that it was primarily the ideas and traditions of those German building craftsmen called to England which brought about the transformation of the fraternities of masons in that country into associations of Freemasons.[6]

[Gierke now discusses 'the influence of the union-system upon the family, especially among the nobility' (chapter 39), and 'spiritual fellowships' ('the church as such', the '*Zunft* of the clergy', orders of knights and beggars, brotherhoods and heretical groups; and 'the significance of the fellowship movement for the Reformation') (chapter 40); then scholarly communities, the universities with their faculties and colleges (chapter 41). He next turns to 'vocational fellowships and fellowships for particular purposes' (chapters 42–3).]

Chapter VI

Political unions, city leagues, the Hansa [44, 45]

The system of political union in general

[457] The system of political union carried the principle, which up until now we have only seen in effect [458] among the citizens of towns and within individual professional groups, beyond the city walls and past the confines of the estates, into *Land* and Empire. By producing, in increasingly wide circles, oath-bound groups, confederacies and alliances, which all exhibited a visible trend towards reconstructing the decaying Empire itself out of these elements as a great federal community, it reached the limits of what a popular movement in the Middle Ages, organised from below, was capable of achieving. The movement towards union never reached its final goal. But within its limits it produced important and far-reaching political structures and it was this movement the nation had to thank if, at the end of the period, something of the unity of the Empire had been saved and given new form. And if the system of union led only temporarily or in isolated cases to real state communities encompassing more than the citizenry of a town, none the less it played a very considerable, and too often unacknowledged, part in the creation of the modern territorial state [*Landesstaat*], which the idea of sovereignty, arising from the ruins of the old imperial structure, led on to victory . . .

The impulse for this movement, too, came from the towns. As early as the [late eleventh and early twelfth centuries] the Rhineland towns, emerging for the first time as a political power in the Empire, appear to have been allied in confederacies. In the further course of the twelfth century, as becomes evident from repeated prohibitions, such associations must have continued to exist, albeit secretly . . . We hear more specifically of German city associations from the beginning of the thirteenth century, when they were prohibited in Frederick II's edicts against cities. A special oath-bound fellowship is mentioned in King Henry's edict (1226) annulling the sworn alliance of the towns of Speyer, Worms, Mainz, Bingen, Frankfurt, Gelnhausen and Friedberg.

[459] With the decline of the Hohenstaufen dynasty, there could no longer be any question of such prohibitions. From now on, the Empire could not even claim to prevent its constituent parts from forming independent associations in order to achieve what the Empire itself could no longer provide. From that time, the countless societies, leagues and confederacies which established and defined the public law of the age began to come into being: at first between towns; then between towns, lords and knights; and soon afterwards between the lords as a group; the chivalric estate; clerics, and even the peasantry; and finally between the totality of all the estates. Their all-embracing significance only came to an end when they had fulfilled their mission and had created or helped to create more secure political structures.

The great multiplicity and variety of the political unions, their vacillation between treaties and fellowships, the transformations experienced, often by the same association, in the course of the centuries, all none the less bear witness to the common basis of union. Thus a number of principles can be established which are equally valid for all.

They all owe their origins exclusively to the free will of the associates. According to the perspective of German law, the free right of union was indivisible from the full freedom. Since the completion of the new structures of the estates, this could not be denied to the nobility, the chivalric estate and the estate of burghers. On the other hand, the other estates denied it to the dependent peasantry, who were deprived of the possibility of protecting themselves from, and representing themselves to, the outside world by the right of protection and representation held by their lord. In fact only a few groups of peasants on the coast or in the mountains, who had remained or become free, were able to take part successfully in the union movement.

... [460] As regards the members of the union, the old tenet, that comrades were equal, was bound to have idiosyncratic effects. Because each lasting political fellowship presupposed or established social and legal equality among full members, in the first instance it was primarily corporations and individuals similar to one another who united under oath. Towns allied themselves with towns, gilds with related gilds, craft gilds with craft gilds, monasteries with monasteries, princes with princes, knights with knights, prelates with prelates. But when, in addition to this, the various estates entered into lasting confederations one with another, and for the first time gave the political union its true value, this did not signify an abandonment of the old principle but that it was being further developed. For the members of these associations were no longer in-dividual citizens, nor was the citizenry united as the sum total of citizens . . . ; rather, towns, corporations and aristocracies were bound together as bearers of a specific lordship within the territory or Empire – as political power units [*Machteinheiten*]. As such they were, or (if we disregard other forms of inequality) became equal. In the case of the political union too, unequals could participate only as fellows with merely protective rights [*Schutzgenossen*]. The important change which this represented even became apparent in language, since it was precisely the term estate [*Stand*] (estate of the Empire, territorial estates) which was used for the individual units of political power. As political power units equal to one another, the estates were elements out of which the fellowship of the Empire or of the territorial estates [*Landschaft*] was constructed . . .

[461] In terms of content, all unions were agreed that they were estab-lishing a community based on peace, Right and common interest among associates; but the extent to which this happened varied greatly and the effects were very dissimilar, internally and externally. Internally, all aimed at the establishment of a communal peace, but sometimes this specific corporative peace [*Genossenfriede*] was only an incidental result of the associations and sometimes, as with leagues for the prevention of warfare, it was their main purpose. We encounter everywhere a community based on Right [*Rechtsgemeinschaft*], but this was only in some unions the actual subject of the contract, as for example in groups aimed at mutual legal protection [*Rechtsschutz*], in agreements which exempted the collective from debt and misdemeanours, or finally in the closest of legal alliances [*Rechtsbündnis*], which declared the civil law of the two cities to be common to both . . .

In the same way the unions' aims towards the outside world varied in extent: defence against, or vengeance for, a breach of the communal peace . . . ; the preservation, acquisition or augmentation of mutual rights or privileges in respect of politics, social standing or trades; the execution of joint undertakings in the sphere of politics or commerce, as for example the conquest and sharing out, or joint ownership, of provinces or castles, the acquisition of advantages in trade or the founding of trading settle-ments, the conduct of war, etc.

Accordingly the means used to realise the aims of the community were bound to be very diverse, and they manifest an incalculable wealth of transitional forms, from simple contractual agreements to fully formed federal organisations. The swearing of an oath or solemn vow was regularly used to strengthen the union. Fines and compensation in a case of breach of contract were almost always included. Further, the collectivity was conceded the right to use positive means to compel an individual to obey. Courts of arbitration or agreements defined in advance, from which there was no recourse, or only limited recourse, to the regular courts, brought the fellowship even closer. The individual often had a firm obligation to put mutual decisions and arbitrations into effect, to help comrades, to resist breaches of the peace; and for this purpose the setting up and provision of a specific contribution was demanded. The corporative character of the union became even more apparent when regular assemblies were required, permanent leadership and committees elected, the representation of the collectivity regulated, and resolutions taken regarding the form, content and binding power of future decisions. In respect of property rights, corresponding measures frequently comprised the levying of regular contributions, the building up and administration of joint assets, and the acquisition and use of mutual rights. Yet such unions, and even those which had a very extensive organisation, were not always formed on a permanent basis, but frequently within a specific time limit; they could be terminated on notice, tacitly or expressly prolonged, or merged into other unions. In this case it was difficult to say whether they continued the old association or founded a new one. A firm conclusion as to the legal and moral nature of the individual associations is made especially difficult by the fact that it frequently cannot be established whether the unifying agreements and contracts of the societies were constitutive acts or only a manifestation of the joint will of an already existing fellowship.

[463] If one considers the inexhaustible number of combinations which were not only possible but actually came about, regarding the variety of the origin, subject, purpose and organisation of the political union, the diversity of forms of the medieval system of alliances and associations in the sphere of public law can easily be conceived. What follows will describe, in terms of their legal and moral content, only the main forms in which political union produced lasting federal organisations based on fellowship, which went beyond a mere contract.

The city leagues

The city leagues were the first to make use of the principle of union in regard to political alliances; the other estates followed their lead . . .

They developed by two distinct routes: one, taken in the West and North, emphasised trade interests; the other, taken in the communities of Upper Germany, emphasised the relationship of the towns to the princes and the Empire.

Thus *the German Hansa*, the final product of the many ramifications of the union movement among the Low-German cities, had no direct connection with the Empire or any territorial state. Despite the political dependence of most of its members, as a collectivity this was a completely independent trading republic. This wonderful fellowship is not only generically unique in history, but provides the particular fascination of a completely singular phenomenon in constitutional history [*Rechtsgeschichte*].

Historically, the Hansa emerged from the fusion of two factors: the unification of mercantile gilds abroad, and the system of alliances among trading towns. It has already been demonstrated above how gilds of German merchants in England, Flanders, Scandinavia and Russia constituted themselves into collective groups [*Gesammtvereine*] at an early stage. Because all Germans living in the relevant country belonged to these collective hansas people soon became used to regarding German merchants trading in the north *collectively* [*insgesammt*] as a single legal and moral entity. Together, they were designated as the 'Common Merchant of the [464] Roman Empire of Alamannia', by which was meant not a mere aggregation [*Kollektivum*] but a collective Rights-subject [*Gesammtrechtssubjekt*][1] – a great fellowship manifested in the gilds at home and abroad only as in its members, which obtained and exercised rights and privileges in its own right [*als solche*]. This collectivity of merchants was increasingly called by the name borrowed from the individual gilds, the *hansa Teutonicorum* or German Hansa.

Independently of this, from the beginning of the thirteenth century, the *towns* in the North and West, as in all Germany, began to form unions, in order to preserve peace, protect merchants and goods, maintain good order regarding courts, customs and coinage, and generally achieve defensive and offensive aims. Hamburg and Lübeck had of old been firmly united in this way: in Westphalia, the cities had been united under the leadership of Soest, Münster and Dortmund since 1253. Cologne maintained close relationships with the cities of the Netherlands, and with Bremen and Hamburg, Braunschweig and Stade, Soest and Lübeck. There were city leagues in Prussia, Saxony and the Marches. Lübeck entered into alliance with the German community in Wisby in 1280 and both allied themselves with Riga in 1282. But the closest association, and one which was frequently strengthened and renewed [465] from the last quarter of the thirteenth century onwards, was the one which existed between the so-called Wendish cities (also called the maritime cities), which counted Lübeck, Wismar, Greifswald and Stralsund among their number and soon Anklam, Demmin and Stettin too.

While established groups of cities associated in confederations were emerging by means of such an extensive system of alliances, and these confederations in their turn were entering into temporary or permanent alliances with each other in the most prolific manner, the idea was developing with ever more compelling power that the collectivity of all these cities was one great Right fellowship [*Rechtsgenossenschaft*]. The unified constitution of the merchants who came from these cities but worked abroad was bound to promote this idea. The rights and interests of all the Low-German cities were of course identical with regard to representation and supervision of the merchants' hansas. But other matters, too, were common to all cities, above all the acquisition and protection of trading privileges, the safeguarding of commerce and resistance to princely encroachments. Finally, Lübeck, in association with other maritime cities, appears to have worked consciously towards collective unity, and to that end to have invited Westphalian, Saxon, Prussian and Livonian cities to joint civic assemblies. Thus, although even now all the initiatives towards joint enterprises, assemblies and revolutions came from individual hansas and separate leagues, and the feuds necessary for the general interests of merchants and cities were also fought by them, none the less at the end of the thirteenth century the idea of a joint city league, though admittedly with no written constitution, appears to have been vigorous and effective *vis-à-vis* both the outside world and [466] the individual communities [*Gemeinwesen*]. A similar course of events unfolded in the first half of the fourteenth century. However, just as the unification of the cities progressed, at the same time their influence on the merchants' associations abroad began to increase. These still appear to be independent corporations: the London Hansa could still count among its members some who did not belong to the civic association, and the name 'hansa' is still primarily used for societies of merchants, although there are isolated instances of references to towns of 'the Hansa' as early as 1330. [467] But increasingly the towns were the chief representatives and therefore the chief supervisors of the counting-houses, courts and gilds. However, the most important factor was that the towns and gilds now began to be seen together as a higher unity which comprised the ordinary merchant on the one hand and the totality of towns on the other, a unity in which the towns and merchants at first appeared to be acting in concert but where the towns soon emerged as the real leadership. In any case it itself was a subject of political Right. People increasingly thought of and called this huge collective union the *common German Hansa* – both a concept and a name . . .

[471] If we ask ourselves, then, what the Hansa was in a legal and moral sense during the long period of its existence, it is scarcely possible to find a satisfactory answer for a single point in time, still less for the whole period. Indeed, it might seem that this remarkable federal community was not a legal–moral structure at all, but simply a historical phenomenon, that the question of its origin, importance and form . . . should be banished from the area of law into that of fact. It might appear that only the individual contracts, agreements and statutes established by the various members of the federation within greater or lesser spheres should be considered and characterised as legal acts. According to this view, while [472] in the historical and moral sense one might recognise a notion of unity at work in all the participants, which lasted throughout the centuries, juristically the overall phenomenon should be broken down into a complex of individual circumstances, into rights and duties resting on specific titles. However, a true constitutional–historical [*rechtshistorische*] understanding could not possibly be achieved by such a fragmented explanation. For that we need the idea, created and yet creative, which with compelling power formed the individual legal relationships in such a way as to group them into a collective entity – a concept of Right which, although it developed gradually, grew invisibly and changed greatly, was none the less a unity and as such had a vigorous existence within the legal and moral consciousness of the people. But this idea of Right, which of course only represents one aspect of the basic principle on which the Hansa rested (this being at the same time political, economic and moral), was nothing other than *the idea of a fellowship based on the free union of all those Low-German communities based on German law which were engaged in trade.*

Therefore the basis of the entire association was and remained the *free will of the fellows*, and this to an extent scarcely conceivable to modern thinking, given the federal nature of the whole. Secession was possible at any time; compulsion to remain was impossible. Conversely, exclusion from the fellowship was the supreme punishment and the sole means of coercion used against a league member. Fines, arbitrations . . . and other punishments were merely attempts to bring the common interest to bear without recourse to the most extreme means; a real federal execution, a positive means of compulsion was never once used. Simply because exclusion from the Hansa entailed exclusion from participation in its common Right and the prohibition of any commerce between a fellow and the one excluded – in other words a commercial ban – the threat and execution of these measures had a more powerful effect than any positive coercion. Declarations of secession, agreements, disclaimers and resignations did not occur until the gradual decline of the federation; in spite of the fact that the association could be freely dissolved, its actual dissolution seemed inconceivable.

The members of the fellowship were those communities whose own will coincided with that of the collectivity: that they should be members. At the beginning, such communities were primarily the merchants' gilds; [473] at the height of the Hansa's development they were these and the towns in close association; and finally they were the towns alone. But even when this last position had been reached, the scope of the membership was always in doubt. During the period of its magnificence, nothing was further removed from the federation than a desire for exclusivity, but at a time when a lively sense of community and great aspirations were still urging all fellowships towards expansion, the powerful centres always left participation in the assemblies and in the Hansa's privileges open even to the smallest towns. In its broadest sense, therefore, the collectivity of all Low-German towns – and the entire citizenry [*Bürgerstand*] of Saxon or Frisian origin – counted as belonging to the fellowship. They could all send envoys to the assemblies and vote; all of their merchants, when they were abroad, enjoyed the rights and freedoms fought for by the Hansa. Therefore formal admission to the association, with the exception of the re-admission of excluded cities, to begin with did not take place at all. Only from the beginning of the fifteenth century did this gradually begin to change. It became usual for admission to be formally recognized; soon obstacles were put in its way and endeavours to limit the number of fellows may be discerned. Furthermore, they began to distinguish lesser fellows from fully enfranchised members; the former did not appear at the assemblies but only participated passively in the Right of the Hansa, and were comparable to the protected members of other associations.

The supreme federal power was vested in the assembly of fellows, the towns; these were represented at the assemblies by councillors as their delegates. Such convocations were scarcely ever completely successful. There was no set regular time for the assemblies and usually the time of the next assembly [*Tag*] was appointed at the preceding one. The representation of the towns was unregulated and quite often the decisions were referred back by deputies . . . Originally the manner of voting was wholly unregulated and even later the principle of a majority only came to be fully accepted in matters concerning defeats abroad. If all this is reminiscent of a merely contractual relationship, there is a distinctly federal principle in [474] the precedent . . . that those cities which did not present themselves had to content themselves with the decisions of those which had, and in the fact (which emerged from the start) that the assembled city envoys, however small in number they often were, took decisions in the name of the Hansa and therefore bound all members of the Hansa unconditionally.

In the same way, the federal entity which functioned above the collectivity of individuals developed from the outset in such a way as to accentuate the natural division of the association into head and branches. Lübeck was always at the head of the league. If this appeared to be a purely factual circumstance, . . . nevertheless the leadership in all the business of the league, the convocation of assemblies . . . fell so indisputably to Lübeck that we can be sure that its leadership was perceived by the consciousness of the age not merely as a fact but as a right; and the duty of members to submit to the collective unity represented by Lübeck was regarded as a legal and moral duty . . .

[475] Assembled and structured in this way, the fellowship (of the Hansa) was primarily active in the interests of trade and shipping, but the purposes of its association were by no means limited to these or connected matters. Like all medieval fellowships, it was aimed at all those purposes of human community whatsoever which seemed capable of being realised by the collectivity arranged in this way better than by individual members (or special leagues). For this reason it seldom interfered where the powers of a single town seemed to be sufficient . . . On the other hand, for a time it combined a very marked political character with its capacity as a trade organisation, and at the time of the Reformation it had an ecclesiastical, denominational character, brought constitutional disputes in individual towns and religious affairs etc. before its forum, and even considered itself competent to intervene at the appeal of the Westphalian cities against the territorial courts. That the League as such was a subject of both civil and private law cannot be doubted. The Hansa always acted as a collective personality [*Gesammtpersönlichkeit*]. And, if it lacked for a long time even a name and never had its own seal, it was always recognised from the outside as a unitary political power which waged wars, entered into treaties, and acquired rights and privileges. The Hansa could not be identified with the sum total of the towns belonging to it, for the simple reason that the rights exercised by the totality never belonged to any of its

members . . . But internally, too, the league as such was the subject of rights under property law, even if here the boundary between the rights of the unity and the rights of the member was shaky and uncertain. The power of the league appeared sometimes to be extremely weak, at other times almost unrestrained. The right of legislation in matters of trade and shipping, jurisdiction over the fellowship, penal authority, and above all the right to demand the provision of a proportionate share in ships and men or impose a federal tax, [476] belonged indisputably to the league. The league was the possessor of the so-called freedoms and privileges of the Hansa, of rights in market-halls and trading posts, of the trading monopoly abroad and so on; individual towns only had a share in this as members of the whole. The Hansa possessed non-transferable rights of ownership and mortgage in castles and palaces, and soon in market-halls outwith its own territory as well. The federation also needed liquid assets so that it could use federal funds to meet the expenses entailed in paying contingents of men, mercenaries, subsidiaries and loans, buying privileges, administering and defending the Hansa's property and meeting exceptional losses and losses for which it was not to blame. However it was not successful in forming a unitary federal budget – and this was much to the disadvantage of internal stability and unity – but stopped short at a very imperfect arrangement, by which the individuals or 'circles' levied dues among themselves for a federal account, deducted their own expenses for equipment and gave the balance to other towns which had raised too little . . .

[Gierke then discusses smaller city federations. Next come federations among the nobility, knights, clergy and peasant unions (chapter 46) and leagues of the public peace (chapter 47).]

Chapter VII

The Empire as union [48]

If the system of union produced an inexhaustible wealth of new political structures from the struggles between the estates, it was bound to be regarded more and more as the [509] source of the state association itself. In fact we see that, after the manifest decline of the feudal system, the old perception of the Empire, as a great lordship association with authority handed down from above in many stages, is replaced by another idea, in which the emperor is only the elected head of a voluntary fellowship for peace and Right, based on the union of the estates.

Alongside the principle of union, a new idea, destined to be victorious over it, had already emerged: the idea of state sovereignty [*Obrigkeit*]. Out of the chaos of lordships, fellowships and mixed associations, which after the dissolution of the graduated structure of the feudal Empire were only linked to each other, and to the emperor, by a diverse complex of fortuitous legal connections, intersecting feudal associations, the fluctuating circumstances of stewardship and privately owned jurisdiction and privileges – out of all these, the territorial domination of individual members of the aristocracy had been ever more securely elevated, from the thirteenth century onwards, as a unified power over a delimited territory. However, even in the North and East, where it was possible at this early stage to cut the nobility and communes off from the Empire, this trend's victories were but incomplete. In the South and West, city leagues and societies of knights still existed with sufficient power to apply the federal principle to the Empire, not below the princes but alongside them.[1]

In the last resort, however, it had long since been decided that the new concept of the state would, under the old constitution, triumph not in the Empire, but only in its fragmented parts . . . Even powerful and prudent emperors could not contemplate replacing the feudal Empire with an Empire-state along the lines of territorial lordship [*Landeshoheit*] . . . The only solution left to them was to place themselves at the head of the leagues and movements prohibiting warfare, and to attempt to extend these into an imperial union. The unresolved question, which for so long prevented a successful outcome, was *how* the imperial union was to be constituted. Who were to be its full members? What position was due to the emperor as leader of the union? By what judiciary were the peace and Right of the union to be administered? How were sentences to be executed within the union?

It was clear from the beginning that the imperial union could not become a confederation of the whole nation, but merely a confederation of single estates. For the peasantry had no part at all in the movement! Yet in the middle of the thirteenth century it seemed doubtful whether even the other estates would find an equal footing in the Empire, and [510] whether the Empire would ever arise from its decline and become a powerful confederation of princes, nobility and cities in which the people were primarily represented as a universal citizenry owing allegiance directly to the Empire. The case of the powerful Rhenish city leagues destroyed such prospects; and each repeated failure to regenerate the Empire by means of city associations, leagues against private warfare, and confederacies, limited the space remaining for other elements in the imperial constitution over against the increasingly exclusive College of Electors and the territorial lords who were also consolidating their power . . .

[511] In general, thought was no longer given to the construction of a powerful federal community, but simply to the association of all direct subjects of the Empire in a union for prohibition of private warfare, different to the usual unions of this sort only in its permanence. But there was disunity over the organisation of the courts of justice . . . It was self-evident that the emperor would become head of the union; but emperor and estates always differed in their opinion of whether jurisdiction should belong to his imperial chamber of justice, to a court of arbitration (as in normal unions), or to a court formed from a mixture of both; and how its competence should be determined[2] . . . [Gierke proceeds to discuss measures for reform of the medieval German Empire, culminating in that under Maximilian I (1495).]

[512] Therefore the new imperial constitution was simply a great peace union of the estates. They had not succeeded in shaping the Empire into a true federal state . . . At the same time [the reformed constitution] was of particular importance because it guaranteed political autonomy and self-administration for the towns and the nobility . . . but as a collectivity allowed them greater participation in the imperial union . . .

[514] The league was renewed for the last time, for twelve years, in 1512 and it was destroyed during the Reformation, when so many political associations were dissolved. But its goal had essentially been achieved: the imperial cities and the knights of the Empire had been recognised in the imperial constitution as part of the Empire, and the Empire had once more been newly established by means of a great confederation of all the estates still in existence. At the same time, of course, for all those who were not directly involved in these unions, this put the official seal on their loss of direct links with the Empire; for those not involved in any way (like the Swiss Confederacy and the lands of the Teutonic Order) it meant complete separation from the Empire.

Chapter VIII

Rural communes and federations: Switzerland and North Germany [49, 50]

The influence of the system of union upon the formation of territorial
states: territorial communities [Landesgemeinden]

We have seen political common life emerge through the power of the
union movement in the medieval town; beyond the towns, associations of
some significance for the state had been formed by means of political
alliances over increasingly wide areas. But of all these fellowships none,
least of all the imperial fellowship itself, led to a true *territorial state*.

In fact over by far the greatest part of Germany the formation of a
territorial state based on a purely communal constitution was impossible,
because none of the rural population had any part in the union movement.
With the division of town and country, the great mass of peasants only
sank deeper into servitude; even the free rural communes (isolated fellowships of the old kind) remained largely without influence on the
movements of the age. When they finally attempted, by means of a violent
uprising, to seize or win back the share of freedom and dominion which
had been taken or withheld from them, they failed because of the superior
power of the higher estates. In exceptional cases some of the peasants on
the coast and in the mountains, and occasionally in some areas in the
interior of Germany, succeeded in developing their own fellowship constitution into a communal constitution, and in asserting or winning political independence in dealings with the outside world. This resulted in the
formation of *territorial communes* [Landesgemeinden], which as territorial
communities [Gemeinwesen] [515] made the idea on which the municipal
constitution was founded permanently or temporarily into the basis of the
state association of a whole *Land*. Like the towns, these territorial communities aspired to unite with others, and they succeeded, where the
leagues of towns had failed, by founding a true federal state.[1]

75

However, the less talk there was of a free politically enfranchised peasantry, the more developments in Germany as a whole, brushing aside nearly all incipient attempts to shape the state differently, moved on decisively towards the victory of territorial independence and the formation of *princely states.* In them it was the individual power of the lord of the *Land* which, by transforming itself into state authority, was an especially creative force and finally became the sole embodiment of the concept of the state. Here too, however, the formation of a pure sovereign state was only the end result; originally the people too were actively involved in creating the territorial state. Since the *Land*, in its division into estates, was constituted along the lines of the system of union, the new territorial estate first emerged as a joint community [*Gemeinwesen*] of the lord and the community of the *Land.* Although the constitution based on the estates was bound to fail because of the exclusion of the peasantry, and the implementation of the modern state be left to sovereignty alone, it was not defeated before it had exercised a powerful influence on the formation of the concept of state in the German territories, the consequences of which have never been entirely eliminated.

In terms of Right, there were three distinct structures through which the system of union directly shaped the development of the territorial state: free territorial communes, federal states and corporations of territorial estates . . . *Free territorial communes* developed chiefly only in the Alps, and on the coast among the Frisians and at Ditmar . . . Their internal and external history demonstrates an even greater variety than that of the towns. But one trend . . . is recognisable in all of them, in spite of its having come to an end or having been prevented from further growth at very different stages of development. There are surprising analogies between the transformation of early Germanic folk fellowships into territorial communities [*Landesgemeinwesen*] and the much earlier transformation of similar fellowships into towns; the process was simply much longer and never so fully implemented.

The external part of this transformation was, as in the towns, the protection or re-establishment of freedom in a Germanic fellowship, whether it was a regional, local or *Mark* community or a free commune. The struggle to distance or remove all lordly dominion [516] which this entailed ended in some communes having full freedom within the Empire; these are comparable with the free cities. In others, which correspond to the more dependent royal cities of the Empire, an imperial stewardship remained, without preventing the development of the communal constitution [*Gemeinheitsverfassung*]. Finally, like the rural towns, there were territorial communes under the dominion of a lord, which were dependent to a greater or lesser extent on overseers appointed by the lord of the *Land*. The characteristic feature of a territorial commune was not the lack of any overlord but that such overlordship stood completely outside the collectivity, the latter being self-contained like a state.

The internal development of the fellowship went hand in hand with this. It produced an invisible unity above its members valid both politically and in private law within the concept of the *Land* which itself had developed from a fusion of territorial and personal associations. This led to the introduction of the concepts, first developed in towns, of a constitution, administration, legislation and supervision [*Polizei*], a unified territorial economy and public law. The old constitution based on judges and magistrates had to give way to a constitution based on a council, which established a board, fulfilling, as the agency of the unified political power at the head of the territory, both representative and executive functions. The leading position in the development was not of course here, as in the towns, completely transferred from collectivity to council; it was less centralised and regulated . . . But at least a partial transformation along the lines of the towns is unmistakable in all territorial communes.

The earliest development of this type took place in the Swiss valley communes which became the core of the later federal state.[2] From as early as the first half of the thirteenth century the valley fellowship of Uri . . . emerges as an organised commune answerable directly to the Empire; in 1231 it was declared . . . free of all subsidiary overlordship. It formed its own territorial commune [*Landesgemeinwesen*] (valley, 'forest', 'locality'): this was represented and governed by a leadership which was both judge and council (*minister vallis* or *Landamann*), had a special seal and was fully manifested in the totality of all valley fellows.

[517] In the same way the collectivity of Schwyz (*cives de villa Suites*), declared . . . free of subsidiary overlordship in 1240, already formed a territorial commune in the thirteenth century. At its head were two (from 1282 four) *ministri vallis* or *Ammänner*, while the *communitas* or *universitas vallis* exercised supreme power as the assembly of the *Land*. The *Land* or 'valley' as a legal personality was symbolised by a special seal, real property and movable assets, and it is assigned, as is a town, its own honour, '*des landes eere*'. As even clearer proof that they conceived of their association in political terms, the commune imposed formal legislation concerning land ownership and a taxation law on its members over its whole area; they thus made the enjoyment of equal civic rights contingent on the fulfilment of equal civic obligations and, like the city communes,

would not tolerate any exemption for clerical landowners. About the same time, an independent territorial commune developed in Unterwald on the basis of its independence within the Empire; recognised in 1240, it was [518] not fully organised in a unitary way like Uri and Schwyz, but divided into a double community, with upper and lower valley communes.

The valley communes and forest cantons, constituted in this way, consolidated and completed their independence during the fourteenth century, sometimes by conflicts and uprisings, sometimes by demanding imperial privileges while gradually abolishing overlordship, and at the same time became the model for a series of neighbouring valley and *Mark* fellowships of the peasantry. Clarus . . . and Appenzell, after experiencing varied fortunes, both arrived at the same goal.

Meanwhile, the internal constitution of all these territorial communes resembled more and more that of a truly state-like community, with modifications required by circumstances, repeating the basic characteristics of the city communes. Above all the invisible unity expressed in the concept of *Land* (valley, forest, locality) emerged more clearly as an ideal collective personality [*ideale Gesammtpersönlichkeit*], which was regarded as the source of the community and the subject of the political and private rights emanating from it. It was the *Land* through its representatives which conducted business externally, acted as a military power, waged wars, [519] entered into alliances, conciliated and mediated, entered into treaties and agreements, acquired rights and took over duties, authenticating them with its seal. Internally, the *Land* was also a political unity, with regard to fiscal, judicial and penal matters and the execution of sentences, and it was the subject and focus of all movable and immovable joint assets, and hence of the territorial budget. *Vis-à-vis* the *Land*, all its smaller sub-divisions (the *Genossamen, Tagwen, Kirchspiele*, farms, villages, . . . etc.) were merely dependent communes, which sometimes did not even have their own boundaries; their main political role was as electors.

At the head of the territorial communes were one or more Ammänner, elected annually in free elections. Having been purely court officials in the old Germanic sense . . . they increasingly became the supreme agency of the *Land*; and, alongside the powers of judging and leading the army . . . they took on the functions of the head of a *Land* government. . . . Alongside them, however, a council became increasingly prominent as it had done in the towns . . . [520] But the *Land* constitution was always very different from that of the municipality, in that the assembly of all fully enfranchised members, which according to tradition always met at convened and self-convening assemblies which every enfranchised inhabitant of the *Land* had a right and an obligation to attend, always retained the predominant importance. Here, under the name *Land* assembly (or, from the fifteenth century, territorial commune), the people themselves directly exercised supreme criminal jurisdiction and right of pardon, by means of majority decisions. They established laws, imposed taxes, took decisions on wars, peace-treaties and alliances, elected officials and courts, allocated membership of the territorial fellowship (the Right of the *Land*) to aliens, and renewed the corporate bond of all members by taking an oath on the Right of the *Land* which was publicly read aloud. They had the wealth of the *Land* at their disposal and so also, like the ancient assembly of landowners, the assets and profits of any common lands of the whole *Land* . . .

Therefore the fellowship of the inhabitants of the *Land*, unlike the municipal fellowships of burgesses, to which it corresponded in other respects, was not entirely absorbed into the agencies of the commune established by it, but itself remained the most important organ of the *Land* it represented. Moreover, just as the citizenry of the towns had around them a circle of citizens who had rights only to protection, alongside the full members of the territorial commune were its own protected members: the sub-tenants and dependants. Among the members of the territorial fellowship themselves, however, there was complete equality of political rights without regard to ownership of property . . .

[521] Free *Land* constitutions developed more slowly and less fully in northern Germany. Friesland had in part preserved its independence from the Empire and sovereign-princely authority, and indeed, even where it was bound to recognise the rights of lordship and stewardship, had maintained autonomy and self-government. Here the old purely comradely constitution in many respects remained operative, and only very gradually absorbed the basic principles of a political community [*Gemeinwesen*] in the new sense . . .

[523] The most splendid example of an extensive free territorial commune was presented by Ditmar, where the whole territory increasingly developed into a free state. It subsumed the parishes (which, although they had initially co-existed almost as small states, independently possessing both peace-enforcing power and courts with discretion over life and death, had disintegrated into family groupings), and also the larger division of the regions, which were also independent. It gradually limited the Archbishop of Bremen's sovereignty to criminal jurisdiction and certain sources of income associated with this . . .

All these territorial communes, whether they were free of external control or dependent, experienced an internal transformation of their nature by which the old Germanic district and court constitution approximated more and more to the constitution of a civic council. Instead of the collective will being simply regarded as the source of political Right, the state, as expressed in the concept of the *Land* and made manifest in the territorial constitution, took on this role. Laws were enacted, justice administered, treaties signed in the name of, for the sake of, or on account of the *Land*. A *Land* seal is the outward symbol of the personality of the common life. Uniform taxation brings about a territorial treasury and fiscal policy. As the subject of private rights, the *Land* is also enabled to take part in and enjoy rights in commerce. But, above all, the agencies of the *Land* take the place of judicial and penal officials, operating a republican territorial government with or without the competition of a lordly official . . .

Finally, in Ditmar the council of [526] the forty-eight developed into a corporation which ruled in exactly the same way as in the municipalities. The real embodiment of the law of the *Land*, which in the towns was the citizenry, was here the territorial commune, the *universitas terrae*, and *meene meenta* or *meene acht*. Thus, just as in the municipal charters, . . . the collectivity of the *Land* is named as having rights and duties, being capable of willing and acting, whenever it is necessary to give expression to the full political and legal–moral personality of the territory . . .

[527] The movement which produced these fully developed territorial communes in Switzerland and on the North Sea was not without parallels in the rest of Germany. But its results were nowhere of great significance. Some of the district and regional fellowships which in Western Germany had preserved continuity of fellowship in complete freedom, or continued it under lordly stewardship, were also constituted as political territorial communes or territorial estates *vis-à-vis* the Empire or their overlord . . . In these an elected agency, in nature and usually in name a council, represented and ruled the collectivity. These areas, some of which were free of imperial control, others under lordly dominion, had the temporary or permanent status of more or less developed territorial communities which possessed their own jurisdiction and had a fellowship-based constitution. The territorial estates of the Rheingau, the Hauenstein Union in the Black Forest, the territorial commune of the abbey of Kempen, the territorial estates of the old lands of Huxori which belonged to Corvey, the *Land* of Delbrück, the communes of the villages belonging to the provostship of Ravengirsberg [528] and in a sense also the region of Altenhaslau and the Forest of Dornstatten are examples of this type of territorial commune . . .

Federal state structures

[530] A federal state entity, composed of several territorial communes which were themselves organised as state communities, emerged first of all in those areas of Friesland which had remained free, by means of the old annual territorial assembly, the *Upstalbeam*, which had originally been attended by all free men, then principally by the magistrates and clerics; it transformed itself into the lawful representative of the allied Sealands. All of Friesland now came to be viewed as the oath-bound peace fellowship of the separate territorial communes, based on a voluntary union, and the territorial assembly as the regular congress of the league, with the judges, magistrates and prelates as the fully authorised leaders of their *Länder*. This federal assembly debated and took decisions on all matters affecting the whole of Friesland, gave judgment in disputes which could not be settled by the judges of the separate *Länder*, and . . . established the common law for all Frisians.

In individual cases it might confirm the will and decision of a commune or *Land*, sanctioning it with the seal of all Friesland. But in general it did not act in the manner of a true unitary state, but confined itself to the common defence of the land and of its external freedom, and to internal peace. For this reason it imposed a duty on each of the individual allies to give armed support to any of the Sealands in case of an attack, or to ward off an injustice inflicted upon them. As in other alliances, the Sealand which was endangered was to issue a formal demand for help; and those who received the demand were to respond within eight or fourteen days on pain of a fine, and not abandon the matter without the joint decision of the assembled armies of the communes. In this way the collectivity acted as an intermediary in the feuds of individual *Länder* with foreign princes or towns. The other Sealands were to use force against any one of the allies [531] which itself breached the peace. However, in so far as no limitations were imposed by the federal law, the individual territorial communes were expressly granted their independence.

Although the free comradely organisation of the Frisians was strengthened both internally and externally by this federal constitution, together with the closing off and internal transformation of the individual territorial communes, so that it lasted much longer than the freedom of other German provinces, in the end it succumbed partly to external attack and partly to internal divisions. The neighbouring princes separated one area after another from free Friesland. Even when the territorial power allowed the free constitution to stand (as happened in the *Länder* subordinate to the Archbishopric of Bremen, the islands and coasts of Schleswig or the

Oldenburg Marches), these areas could only maintain the status of independent regions; they were incapable of developing into states . . .

The federal ideas of the tribes of Friesland and Lower Saxony were of lasting importance, if not for Germany, at least for its closest neighbours in the North, since the same ideas which had come to life early among the Sealands of Friesland were influential in the later formation of the federal state of the Netherlands. Consequently, the form of federal unification of larger *Länder* or provinces formed here, as there, the starting-point for constitutional development.

A federal republican state emerged in Switzerland in quite the opposite way, namely from the political unification of a wide assortment of large and small districts and towns. It, alone of all the German confederations of this time, led to the creation of a real state without the intermediary of the supreme territorial power. [532] In spite of the fact that the various alliances, unions and peace unions from which the Confederation emerged differed in no way from the countless similar unions of that time, and although the organisation of many German city leagues, and alliances among the nobility, was much more secure and unified than that of the Swiss Confederation until well beyond the Middle Ages, the difference lay in the fact that the core of the latter always remained an alliance of *Länder* and that from the beginning it was of importance not only in terms of the *estates*, but in terms of *territory*.

Moreover, for the whole of this period, the thirteen cantons . . . did not have any unified federal charter. Indeed they were not all united, but variously and unequally allied on an individual basis. All of the other cantons were allied only with the three forest cantons, whose old, oft-renewed alliance was extended for all time in 1291 and consolidated in 1315. On the other hand, Zürich had allied itself with Uri and Schwyz in 1291 for a period of only three years, and only entered into a permanent alliance with them and Lucerne in 1351 . . . In 1352 Clarus, having been conquered by the alliance of the forest cantons and Zürich, was forced to enter into an unequal alliance with them. This was only changed into an equal one in 1450 (back-dated to 1352); on the other hand, it had already allied itself on an equal footing with Zürich in 1408. The town and office of Zug entered into league with the forest cantons and Zürich in 1352. Bern entered into what was, in many respects, a loose association with the three forest cantons in 1353, and then took on the obligation of notifying Zürich and Lucerne whenever it issued any demand for help; which Zürich and Lucerne bound themselves to respond to any such demand in separate charters. In 1481, Solothurn and Freiburg joined their eight regions which were variously allied to each other, and in 1509 Basel entered into league with all ten. Schaffhausen united itself with Zürich, Bern, Lucerne, Schwyz and Clarus for a period of twenty-five years in 1454, renewed the contract in 1479, when Uri and Unterwalden also took part, and was formally admitted in 1501. After Appenzell had formed very unfavourable alliances in 1411 and 1452, it was admitted on equal terms in 1513.

All of these federal alliances varied in content. The duty to provide mutual support in case of war and maintenance of peace among fellows was established to the same extent in all of them by means of courts of arbitration and coercive regulations. [533] . . . But the provision of help was sometimes restricted to defined contingencies or . . . to certain geographical limitations, or was only to be given after a thorough examination by deputies, and deliberations . . . Changes had to be sanctioned unanimously, although, in the alliance with Appenzell of 1411, the forest cantons reserved the right to make changes unilaterally. In the same way some, but only some, of the members were occasionally denied the right to enter into further alliances without the approval of their fellows (e.g. Clarus in 1352. The confederates were also unequal in many other respects: after the treaty with Zug, Schwyz was to elect the former's *Amman*. In other treaties there were, in addition, regulations on trade, business, civil and penal law, mutual conquests, etc.

In spite of this, all these *Länder* and towns saw themselves increasingly as fellows bound by oath, and at their assemblies they gradually formulated a federal law and federal legislation. As early as the fourteenth century, joint statutes were enacted against the immunity of the clergy, against forbidden forms of self-help and unauthorised attacks; regulations were also made for internal peace, domestic law and martial law. At the same time, the right of intervention by the sworn fellowship in internal conflict within a canton was gradually being established. From the beginning of the fifteenth century, the assemblies of the eight cantons allied at the time became increasingly frequent, but regular sittings and formal federal decrees did not start until 1481 . . . Genuinely federal laws are not found until 1472. The basic principle that the estates which were in a minority must comply with those in the majority, in cases concerning the honour and well-being of the Confederacy where there was no conflict with the alliances nor with tradition, was not established until 1515 . . .

[The tendency to concentrate the various rights of lordship into a single territorial sovereignty and the tendency to unite the estates in the manner of a fellowship into a single territorial community both contributed towards the German territorial state.]

Chapter IX

The estates, representation and the territorial state
[51]

[534] In Germany true states never (apart from the above exceptions) resulted simply from the unification of the members. But the significance of the system of union as a contributory, if not as the sole, factor in transforming the territories into *states* during the fourteenth and fifteenth centuries can scarcely be overestimated! The source of the German theory of the state should not be sought in the development of territorial dominion alone: alongside and in conjunction with it, the development of the *territorial estates* [535] was an equally important element. But, if the former implies the transformation of dominion into *sovereignty* over a *Land*, the latter, in so far as it is considered in relation to sovereignty, implies the organisation of the *Land* by means of the *comradely union of the estates*. The *Land* and its Lord became the juxtaposed bearers of political Right. Their combination displays the German state as it emerged from the close of the Middle Ages.

Thus from the thirteenth century onwards two trends run parallel in all the territories. They engage in much conflict and confrontation with one another, but by the very violence of their struggle they only hasten the achievement of their mutual goal – a state. One of these trends is the endeavour of the princes to become territorial lords. The great power which had been vested in princes, individual counts and free lords from as early as the beginning of the thirteenth century, and in particular after the decrees of Frederick II, was still, in the fourteenth century, nothing more than the aggregate of dissimilar rights over individuals and areas, each of which rested on a specific basis in law. As far as individuals were concerned, some were only entitled to the powers of old imperial offices, whether of the rank of duke or simply that of count, and to rights of jurisdiction, military levy, the maintenance of law and order and attendance at court; others had rights of usufruct and rights of lordship which they had acquired by chance; and still others had feudal rights as lord or liege, rights of stewardship or protective or territorial rights of their own. In terms of land, some had allodial rights to land, or held it as fiefs from the emperor or other estates . . . [Similarly in some cases] allodial lands[1] were held by lords, knights, those of juryman status [*Schöffenbar*][2] or free peasants. All these personal and real rights could intersect in many places, indeed the same piece of land could belong to different territories. The territorial lords were now attempting to define and draw together both land and people internally and externally as a unified sphere of lordship . . . [536] At first this only represented the greatest possible concentration of the Right of Lordship in one hand. But soon, and with ever increasing clarity, a higher philosophy emerged. The territorial lords began to see themselves as the embodiments of a state power which was *in its nature unified* and inalienable and indivisible for the sake of the public good – in other words as sovereign powers . . .

Another trend was active in opposition to the endeavours of the territorial lords. This aimed to preserve the independence manifested in the general and special assemblies of the *Länder*, at diets of knights and territorial gatherings [*Landdingen*], in the lordly and comradely associations. It finally brought about the unification of all engaged in the common pursuit of this goal, and of the units of power in the territory which were sufficiently strong for the purpose, in *corporations of territorial estates*. The participation of [537] subjects in the affairs of the collectivity was as old as German public law itself. But, while it had been visible during the time of patriarchal freedom in the general assemblies of the free members of the nation, and then in feudal times in the assemblies of the great men of the land, feudal courts, diets of knights and great vassals, because of the power of the system of union it now suffered a complete transformation of its nature and form, for the third time.

At first, of course, aspirations towards independence and freedom appeared as the aspirations of the *individual* lords and local communities who lived in the *Land*. But the nature of the matter and the spirit of the age soon led to their *unification* in order to reach the common goal by communal methods. But while first of all the members of the same estate, and then the estates themselves, allied themselves with one another, took oaths and formed brotherhoods within the fellowship whose existence was in this way prolonged, the idea increasingly gained ground that they were not simply the sum total of individuals with a number of rights – some mutual, some specific – but a unity, representing the *Land* itself. They characterised themselves as the *Land*, as the *common estates of the territory* [*gemeine Landschaft*]. By *Land* they meant the aggregate of personal and territorial spheres of Right, in opposition to those of the lord, organised into a vigorous collective unity, the embodiment of which was manifest in the totality of the independent political units organised as fellowships – i.e. the estates of the *Land* – while the individual subjects or citizens of the estates took part in it indirectly as protected members.

The lord of the *Land* and the estates became, therefore, two powers independent of one another, neither deriving their rights from the other. But the unavoidable necessity that they should co-operate, and the correspondence of their rights and duties was bound, at the same time as they were formed, to lead to both of them recognising a mutual source, a unity which stood above them both. Under the influence of the idea of the public good of the whole *Land*, which was equally stressed by both powers, established by both as a precept and equally represented by both, such a unity emerged more and more clearly defined as a broadened concept of the *Land*: the *Land* as *state*.

In this way the idea of a state, which had until then only been realised in the cities, was perfected in the greater sphere of the *Land* . . .

[Gierke discusses 'the constituting of the territorial estates', namely the 'Fellowships of the estates (or classes: *Stände*)': prelates, knights and lords, cities, peasants.]

[561] In whatever way the development may have taken shape, it always and everywhere resulted [562] in the establishment of a fellowship based on German law (*deutschrechtlichen*], a corporation [*Körperschaft*] of the estates, which, until well into the sixteenth century, had its basis in the idea of free association, and in which the subjugation of the members to the collectivity was the consequence of their own free will, while the association on the other hand, was held together by a series of the most important of the powers acquired by the corporation as such, and individuals only shared in these powers as members of the association.[3]

As will have become clear from the details already given, this fellowship was organised internally in exactly the same way as other voluntary associations. Its fully enfranchised members were the individual estates, which, for their part, were also linked in smaller fellowships (*curiae, corpora, collegia, Bänke*). The only way of gaining admission to the fellowship was to enter and be accepted into the association. The condition on which admission depended was qualification as an estate, that is, as an independent unit of political power in the *Land*: this almost always necessitated independent dominion over an area of territory within the *Land*. But the point had not yet been reached when the estates were the appurtenance of individual pieces of land . . .

The estates are united to each other as fellows and have corporate duties . . . To keep the peace and [563] to bring their disputes before their fellows, to offer loyal assistance and to stay true to each other, to submit to the decision of the collectivity, to risk life and limb in aid of other members of the estate [*Mitständen*] against miscreants, outsiders or even the prince, to take no individual initiatives or decisions in the affairs of the territory, even to pay contributions on demand for mutual enterprises – the estates tied their written or unwritten constitutions to all this and to much that was similar. The supreme power of the fellowship was vested in the assembly of full members, in the totality of all estates in the case of affairs concerning the collectivity, and in individual legislative assemblies where only the affairs of an individual estate came into question. The fact that the representatives of the bishoprics and communes were accountable and bound by instructions was a necessary consequence of the fact that not they but the juristic persons they represented were the subject of the Right of the fellowship; it was understandable therefore that voting by proxy was permissible for other estates as well.

None the less, from being the meetings of single, independent individuals these assemblies became the embodiment and agency of a collective personality with its own rights. This development was increasingly evident in the growing acceptance of the principle of majority voting: this was finally enforced even in resolutions about taxation which had initially been regarded only as grants made by individuals . . .

The pressure for unity over diversity came to the fore even more in that the territorial estates set up the 'broader' and 'lesser' committees which later attained such great significance and threatened the estates themselves. In the course of time these became true collegial agencies of the fellowship; and, although they acted in its name, they were none the less independent and often even had the right of co-option. They functioned as advisory or juridical authorities, or again as representatives of the estates if these had not assembled. In this case they themselves had to safeguard the estates' interests, accept complaints on their behalf, give redress, and decide lesser matters. In cases of emergency they had to convoke and lead the assembly . . . Sometimes they were the fiscal authority for the collection, use, or supervision of agreed taxes, the administration of the estates' budget and [564] the settlement of territorial debts. Sometimes they functioned alongside the prince, or in his place, as a council ruling the territory.

It was the collective personality of the association of estates organised in this way, not the sum total of participating individuals, which was the subject of the political and private rights of the estates of the *Land*. Originally of course only individual freedoms and privileges had a basis in law. For a long time after unification, the rights granted to, or obtained and bought by, the collectivity of the estates were valid as joint rights in the old sense, so that all as individuals had as much of a share in them as all together. Through the influences of the union movement and the model of the towns and other corporations, the view increasingly became established that, independently of the rights and privileges of individuals, there existed rights pertaining to the territorial estates or to a court as such, the individual only participating as a member of the collectivity and according to the terms of its constitution.

These territorial estates, which represented an entity in law not only *vis-à-vis* their members but also *vis-à-vis* the territorial lord, were as such just as much *inhabitants* of the *Land* as the individual estates: that is, they were subordinate to the rights of dominion of a prince. However, this subordination was based on a quite specific legal and moral relationship. This stipulated for both sides rights and duties, established partly by tradition, partly by explicit treaties, acts of union, charters of privilege. The obligations of the territorial estates were terminated by a breach of these rights by the lord; this accounted for the right they had, to pay homage only when their privileges were confirmed. It accounted for the enhanced rights enjoyed in Bavaria, Pomerania, Brandenburg and many other places, which allowed revolt and resistance even to the point of electing another prince. That this resistance [565] could be undertaken with arms was the natural consequence of the right to bear arms and conduct feuds, implicit in full freedom. Consequently, the territorial estates could wage war on the territorial overlord as an independent political power; they could negotiate and conclude settlements and treaties. The right to assemble on their own initiative, and to form unions and alliances, and the autonomy which was manifest in the independent creation of an organisational structure, were the natural attributes of free fellowships . . . The territorial estates' own [566] budget, from which the expenses of the fellowship were covered and officials employed and paid (and, in cases of emergency, even troops procured), was the free property of the territorial estates, which in all other respects too had the rights of an independent subject in private law. They were completely capable of conducting business and commerce on their own behalf . . .

[567] Internally, there was scarcely any branch of administration upon which the estates were not authorised to act as advisers, obstruct proceed-

ings, or to act in a supervisory or independent capacity, wherever the welfare of the territory seemed to demand it, or wherever important secular or spiritual interests of the territory were concerned. The establishment of peace and [568] law and order was to a great extent in their hands. They intervened at an early stage in the regulation of coinage, they restricted the prince in his choice of servants and officials; and they safeguarded the ecclesiastical and religious interests of the territory. Finally, in many territories, the estates practised what was in effect joint government, gaining a greater or lesser degree of influence over the appointment and powers of the councils of territorial lords, and in the end transforming these into pure committees of the estates, elected by the estates, which not only safeguarded the interests of the territory against the prince but made him dependent on their agreement or even bound him to their decisions. They could therefore no longer be regarded as princely councils but as *joint territorial councils with a share in the government*.

They cared for the good of the *Land* jointly with the prince if one existed. When there was no prince the sole and complete government of the *Land* devolved on them. There are instances, when the throne was vacant, of the estates setting up a regency endowed by them with full powers, [569] which ruled the *Land* as an aristocratic corporation. We see them acting as guardians or joint guardians of a prince who had not reached his majority, and in this case they took an active part in choosing the co-guardian. We see them taking the final decision in cases of disputed inheritances, regulating the negotiations for dividing inheritances, or disposing of communities among several princes. There are cases where they were empowered to elect a new territorial lord where there was no agnatic heir entitled to inherit.

Of all the rights the estates enjoyed, however, by far the most important, on which all the others were established and from which they developed, was the right to approve taxes. This included the authority to co-operate in the raising and administration of the approved taxes and to supervise their use. At the start of the development of the territorial estates . . . it goes without saying that a prince who wanted to demand more, in any respect, was dependent on the good will of the subject who had to produce more than he was [570] obliged to. This was the case when the prince claimed some personal service to which he had no right, and in particular when he called for military service over and above the specific military duties of the vassals and warriors . . . It was also the case when he demanded financial contributions for which there was no obligation based on tradition, treaty or a specific condition of lordship binding on all inhabitants or individuals. In such a case, he was obliged to approach all individuals whom he required to pay an extraordinary levy or tax, with a request for their approval. It was a matter for the free will of those approached whether they granted or refused the request, whether conditions were attached to granting the request, and if so of what sort, whether they wished to be guaranteed freedoms and privileges in return or to 'buy' concessions, and if so of what sort. However, since it was no longer individual persons or communes who were approached about the tax and gave it approval, but increasingly the assembled members of an estate or all the territorial estates – and they, on the contrary, did not act as individuals but as a collectivity in confirming or granting rights or issuing declarations to the effect that the approval was granted only out of good will, 'by love not duty', and that it did not form a precedent for the future – the view gradually developed that taxes were not to be granted [571] by individuals but by the collectivity of an estate of all estates *as such*.

Admittedly, in many respects the view that the collectivity only represented the sum total of all individuals, and that therefore each individual could withdraw from the joint decision at will, persisted here far longer than in any other context. But the opposite view was bound to develop at an early stage, by virtue of the fact that when approval had been granted, the collectivity did not leave the execution of the decision to the individual but nominated a committee which managed or at least supervised the levying of the tax in the name of the whole corporation, delivered the money raised to the territorial lord or safeguarded it, until it was needed, in special territorial coffers, and administered it as the property of the territory.

Finally, after every assignment of money to the prince, the committee checked that it was used for the purposes for which it was intended, or else demanded that it should be accounted for. This supervision extended to the point that where concessions had been made for war, a committee of the territorial estates paid the wages themselves, kept the key to the armoury where the equipment bought with the money raised in the *Land* was kept, and was at the side of the territorial lord during the conduct of the war itself as a council of war, advising and restraining him. Thus the granting of taxes itself was also bound to be seen increasingly as a matter for the corporation, and to follow from a majority vote in the individual legislative courts or even among the courts themselves.

Although the collective rights of the estates in matters of warfare and taxation became in this way the rights of the territorial estates as a corporation, as a unity, this did not at first mean that the old relationship between the estates and [572] the lord had changed. The lord was now faced not with individuals and fellowships but with a territorial community, in which all their rights were concentrated. At this time there was no question of the idea of a unified state fiscal policy whose extent is regulated by the needs of the territory. Rather, the princes and the territory are two co-existing Right-subjects who use the funds raised jointly for the purposes of the community according to the terms of a contract between them. At the same time, the relationships between the *Land* and the prince, founded on loyalty and protection, still required that in a case of real need the estates could not refuse to assist the prince as long as he respected their rights. His personal needs and those of the *Land* were always identical, or rather the state had as yet no requirements of its own; there were only those of the lord of the *Land*.

But the more frequently the prince demanded to levy a tax and the territorial assembly debated it, the more both demand and debate must lead to the motives for the approving or failing to approve the tax being sought in the common and similar needs of the *Land as a whole*. The idea that the *Land* had needs which were distinct from the personal requirements of both the lord and all individual subjects or territorial estates was bound to develop an idea of the *public good* which had to be complied with under all circumstances. This had already been recognised as the ultimate aim of co-operative endeavour in the realms of administration and legislation. This was bound to give rise to the view that the prince and the territorial estates were *obliged* to co-operate in cases where the needs of the *Land* demanded it – the requirements of the *Land* naturally could also include the personal needs of the prince and his household. The only questions which had to be asked, therefore, were whether such a requirement existed and how taxes could be raised, administered, spent and supervised in the best interests of the *Land*.

However, this view of Right, with all the consequences which flowed from it, formed only the final stage of an entirely new conceptual structure which had been developed over a long period in all areas of law and which transformed and perfected the essence of the territorial estates. It was a symptom of the *concept of the state* which was gradually coming of age . . .

In the early days of the estate constitution there was still no concept of the *Land* as a state, that is, as a unified community like the towns. Lordship and the territorial estates [573] were two co-existing Right-subjects, who, though linked together by the most diverse legal and moral connections, were not members of a higher unity distinct from themselves.

Lordship consisted of the lord, who was its representative, and the *Land* and people, who were the members of the association . . .

Since the idea of representation was everywhere in the ascendant, the unification of the estates into one collectivity produced the idea that, although the individual members of the territory were always primarily represented by the individual estates to which they were subordinate, at the same time the collectivity of all those belonging to the territory was represented and symbolised by the fellowship of the estates itself. As soon as this idea had prevailed – and this was often the case even before the beginning of the fourteenth century – *the Land itself* became the subject of Rights; the territory as the aggregate of all the spheres of personal and property rights, organically conjoined to form an independent unity in opposition to the lord, came increasingly to bear the same relationship to him as the town had to the town lord in the first days of the civic communes: it became an *organised territorial commune [Landesgemeinde]*, manifest in the assembly of the full members.

The collectivity of the estates was by this stage [574] fully entitled to act in the name of the *Land*, indeed to call itself pre-eminently the *Land* or the estates of the *Land*. For, in the same way that the town was manifest in its burgesses, the *Land* was manifest in the estates. It transacted business and expressed its will through them, through them it acquired rights and undertook obligations. Privileges and bonds were issued, rights and freedoms given, oaths and vows taken, not to the estates alone, but – alongside the prelates, lords, counts, freemen, knights, vassals and towns – to the rich and poor, noble and commoner, cleric and layman and to all the *Land*, or simply to the common *Land* or the land and people. As early as 1307 the Dukes of Munich and Ingolstadt sold their coins to 'the lords, the prelates, the counts, freemen, servants, knights and their equals in town and country, citizens, masons in the town, markets and everywhere in all our land of Bavaria'. The freedoms and rights of the *Land* were protected and defended by the estates; the estates assembled for the sake of the *Land*, indeed all the people of the *Land [das gemeine Land]* appeared to be assembled in them. Their grants of taxation, acts of homage and vows counted as having been made by the *Land*, by 'all the lords and the poor people of all the *Land*', their treaties were 'territorial treaties' [*Landesverträge*], their leagues 'territorial alliances'. The league of 1394 described itself as 'a union and alliance of the counts, free knights and squires, towns and markets, *land and people, rich and poor, noble and commoner*, all bishops, abbots, prelates and all spiritual orders in the land of Lower Bavaria'. Frequently, moreover, freedoms and privileges were expressly given to the estates for all the inhabitants of the *Land* (as in Lüneberg all manner of rights, jurisdictions and traditional usages were granted for the whole territory). [575] The estates might even describe themselves as representatives of the common *Land* or of the people.

Even greater proof than these phrases is given by the powers which the estates assumed, not only in the protection of the whole *Land*, but in the representation and protection of every single member of the *Land* if their rights had been infringed. But the greatest proof lies in the way that they actually concerned themselves not only with their own interests but with the interests of the collectivity. At the time when they were at their height, the idea of the estates as a privileged corporation separate from the *Land* was totally alien to the territorial constitution. But of course the idea of representation of the *Land* through the estates was essentially different from our present system of popular representation. First – and here the whole structure of the constitution precluded any development – the old estates of the *Land* were the representatives of the *Land in their own right*, they were not the instrument [*Organ*] but the embodiment [*Träger*] of the Right and unity of the *Land*; their relationship to the *Land* was not, we repeat again, like that of the *council* (or at a later date, the greater council) but like that of the *full burgess community* to the town.[4] Secondly, however – and here there was further development, although in a different sense from today's – the legal unity manifesting itself in the estates of the *Land* [576] was a *distinct territorial commune, constituted in both political and private Right as a collective personality in relation to the territorial lord and his entire lordship association.*

Such a concept can perhaps still be recognised in our non-juristic language, but it is not recognised by a single currently valid law, nor by the more advanced legal consciousness of our age. For the *Land* and people [*Volk*] to have an independent personality in law, existing inside or outside the state, in antithesis to the state government – that is inconceivable for us today. The state itself is for us the whole people – governing and governed – organised into a political and juristic unity . . .

From the fourteenth century the commune [of the *Land*] had been beginning to come to agreement with the lordship of the *Land* concerning the concept of a state standing over them both. When both powers co-existed independently, were incessantly in dispute about the interpretation, extension and renewal of their treaties, and fighting about the necessity of laws, impositions, taxes and wars, what was then the final form for a decision, the ultimate judgment for or against, the final goal of all efforts within their unions, if not the public welfare of the whole *Land*?

If, however, there was a public interest which coincided in its entirety neither with that of the *Land* commune nor with that of lordship, then there was a higher unity above both of them – a state. If there was a state, then the territorial commune and lordship were no longer simply two individual units, associated by complex legal connections, but members of the state which was equally manifest in both of these elements. The two units, therefore, were no longer acting simply for themselves; both were also working for the state. Their agreements in political affairs were now no longer simply treaties, but constitutive policy-making deeds, their provisions about peace, law and public morals were no longer [577] legal transactions, but statutes. Treating the *Land* according to the principles of private law, dividing and selling part of it, must now be restricted for the sake of the welfare of the *Land*. The fragmentation of lordship into a series of single powers had to give way to the unitary concept of a state power of a purely public-law character, composed on the one hand from the concentrated territorial sovereignty and on the other from the unified practice of territorial Right. Both the lord and the community of the *Land* were now the instruments [*Organe*] of the *Land* as a whole, and they also represented it in its totality on their own, where the constitution allowed for this . . . [579] The council, too, established with the participation of the estates or by them alone, increasingly became an agency of the state; and the whole administration in all its branches – particularly in bureaucracy [*Polizei*] and military affairs – was increasingly transformed, along the lines of the model which had already been implemented within the more restricted spheres of the city communes, into a unitary state administration, differing only in the greater numbers of its agencies.

This development did not, of course, progress evenly in all *Länder*, nor was it anywhere complete as early as the end of the Middle Ages. In particular, it nowhere reached the point at which the separate legal and moral entities – the territorial lordship and the estates of the *Land* – were completely fused in the new concept of the state. For, as long as the estates claimed an independent status not derived in the first instance from the lord of the *Land*, the state remained a two-fold unity. But when, in the following centuries, the inevitable consequences of the increasingly powerful idea of the state demanded to be realised as a *unified whole*, the estates had declined too far internally and were too powerless externally to lay claim to their share in the state. They were more and more pushed aside by the territorial lord [*Landeshoheit*] from the realm of public law into that of private law. He alone took full and complete possession of the idea of the state; they became privileged corporations.

In most *Länder* the territorial estates now wholly ceased to be a territorial commune, representing the territory or people in a characteristic way. Petty and cowardly, they acted only for themselves . . .

[580] Here our aim has been, first of all, to follow the rising trend of the development of this idea in more detail and to demonstrate that the idea of the modern state did not by any means arise solely from regional independence and the idea of sovereignty, but from these in conjunction with the territorial estates, which developed truly magnificently [581] under the influence of the idea of union. The German concept of the state could scarcely have been formed by territorial sovereignty alone, which for its part was not hindered but hastened in its development by the estates . . . This is a concept which differs fundamentally from the notion of the state held by the ancients, above all in its recognition of public law as law – the valuable outcome of the long ascendancy of private law.

Chapter X

The peasantry and rural fellowships [52, 53]

Fellowship in the countryside: the system of union and the rural communes [Landgemeinden]

[581] We have now reached the point at which the system of union had achieved the greatest results of which it was capable. From their simple beginning, the gilds, alliances and brotherhoods, which the mighty Carolingians, with a premonition of the danger threatening the concept of lordship, tried in vain to nip in the bud, had fundamentally re-created the whole public and private life of the German people (and that of all European nations in a slightly different way!). They passed a little-remarked, obscure childhood in the dark centuries which followed the decline of the Frankish monarchy; then, while the feudal empire and hierarchy were perfecting the most magnificent of all organisations of which the all-powerful concept of feudal service was capable, they slowly trained a new class which was destined to be the embodiment of a later stage of civilisation. Finally, in days when all institutions which derived their authority from above were disintegrating, they created an astonishing wealth of new structures from the chaos into which all that was old appeared to be dissolving. In these the nation constituted itself once more from below and within by means of the freest kind of spontaneous activity.

In free civic communes [*Gemeinwesen*] [the gilds, alliances and brotherhoods] developed the most ancient state association in German law on the basis of self-government and consensual justice [*Recht*]. The increasingly flourishing groups of citizens were securely organised into gilds and, along with political and religious unification, trade and commerce were organised as fellowships. From their base in the towns they made their mark on all the other estates. Within the nobility, along with a series of loose associations, they produced a movement towards the reconstruction of the

96

family as a fellowship. On the basis of a number of less than [582] perfect communities, they organised the newly emerging lesser nobility into chivalric associations. They took root among the clergy and brought the system of religious fellowships to their zenith. They prepared the way for learning. Every profession, old or new, known to the people, from the duties of the lords to the despised skills of the travelling entertainers, from the office of the clergy to the trade of robbers and beggars, from the old service of the shield to the new rank of mercenary, from the great art of the stone-masons to simple wage labour, from great merchants trading overseas to the small shopkeeper, from teaching posts at the university to the school of fencing, from the industrial trade of the miners to all branches of craft, from the vocation of the seamen scattered over the ocean for the greater part of the year to the countless convent-like communities of the charitable and pious, from the art of song to the sturdy profession of archer – all these were structured in fellowships by the system of union, creating higher and more general associations of fellows in looser or more tightly knit forms above the corporations, gilds and fraternities.

In matters of detail, the diversity of life had already begun to split the firm professional fellowships and communities into different branches, to separate out spiritual and temporal, municipal and commercial associations, and head and branch ones. It had begun to prepare a system of association for single purposes in conjunction with common-property groups and contracts. But, above all, the system of political union created and dissolved association upon association in an inexhaustible wealth of forms among the various parts of the *Länder* and the Empire, until a secure organisation of public law emerged from the confusion of alliances, confederacies and societies. The great trading republic of North Germany arose from merchant and city leagues. Civic alliances formed in all parts of the Empire and led the political movement towards unification. At their side were leagues of princes and lords, societies of knights, unions of prelates and clerics. The estates attempted to create a higher legal order in the leagues for peace. On many occasions the final goal of union – a federal community within the Empire – was within reach; and, if the Empire did not achieve the status of a unified state, a lasting imperial union with certain political functions was at least saved. On the other hand, the system of union did achieve the true significance of a state in the *Länder* by creating some free territorial communes, by drawing some of these together into a federal state, and finally by helping to create in the *Länder* the princely state governed by a lord. This was achieved by means of the development of the territorial estates, which the system of union had produced and whose form it determined.

But here, of course, union came into abrupt collision with the new concept to which it soon deferred in all areas and by which it was soon to [583] be defeated. For, in opposition to the idea of fellowship which had been rejuvenated by *union*, the idea of lordship was gradually no less vigorously rejuvenated through the concept of sovereignty [*Obrigkeit*]. This encompassed land and people equally. In opposition to the legal and constitutional structure emanating from within and from below, it established a state authority which created a unitary coercive Right and an organisational structure from above and from without. This was ill-disposed towards political independence and committed to a system of guardianship [*Bevormundung*] which monopolised care for the common good. But, in return for this, it endeavoured to impose the same law for all in place of the structure which existed under the estates, and universality in place of overbearing individuality. However inexhaustible the power of the medieval system of association appears to be, it is unable to defy this new, superior idea, all the less so because, in the same gradual process by which the system of sovereignty unfolds, the system of fellowship is decaying internally.

As early as the fifteenth century it was evident that the creative power of union was in decline; in the sixteenth century the fellowship movement definitely ceased developing; corporate life became atrophied in its traditional forms. From then on, the complete corruption of the fellowships proceeded unabated: they divided the estates, which they had earlier sought to unite, in an increasingly pronounced way, restricted the sphere of their associations more and more tightly, increasingly found their aims in narrow, petty issues, and increasingly raised the particular above the universal. A system of privileged corporations encompassed the whole nation: from being vigorous members of a great national organism, corporations had become purely individual organisms. This threatened public life with fragmentation, contraction and decline, until finally only the supreme authority raised to the level of princely absolutism was capable to leading the concept of universality to victory by means of the merciless destruction of the associations which held the middle ground between state and individual.

If the final reasons which made events turn out as they did are as unfathomable as the obscure twists of the whole history of civilisation, the most important of those causes which can be identified as combining to bring about this final result is undoubtedly the fact that the part of the population engaged in agriculture had no share in the new political structure of the age. For a great free state could never be brought forth by cities, however free and flourishing, and an aristocracy, however mighty, if they were not supported by a peasantry organised as a collectivity and taking an active part in the state, with equal rights in public law. Without such an arrangement, the structure formed by the estates, rather than being an organisation of all the nation, must necessarily lead to the division of the nation into privileged and oppressed classes [*Klassen*]. The proof of this assertion is given, piece-meal, by observation of the isolated exceptions which themselves prove the rule up to a point by their singularity.

All that now remains is to give a positive demonstration both of the continued existence [584] of the older rural system of fellowship, which was not developed either internally or externally by the new idea of Right, and also of its general exclusion from the union structures . . . A more detailed treatment of the constitution of the rural communes . . . will therefore be given here, since the internal structure of the rural fellowships remained throughout the Middle Ages fundamentally the same as it was shortly after the migration of the Germanic tribes. At the same time, a description of rural fellowships in modern times will be included, in so far as its form endured unchanged into the seventeenth and eighteenth centuries.

It must be said that in this instance a summarised discussion presents its own difficulties. Rich and varied in form and content as medieval associations were in all their ramifications, the countrymen's system of fellowship surpasses all in rich variety of forms. All the other fellowships did indeed live their own lives and develop their own law; but among the other estates lively intercourse, and a comprehensive exchange of ideas between them, produced a degree of similarity in their aims, and hence gradually a definite series of clearly defined legal institutions. The fellowships of the countrymen, on the other hand, persisted in an isolation which scarcely permitted the influence of neighbouring sister organisations, still less the reciprocal influence of distant areas on each other. Hence a varied mixture of constitutional forms arose, encompassing not only the application of the same principle to differing conditions, but totally divergent principles. The basis, organisation and legal–moral significance of the fellowship was unevenly constituted depending upon diversity of origin, of geographical location, on whether land was originally German or Germanised, on whether there were scattered or village communities, on how far *Mark* lands had been parcelled out, and on whether the lord's rights over land and people were public or personal, stronger or weaker, and so on. But they often varied without any discernible reason in areas which were close to each other. They varied in terms of the relationship within them between personality and property, between public and private Right, and between collectivity and directorate [*Vorstand*]. The ways and circumstances, in which in many places the old fellowship and the old joint property began to be transformed from within into a comradely community and communal property, also varied. Even greater differences emerged, however, when state power confronted these varying circumstances and, by intervening to restrict and regulate them and make them more uniform, attempted to produce a commune which was a political administrative district. For now there was not only a confrontation between a trend from [585] within the commune and one acting on it from outside, but there was a dual tendency within the community itself. On the one hand, this slowly accomplished the formation of a new structure; and on the other it calmly continued to spin out contradictory forms which had arisen from the spirit of centuries long forgotten. Cut off from the public life of the nation, and fearing all innovations because for a long time their only experiences of innovations had been bad ones, the peasantry made an obstinate attempt to cling on to the remains of its comradely constitution, or to improve it on its own, without being able to revive it inwardly by imbuing it with a new spirit. It is often difficult to recognise the influences at work in the mixture of old and new principles and forms developing in this way, and in the direct juxtaposition of modern and ancient concepts of Right, long since lost among other groups of people . . .

The rural fellowships[1]

The fellowships in which the rural population lived during the Middle Ages and at the beginning of modern times may be separated into different types, first [586] by the nature of their land, and secondly by their relation to an overlord . . .

[Gierke argues that nearly all rural fellowships 'remained fellowships with a collective Right in the old sense', were 'basically untouched by the idea of union', and failed to develop 'an independent collective personality'.]

[589] Therefore none of the rural communes of this time were based on the consequence of a freely chosen act of will or of political necessity; rather, the traditional personal community of fellows, on one hand, and their collective real Right in their lands on the other, were the basis of their association. Both spheres of law influenced the other, conditioning and defining each other in a multitude of ways. However, they always remained two separate spheres which did not intersect in any way, and did

not combine in an invisible unity which fused them together . . .

Rural lands [*Mark*] were never, therefore, like the area of a town, a territory in the political sense. They were certainly a single unit in geographical and property terms . . . Yet their unity was purely natural, and to a certain extent geographical; it was based on the nature of the land itself, and not on the fact that it was the basis of a self-contained community [*Gemeinwesen*]. Hence, while the town's rights of ownership in its lands could be divided into political dominion and private ownership, in rural lands the old title of ownership (encompassing the rights of both public and private ownership) persisted, until the territorial overlord was able to assemble the land rights he had acquired . . . into a regional supremacy, confine the communes to owning land purely as private property, and was thereby able to destroy the constitution of the rural fellowships at source . . .

In completely the same way, the *fellowships of the countrymen* remained collectivities of persons, which, because they were identical with the sum total of all individuals, could never isolate themselves as political communes in relation to the public or lordly authority . . . Thus, alongside the dependent position of the collectivity, the individuals always continued to be in a position of direct dependence; in matters regarding an act of public or lordly authority – taxation or seizure, judicial summons or the execution of sentences, or military levy – the official or lord could first [591] approach the collectivity with a request for settlement or he could equally well proceed against the individual directly. The towns, on the other hand, after they had become communes, were the necessary mediators in all matters between their citizens and the emperor or territorial lord. In other words, in the rural communal fellowship there was neither communal land nor communal rights for the inhabitants, but collective rights to the lands and personal rights to the fellowship . . .

[633] If, after this exposition, we review the position of the rural population in conjunction with what has been said before, and with regard to conditions created, on the one hand, by the medieval system of union and on the other, by territorial sovereignty, already engaged in violent conflict with the former, [634] we are able to give roughly the following picture of the end of the Middle Ages. A unified peasantry had come into being, separated from all fellowship-based association with the privileged estates. Existing, with only a few exceptions, in a state of serfdom, in most *Länder* this peasantry had no political rights in church or state. The peasantry admittedly still possessed extensive self-administration and autonomy in its own affairs. It lived in small local community fellowships, and

occasionally in larger ones, regulating the affairs of the fellowship independently, continuing to develop its own law according to its own needs and wishes, and administering justice in the old way. Yet these fellowships took little part in the great intellectual movements of the time and were therefore incapable, by means of their own strength alone, of becoming communities based on fellowship [*genossenschaftliches Gemeinwesen*] in the way appropriate to the age.

It is of course possible to find the beginnings of an inner transformation of the fellowships into communal organisations [*Gemeinheiten*], especially in places where the peasantry still took part in public life. The development of local rights of citizenship, instead of the rights of fellows based on the local communal lands and personal legal obligations, the fusing-together of the property-based and personal aspects of law into territoriality, the divorce of public and private law, the formation of communal assets and a communal budget, the institution of communal imposts and communal services for public needs, the founding of a common constitution by the creation of true agencies of the local community in local directorates and community councils – this and much more, which can be summed up as the emergence of an invisible community distinct from the collectivity of fellows, was in a few places the result of a movement which had come to life within the fellowship itself. And this movement was evidently identical with the union movement which had long since dominated the other estates. But much was still missing before such a transformation could achieve a more universal significance. While here and there local, parish or bailiwick communities in the countryside, and even peasant or village communities, were formed in the same way as municipal communities, on the whole the rural community remained simply a land-based fellowship in the old sense.

But, because the local rural communities continued to be excluded from the new fellowship-based organisation of the people (now structured in estates), lordship over land and the territorial domain which developed from this had the most distinct advantage in its never-ending battle against their independence. The might of the lords advanced irresistibly against the elements of fellowship within the rural constitution. Since the peasants had been robbed of the right to bear arms, freedom and real property had become rare among them. The lord's judges and officials pushed their way into the fellowship; lordly decrees began to limit the voluntary arrangements, while compulsory labour and levies – [635] the necessary consequence of serfdom and dependent ownership – were continually increased. The development of the towns brought only disadvantages to the rural population, by drawing away the free elements of the rural population and cutting it off from the new branches of commerce. The advent of exclusiveness in the lordly and chivalric estates, the formation of the territorial estates, and all acts of union which proceeded without the participation of the peasantry, endangered rural freedom more and more decisively. The learned lawyers who were crowding into the court-rooms and councils of the princes were already beginning to apply Roman law, which did little to favour community freedom, to the circumstances of the peasantry. In short, having already excluded it from public life, everything united in an unchecked advance to curtail the peasantry's fellowship-based independence in the affairs of its local lands and villages.

The rural folk did not submit without violent resistance and, latterly, armed conflict. Complaints against the violent extension of territorial lordship by the princes had been resounding since the thirteenth century. The following centuries witnessed bloody revolts by oppressed local communities. Finally, when, along with the spiritual liberation of the German nation, the desire for freedom in this world was stirred up in it even more strongly than before by the Reformation, the rural population in nearly all of Germany gathered together its remaining strength for the great attempt at freeing itself in the Peasants' Revolt (1525). The goals of this [636] movement, as formulated in the twelve articles[2] which were accepted by almost all of the rebelling bands, were lacking in neither historical nor internal justification. They demanded the free election and deposition of clerics by the communities (article 1); independent management of matters concerning timber and the *Mark* by persons elected by the local community (article 5); the abolition of tithes paid in the form of livestock, and the use of the great tithes for the vicar, the local poor and other communal needs (article 2); the annulment of any serfdom (article 3), and of its distinguishing feature, the right to reclaim lands after the death of a serf (article 11); redress for arbitrary punishment, and the institution of impartial justice (article 9); the removal of dues and services introduced, or arbitrarily increased, in the face of tradition and existing agreements (articles 8 and 9); the reduction of exorbitant demands for compulsory labour (article 6); and, finally, the return of communal rights of exploitation of water and forest (especially of hunting and fishing) (article 4), of timber-felling and ownership of the common land [*Allmende*] which the prince had taken illegally (articles 5 and 10). The peasantry, however, lacked a secure collective organisation which would have been able to ensure victory. The uncohesive movement, lacking an overall plan, succumbed to the combined might of the princes and nobility. The defeated rural population realised that its situation had scarcely anywhere improved and had in many cases become worse.

By 1525 it had been decided in Germany that freedom was only possible through the intermediary of absolutism. However abundantly the system of fellowship might flourish, from the time of the failure of the last violent attempt of the German peasants to enter the ranks of the privileged estates by their own strength, the nation became divided into privileged and oppressed classes. The consequences were soon to emerge in the degeneration of all fellowships into chartered corporations, which in the long term were incapable of standing their ground in the battle against the new idea of sovereignty.

[For further discussion of rural fellowships, see chapter XII.]

Chapter XI

Corporations and the sovereign state 1525–1806; the modern association movement, 1806 onwards: introduction [54]

The nature of sovereign power, of the chartered corporation and of free association

[638] From the Reformation and the Peasants' Revolt until the dissolution of the Empire (1806), we have posited a fourth period in the legal and moral history of German fellowship, in which the concept of sovereign power [*Obrigkeit*] is the dominant principle and the system of fellowship increasingly turns into one of privileged corporations. The idea of modern free association only begins to emerge towards the end of this period. Then, in our century, it develops so great a transformative, regenerative power that it seems justified to see in this idea the formative principle of the fifth period, at the beginning of which we now find ourselves. We will attempt, first, to sketch the nature and history of these ideas in very general terms.

The *privileged corporation* [*priviligierte Korporation**] differed from the medieval fellowship more in its inherent nature than in its name and form. The transition from the medieval to the early modern was very gradual and almost unnoticeable. In general, its nature lies in its being a corporation whose form is determined and conditioned by a privilege or by the sum total of privileges to which it is entitled. In earlier times, too, fellowships had sought and received countless privileges; but the privilege always existed only for the sake of the fellowship and served its purposes. Now, conversely, the corporative group was simply a means of exploiting the privilege, it existed because of and for the sake of the privilege; indeed it often seemed nothing more than an *incorporated privilege*.

[639] The group of fellows now no longer had its basis for existence within itself; the privilege, the concession, and thus a higher will, gave it existence, but the corporation took not merely its existence, but in-

creasingly also the form of its being from something outside itself. It became basically an *institution* [*Anstalt**], for which the circumstance that its substratum was an association was not of intrinsic relevance.

The composition and structure of the corporation were based purely on private right. Membership was regarded, and treated, as a share in the privilege and could be acquired and lost accordingly. Special positions and often even offices within the association were conceived as special rights deriving from the privilege.

The *legal and moral* significance of the corporation dwindled correspondingly. Its chief importance lay in the maintenance, exploitation and augmentation of the privilege. But, because the privilege was conceived only in terms of profit – and therefore increasingly treated as a private Right even where its content was in reality public in nature – the corporation declined, even without outside interference, into an institution based mainly on private law. In dealings with the outside world, this resulted in all fellowships withdrawing from public life; in corporative egotism, and a consequent desire for monopoly and exclusivity in relation to non-members; in a narrow-minded isolationism *vis-à-vis* other associations and estates; in the limitation of corporative laws to those types of corporation present at a given time, with a total lack of a new creative form of association coming from below. In relation to the state, it resulted in a desire to have rights without undertaking corresponding duties – the one-sided tendency of the corporative consciousness itself to perceive the corporation as a unique individual, where it had formerly perceived itself as also being a member of a higher universality.

Corresponding changes took place within the corporation: the collectivity lost its former unity, not to become a higher entity existing above the individuals, but to stand alongside them as a limited subject of private Right and consequently as a mere individual. The corporation entirely stopped being a community [*Gemeinwesen*] in miniature; its religious and moral elements disappeared; the fellows did not see themselves as members of a greater whole, but merely as private individuals with a specific share in the incorporated privilege. The corporative sense of community disappeared and communal life atrophied in dead formalism. Instead of continuing its organic development, the corporation finally began to ossify. In the end it completely stopped being a vital organism and became a legal mechanism [*Rechtsmechanismus*] which could be constructed at will.

[640] *In historical terms* these changes took place very gradually, in correspondence with the transformation of the German people as a whole.

In the fifteenth century it was already noticeable that the union movement had come to a standstill, although this was interrupted one last time, violently but unsuccessfully, during the first quarter of the sixteenth century. The century following the reformation shows a distinct decrease in the creative power of the nation. A certain amount of fatigue was understandable after the elevation of the national spirit. The suppression of popular movements in countryside and towns separated the mass of the people more sharply than before from the privileged estates. Even among the latter, however, those who had previously been the main embodiments [*Träger*] of the developments towards freedom – the burghers and knights – declined in importance and became less independent, under the influence of the change in the nature of warfare. The predominance at this time of an inclination towards spiritual and religious interests, the beginnings of humanistic education, the strongly awakening need for a personal spiritual and emotional life – all these diverted interest from public matters. It almost seemed as if in the sixteenth century, as later at the end of the eighteenth, the power of the nation was so exhausted by single important personalities that the innate creative power of the people receded before the activities of individuals. As the participation of the collectivity in the management of large and small circles of fellows decreased, so interest in public life, political understanding and love of freedom lessened in turn among the majority, until finally the long period of disuse sapped even the capacity for self-government. And so the corporative organisation handed on from the Middle Ages began to atrophy; the formation of new fellowships faltered, and the transition from free fellowship to chartered corporation was complete.

Although it was clear, even at the beginning of the seventeenth century, that the construction of the modern state was based solely on the sovereignty-principle [*Obrigkeitsprinzip*] embodied by the princes, the political power of the people and the vitality of its corporate organisms were still significant enough for it to appear possible that, as in England, the concept of the sovereign state might enter into a compromise with the notion of corporative self-determination and self-administration, that, alongside a strong unified state, the participation [*Betheiligung*] of the people in the creation, pronouncement and application of law, together with freedom of movement in hereditary or chosen spheres of community, could be preserved for the German nation as well. The terrible national disaster of the Thirty Years War (1618–48), which ruined the nation externally and internally for more than a century, destroyed such possibilities. The decline of the German people was so profound that rescue could only be hoped for from the intermediate step of a merciless [641] absolutism.

In the period from 1648 to 1750 there was scarcely any public-minded spirit. Anyone who compares the documentary testimonials of this time with earlier ones asks with painful astonishment whether this can be the same nation, so changed is its soul. The sense of nation is almost entirely lost and the idea of the state is dispersed throughout countless small princely courts. The chivalric spirit of the independent nobility is perverted into pride of caste towards inferiors and lackeyism towards superiors; the proud sense of citizenship has become a worthless narrow-mindedness. The magnificent spirit of commerce has turned into a debased shopkeeper mentality, and pride in craft has turned into a notorious exclusivism. For the peasant engaged in compulsory labour and the payment of rent, the last memories of the old freedom now disappeared. There is scarcely a prince or thinker whose vision extends beyond his own land, town or trade. Scarcely anywhere are motives other than petty and short-sighted self-seeking understood. Scarcely anywhere does public life (or what is taken for it) revolve around a goal apart from that of maintaining and augmenting bought or inherited privileges. The people have become the sum of all individuals; the concept of community [*Gemeinheit*] is almost lost to them. So lacking was the age in a sense of community [*Gemeinsinn*] that the much-used proverbs *communio mater discordiarium* (community is the mother of discords) and *negotia communia communiter negliguntur* (common matters are neglected in common) were confirmed every day. Even the word 'common' gained the pejorative sense which persists today.

The sad receptacle for such contents was the system of corporations; in this period their corruption and decline reached its peak. When the nation gradually revived in the second half of the eighteenth century, with the intellectual blossoming of science and art, with the great deeds of individual princes – above all of those who enabled the Prussian state to become the leader of Germany – and with the gradual re-awakening of the German spirit, the old corporations were too set in their ways to be the agent of the new public-spiritedness, or conversely to have new life breathed into them by it. Instead, the new movement itself brought about their downfall; it had to do so, in order to prepare the ground for reconstruction. Some corporations succumbed to the storms transplanted [*sic*] on to German soil by the French Revolution. The majority did not die, or were not abolished . . . until much more recently, in about the last twenty years. A few saved themselves by modifications appropriate to the age.

Others still, even today, prolong their existence in the old way.[1] But a sharp divide separates the modern system of fellowship from the remains of the chartered corporations, whose time of greatest prosperity was also a time of national decline.

The concept of sovereign power, which was given the task of [642] forming the new structure of state and Right, in opposition to the declining system of corporations, had gone through various stages of inward and outward development. The *essence* of this concept, however great the difference in other respects between Luther's demand for obedience, the 'l'état c'est moi' of Louis XIV and Frederick the Great's 'first servant of the state', has remained the same in spite of progressive clarification and intellectualism. Indeed, it applies equally to all the diverse political constructs of the philosophers of the seventeenth and eighteenth centuries and to the idea of the state found in the French Revolution. The characteristic feature of this concept is that it sees the state as something apart from the people. In the abstract formulation of this state, it concentrates the sum total of all public power within a distinct sphere, territorially and personally enclosed. It concentrates the Right and duty to represent the common interest (*salus publica*) against special interests . . . to create Right and public order, and to regulate the relationship of member to whole in a necessary unity, to such an extent that sovereign power becomes the visible representation of the abstract concept: apart from the state there can only be individuals.

If we consider the particular form assumed by the concept of sovereignty in Germany, we recognise it as a heightening of the old concept of lordship in just the same way that communities had previously developed from a heightening of the old fellowships. Hence community [*Gemeinwesen*] and state sovereignty have much in common – above all a truly state-like [*staatlich*] character. In both, the idea of an invisible entity has replaced that of an entity discernible by the senses; collectivity or lord remain only as visible representatives, as the physical manifestation. Just as in community the collective Right can be encompassed within a single concept, so too the Right of lordship in the authoritarian state is encompassed in a single concept, all of whose attributes are necessary; and therefore in both cases the alienation, division and fragmentation of public power on the basis of private Right gradually cease. In both cases the distinction between public and private law develops. True agencies of the unified subject of state power take the place of those who owned public power, whether in their own right as feudatories, or as those to whom authority had been mandated. In both cases, finally, the individual's characteristics as a member of the whole became distinct from his characteristics as an individual; and, as had happened in the case of civil law, it becomes possible here too, in the concept of the subject . . . to separate the *public* duties of obedience, service and taxation from those obligations to undertake duties, give service and pay dues which were based on a *specific* title.

Greater than any such parallels, none the less, are the differences between the legal ideologies [*Rechtsgedanken*] of community and of sovereignty. In community, [643] all had a share in the representation of the unity; in the sovereign state, unity is represented only by an individual, or in exceptional cases a group of individuals. Thus in community, unity is collective, dwells in the collectivity and finds its highest expression in the collective will; whereas in the sovereign state, unity is alien to the collectivity, exists for itself and takes effect through an individual will set above the collectivity. Therefore, while the communal constitution determines the organisation by means of which the collectivity *governs itself*, the sovereign constitution contains within itself the organisation by means of which the collectivity *is governed*. The concept of *citizen* unites political rights and political duties, lordship and obedience, active and passive participation in the common life: the *subject* is a legal subject only in the sphere of private law, in public law he is merely the object, he is to the state as the layman is to the church.[2] The common life demands that the citizen participate in administration, adjudication and legislation, and inclines towards the principles of election, collegiality and majority voting; sovereignty strives towards the exclusion of subjects from public life and favours centralising administration by means of nominated unitary agencies.

If, then, the principle of sovereignty strives towards the realisation of the *absolute state*, it is at the same time a *supervisory* state [*Polizeistaat**].[3] For, since the concept of *the public good* is regarded as supreme, concern for the public good or positive intervention [*Polizei*] are bound to count as the functions of the state, for the sake of which all other functions exist. If, then, existing law comes into conflict with the public good, it must give way unconditionally; even state treaties, privileges and well-established rights become invalid where they are prejudicial to the public good.[4] Since the representative of the public welfare – the sovereign – has the exclusive right to verify and decide whether such is the case, the principle that *salus publica lex suprema est* (public safety is the supreme law) is a convenient argument for justifying all breaches of law [*Recht*]. Despite flying in the face of ancient tradition and many of the practices of the imperial court, sovereignty as the representative of *Polizei* recognises no limitations on, or even protection against, its powers in Right. Rather, the sovereign state increasingly moves *above* and *beyond* Right and becomes the opposite of the *constitutional state* [*Rechtsstaat*] foreshadowed in the communal system [*Gemeinwesen*], which exists within the law and accepts that law sets limits on its freedom of movement – its organism itself is law – and which strives as its ultimate goal for the unity of state and Right. The sovereign state not only wants to control all powers, it wants to control them exclusively. The recognition, implementation and protection of what is required for the common good is not simply its Right and duty, but the *monopoly* of the sovereign. The subject as such may see to his own individual affairs, but he is neither capable of keeping universal affairs under his control, nor empowered to so do, unless [644] he is endowed with the superior insight, common sense and political authorisation by a state office. Therefore, while the office is almost like ecclesiastical ordination in consecrating the individual to a higher status, the common subject, even though he has attained his majority in terms of private law, remains politically a minor until the end of his days.

Even private affairs are supervised, directed, restricted and regulated wherever they encroach on the public interest – and whether or not this is the case is adjudicated at the discretion of the sovereign power. It is the Right and duty of the state to prescribe, enforce or restrict, in every detail, the economic activity of the individual for the increase of national wealth, to standardise trade and commerce by means of statutes, taxes and regulations, to tax unproductive consumption by means of sumptuary laws, to prescribe the country's manner of building by cultural decrees, and to prevent idleness or the incorrect use of labour by threats of punishment. In the same way as it attempts to be the guardian of economic life, it seeks also to be the guardian of the life of the intellect, to prescribe its direction and to limit its own vitality. Indeed, if at all possible, the subject is to be regulated even in his social and recreational activities, each one's rank and entitlements being determined by the sovereign power. From this it emerges that the authoritarian state is a *tutelary state* [*Bevormundungsstaat*], and also that it inclines towards bureaucratic over-government, centralisation and standardisation.[5]

From such basic principles it follows that the relationship of the sovereign power to the system of fellowships is one of total antagonism. Of course, the sovereign state is as little able to do without articulation into lesser associations as the system of fellowship, nor is it able entirely to suppress associations which are outwith the state. But, while the free system of association in German law recognises the lesser associations of its citizens as communities homogeneous with the greater whole, and allows them independent life even while it uses them as building blocks for the overall structure, sovereignty endeavours with steely single-mindedness to reach a two-fold goal: first, to absorb all the public significance of communities [*Gemeinden*] and fellowships into the concept of state, and secondly to reduce whatever remains in these groups of innate importance to the level of a state-owned capacity. All corporations, therefore, in so far as their nature is based on public law, are to be considered *components of the state* – whether as divisions of the state territory or as its subjects, as administrative districts or as state institutions . . . [Otherwise] they are to be *private associations*, which, as a result of a specific state charter, have the right to be regarded within certain confines as unitary subjects of private rights. In this way, the autonomy, jurisdiction and self-administration of associations of fellows are annulled; whatever remains of these things *de facto* is either assumed to relate to private law, or explained as originating from a special commission of the authorities [645] and accordingly treated as a right which derives from outside the group. Even in the law of property the corporation must pay for its legal personality with the utmost dependence. Its existence is tolerated and standardised from above; and its standing is far behind that of the individual, for it is not even regarded as having reached its majority in private . . .

The dissipation of all local communities and fellowships into the concept of state on one hand, and into the concept of the individual on the other, is only a symptom of a more universal tendency which aimed also to achieve, alongside the absolute state, *absolute individuality*.[6] This tendency, which begins with the slow emancipation of the individual, in all spheres of life, from the Middle Ages onwards, but has only been consciously active since the second half of the last century, sets as its ultimate goal a condition in which *apart from the state there are only individuals*. Hence there are no intermediate links of any kind between the supreme universality of the all-caring state and the sum total of single individuals, comprising the people [*Volk*]. Such connecting bodies as there are count only as local manifestations of the state, or as themselves individuals. This last goal, which came close to being realised in France by means of the Revolution, was never achieved in Germany, least of all in practice . . .

Since the authoritarian state, single-mindedly pursuing its own ends, worked against all particularities which stood between it and the individual, it achieved for all its subjects *individual freedom and equality under the law*; this has been almost perfected today.[7] *Individual freedom* was bound to result if the state destroyed the lordship associations contained within it, as it had the fellowships, and annulled any indirect or private subjection which was incompatible with direct subjection to the state. Not until relatively late did the absolute state perceive this great and fruitful consequence of its basic principle. But it did – and thereby accomplished one of the greatest deeds of history. The liberation of the peasantry at the end of the [eighteenth] century and the beginning of this, atoning for the injustice of centuries, produced for the first time states in which there were only free men. Hand in hand with universal freedom went the legal *equality* of all. For the political and legal equality of subjects was the beneficial consequence of the destruction of the medieval corporations and lordship associations, based on the estates, and of the final levelling of the estates themselves.

This represented an immense step forward from the medieval gild-state. [646] For in spite, or rather because, of the equality established between those most closely associated, the gild-state was based on the utmost inequality under public law, since, alongside the full members, there were lesser associates and protected members . . . Even if in the Middle Ages the high regard for the unconditional correspondence of Right and duty counterbalanced this inequality before the law, it held within it the seed of the downfall of the old fellowship system. There was, on the other hand, from the very beginning a tendency inherent in the idea of sovereignty to subject all members of the state to the same authority, the same law and the same courts; and to afford them all the same measure of protection, representation and care for their welfare. The realisation of this idea came late, and even today has not been fully implemented.

Yet the freedom and equality aspired to by the absolute state were only the freedom and equality of *subjects*. The content, therefore, was exclusively negative and the participation passive. A further development, by which the *freedom of state citizenship* was added to individual freedom and the equality of subjects was increased by equal participation in active political rights, could not be accomplished on the basis of the sovereign-state concept. It was initiated by the new political philosophy of our century, which transferred the state back to the people. This one-sided tendency to place state absolutism and absolute individuality alongside one another, without any intermediaries, can be overcome in the same way. Necessary as this is for political unity and equality, it is the death-knell of all true freedom, since its ultimate consequences are *centralisation of government and fragmentation of the people.* In Germany, we were protected from such a danger, the scale of which could be seen in France, by our sense of fellowship. This had never completely died, and with the awakening of the nation's vigour [*Volkskraft*] it became more powerful than ever.

If the actual reason for the victory of the principle of sovereignty lay in its own inner strength and the weakness of the privileged corporations, certain external forces . . . were of great significance for the form its victories took. The decisive factor was the political fate of the German nation. Since everything was uniting to fortify the territorial lord at the expense of the Empire and of the other estates, the form of constitution which was most favourable to the concept of the sovereign state, and most hostile to corporative self-management, was elevated to be the standard, legitimate form. It is of course true that in the city communities, in so far as these achieved the rank of states, the communal constitution [647] gave way to an authoritarian constitution in which the privileged body merely took the place of the prince; and that the principle of sovereignty even penetrated the territorial communes of Switzerland. But the real representatives of the new idea were the territorial lords; each victory of the territorial lords, therefore, was a victory for the system of sovereignty and a defeat for the order of fellowship.

Of hardly less importance was the alliance of the sovereign-state concept with Roman law. The nobility and people had good reason to hate and fear the foreign system of law; the violent popular opposition which, at the end of the fifteenth and beginning of the sixteenth centuries, attempted to remove lawyers trained in Roman law, can be explained more easily than can the speedy defeat of this rebellion. For, once the reception of the alien system had been decided, and (more importantly) more and more learned jurists were giving decisions in consultative and administrative agencies as well as in the law-courts, the power of the princes had gained a keen-edged weapon against the freedom of the people. The Roman lawyers unhesitatingly applied to conditions in Germany not only private law but also, whenever it appeared advantageous, the constitutional tenets of the *Corpus juris*; and they justified earlier arbitrary acts by citations or analogies from Roman law. At first only the emperor was for them *princeps* in the Roman sense, but soon they imbued the territorial lord with the same attributes . . . and indeed declared him emperor in his own land[8] . . .

Administration by the sovereign (instead of self-management), unified state legislation (which pushed aside autonomy), sentencing by state officials, centralisation and uniformity as goals, bureaucracy with its principles of secrecy and of committing everything to paper, in short the state itself, separate from and independent of the people – all of these found in Rome's old age a model which could be lived up to only with difficulty. Only in paternalism and over-regulation could the German sovereign state, with its modest circumstances, improve upon Justinian's Empire. In particular, Roman law encouraged the tendency of the supervisory state [*Polizeistaat*] to elevate itself above the law. For, in the Roman view of the status of public and private law, only the latter was recognised as genuine law; the former was simply an administrative structure, which recognised law, and legal protection of the citizen against the treasury – but never against the state and its agencies.

If German state absolutism found support in Roman ideas, Roman law was incomparably more important for pushing ahead absolute individuality. [648] The late-Roman state consisted (apart from slaves, who for it were not persons at all) only of a sum of individuals, equal to one another, but for public affairs with no further organic connection among themselves, but rather mechanically divided, and forming individual associations, at most, for separate private-law purposes.[9] The greatest possible centralisation thus corresponded to the most extreme fragmentation. In their defence of sovereignty in conflict with the communes and fellowships, therefore, lawyers trained in Roman law need never be short of a legal text. In reality, admittedly, it was no easy task to force the inexhaustible wealth and vitality of German fellowship groups down into the position occupied by municipalities, colleges and institutions in the soulless imperial structure of the East Roman Empire. But a theoretical formula for it was soon found in the *universitas* or *corpus* – the association with a mystical, moral, juristic personality![10] This entailed exclusion from public Right, restriction to right-subjectivity [i.e. legal personality] for the purposes of the law of property through a state-granted concession revocable at any time, eternal minority, and an internal organisation based purely on private law, involving the reduction of the collective entity to an individuality entirely distinct from the collectivity. The effectiveness of this new formula for the slow transformation of the fellowship system cannot be underestimated. Roman jurisprudence . . . helped also to smash the estates, emancipate the individual, and finally to bring about the freedom and equality of subjects. The peasantry, not least, however badly they suffered under the application of Roman law – unintelligible to its members – is indebted to it for finally gaining not only full personal freedom but also full ownership of their lands.

One need only say in passing that the *theological* perceptions of both the old and new church remained almost constantly favourable to the concept of the sovereign state; in tracing sovereignty back to divine institution, it exercised a powerful influence. Ever since *philosophy* had drawn state and society into its orbit, philosophical systems, however much they might differ from one another, were all no less helpful to one or other aspect of the tendency of the age: they promoted either state absolutism or the emancipation of the individual. Their very dependence on ancient culture and the political theory of the ancients encouraged this; the spirit and needs of the age encouraged it even more. While there were of course various 'institutional' theories [*Anstaltstheorien*], regarding the state as of divine or human institution [649], reflections on the origins of the state increasingly gave the victory to theories of contract.

Those who came up with a contract of submission were entirely favourable to state absolutism; theories of a contract of society, on the other hand, made the state the product of the will of the people, but still posited the state as something separate from the people. Philosophical theories about the ends and the corresponding arrangement of the state all drew very different boundaries between state and individual, ranging from almost complete destruction of the state to almost complete destruction of the individual; but they all agreed in seeing the state (in so far as they recognised it at all) as a power separate from the people, and the people (in so far as they acknowledged their existence) as the sum of all individuals otherwise not united in any way. Theories of the state, since fundamentally they identified the state with sovereignty and the people with the sum total of subjects [*Summe der Unterthanen*], were far removed from recognising the state as the organised personality of the people [*organisierte Volkspersönlichkeit*]; and, most importantly, none of them permitted between individual and state the existence of self-substantive intermediaries with the status of lesser commonalties [*Gemeinwesen*]. From standpoints ranging from Hobbes to Rousseau, they all declared themselves against any separate independent grouping within the state and therefore against the citizens' rights of free association; and in Germany, before Hegel, there was scarcely any system of political ethics [*Rechtsphilosophie*], least of all that of Kant, which recognised any independent communes or fellowships within its system. Here the ideal states that were proposed differed little from existing states. Some aspire to a supposed state of nature, in which the polity is to be dissolved into individuals, while utopians preach state absolutism with progressive intensity until finally, in communist ideals, not only the political but also the private-law personality of all individuals is destroyed in favour of an all-caring state.

When, therefore, the theories of the philosophers were put into practice in the *French Revolution*, and thereafter the direct influence of the ideas implemented in France began to be felt in Germany, it became clear that the Revolution did not overcome the old dualism of state and people. [650] Although, with the establishment of an absolute state and the recognition in state and law of the absolute individual, it realised unity and equality; nevertheless, by transforming the state into a machine and not recognising lesser organic associations, the Revolution had undermined the active freedom of the people. That is why the transition of the [French] republic into an imperial state could be achieved so easily, and why in Germany absolutist territorial lords could implement the revolutionary legislation without this being any more than a sudden advance towards the goal to which the authoritarian state had until now been slowly travelling.

Lastly, from the eighteenth century onwards, the influence of *theorists of national economy*[11] also worked towards an authoritarian design for the state system. For they had proved – rightly or wrongly – that existing economic circumstances were preventing the maximisation of national prosperity, and had shown that these could be transformed, and how this could be done. This caused governments to intervene from above in the private lives of individuals, fellowships and communes – furthering, restricting and transforming them. In this way . . . the package of sovereign institutions was being elevated into a principle, and the struggle began against economic organisms originating in the past, in particular the agrarian community and the gild system, which were regarded as fetters upon a freer economic development.

In historical terms the development of the concept of the sovereign state proceeded in several phases. In the German cities and *Länder*, the concept of lordship was transformed into that of state sovereignty as early as the fifteenth century. The Reformation was epoch-making, because it gave the state sovereign power in the church and in matters of belief, contributed to the increasing decline of the Empire, and because of the whole tenor of church development after the unsuccessful popular rebellions. From then until the Thirty Years War, the sovereign state made steady progress, concentrating and developing its powers. Yet to a certain extent a balance of power existed between it and the older associations, which were initially only restricted, not annulled. By developing in detail the system of custodial intervention, territorial sovereignty was the only positive force at work from the Peace of Westphalia (which formally sanctioned it) until the middle of the eighteenth century. Meanwhile the powerless people scarcely attempted to save their political independence in communes and fellowships any more.

The second half of the eighteenth century brought two-fold progress.

First of all, state absolutism was perfected: by overcoming the pettiness which had attached to it until then, it created, [651] especially in the Prussian state, a secure and powerful unitary state ruling a large section of the German people. This unitary state, although initially independent of and in opposition to the people, increasingly enabled the political confidence of the nation to re-establish itself. Secondly, with so-called enlightened despotism, the state began to work consciously for the emancipation of the individual, complementing absolutism, and for the levelling of estates and the equality of all before the law.

The victory in principle of the concept of the absolute state and of individualism was determined when the storms of the French Revolution were carried over into Germany, when, following the dissolution of the Empire, territorial dominion was transformed into sovereignty, and the revolutionary legislation completely or partly adopted. From then till now it has been a question of slow progress towards the realisation of both principles in detail, which today is almost complete. The idea of the absolute state has more and more asserted itself in a state unity carried virtually to the point of centralisation, in the formation of modern administrative organisations, and in a levelling-out of local differences in public law, verging on standardisation. On the other hand, the barriers which separated the individual from direct contact with the state, and produced inequality in public Right were increasingly disposed of: privileges and exemptions, the estates' prerogatives, patrimonial powers, differences occasioned by religious creed, trade and business monopolies, and the inequality of public impositions, were increasingly abolished. At the same time, the old associations which fettered the individual in agriculture, trade and status were broken up or robbed of their binding power.

If, in all these areas, modern developments appear to be solely the result of ideas which had for centuries been determining the direction of the sovereign state, and whose realisation is brought nearer, consciously or unconsciously, by each step forward, in our century quite a different principle is at work. It works partly in association with older ideas and partly alongside them. The value of our modern upheavals would in fact be very questionable if they were influenced solely by that power which used its positive creative energy only in favour of unconditional state unity, and whose effect on all other organisms was only to negate and dissolve them; and if their inevitable result was a one-sided culmination in a centralised and mechanistic state and an atomised people. We owe the fact that such is not the case, and never will be, to the reawakened [652] *spirit of association*. By endeavouring to fill all public associations from below with an independent communal life and by building together the particles, into which the nation had threatened to disintegrate, into countless new combinations, organic in structure and containing inherent vigour, this is the real positive principle which shapes the new epoch for the development of the German law and constitution in our century. It, above all others, gives us a firm guarantee that the epoch will not represent the old age of the German people, but rather the full bloom of its manly vigour.

The *modern association movement* is still so much in its early stages that its nature can scarcely be defined and it has no proper history of its own. It ought to be clear, therefore, that it is in essence a new and distinctive phenomenon and that its development will be ever upwards.

The essence of the modern association movement clearly brings it much closer to the medieval union movement than to the privileged corporation system of later days. In most points it is the direct opposite of the latter; while in relation to the medieval system of union, it is but a higher stage of development of the same principle. Thus the modern system of association offers many analogies with the medieval system of union. It too comes from within the people and builds upwards from below. It too is an expression of the awakening national consciousness and the vigour of the people [*Volksbewusstsein . . . Volkskraft*] with quite free self-help creating forms of the self-determination and self-management they have longed for. As the medieval union was set against the idea of lordship and service, so the modern association sets its face against the idea of a sovereign standing above and beyond the whole. Likewise, it is combated, restricted and prohibited by representatives of the old principle, who cannot however quite succeed in smothering the new idea. Modern association, like union, is rooted in freedom; and it too tries to build ever wider spheres on to narrow ones. The privileged corporation's corporative separateness, exclusivity, rigidity of form and privatisation of public rights is no less alien to it.

In contrast to the pronounced corporate forms of the intervening period, the modern association, like the medieval union, has an air of constant flux – the essential mark of a time of strong growth. Hence it is rich in transitional forms and intermediate structures, in short-lived phenomena which exist only to pave the way for a fuller legal structure, in a wealth of intersections and combinations which it is difficult to systematise. To an even greater extent than in the Middle Ages, countless forms of community [*Gemeinschaft**] emerge from the modern association. These almost fill the gulf between the conceptual opposites [653] of a personal society (or proprietorial community) and a fellowship endowed with an independent legal personality (or living community). Just as, lastly, union had the dual effect of remodelling fellowships based on necessity and recreating fellowships based on will, so that no clear boundary could be drawn here, so too the modern system of association operates in both areas with no clear demarcation.

There are, however, alongside these analogies, fundamental points of difference between the modern phase of the fellowship system and its medieval manifestation. The higher development of public and private life on the one hand, and the more precise definition of legal terminology on the other, along with the multiplication of forms, has brought about a division of the fellowship system into many branches. Although there are links between these, they are much more sharply distinct from each other than were the medieval forms of community. In the first instance, groups with their own legal personality emerge in distinction to mere communities and societies. Among the former, groups comprising states, whose existence is independent of free will, are much more distinct than before from freely formed associations. Of the utmost importance is the fact that public and private law have separated out, so that groups with importance in the public sphere are put together and organised on principles of public law, and private-law corporations on principles of private law. The danger of their being transformed into privileged corporations thereby disappears.

But the most important difference between the modern and the medieval is that, through the continued splitting-up of group life, fellowships are formed more and more for single purposes; so that finally, in contrast to the medieval tendency to extend each group of fellows over the whole person and simply make it into a community [*Gemeinschaft*], the opposite tendency has prevailed: *the purposes of each individual association are precisely defined*, and its organisation adapted and its significance limited accordingly. Even the highest association – the state – has its purposes, and therefore the limits of its scope prescribed by this modern trend. The purposes of local communities [*Gemeinden*] of higher or lesser degree are defined even more precisely; indeed in many cases special groups resembling *Gemeinden* are set up for specific purposes. The same goes for the church and other public bodies. It is, in short, the general rule today that freely formed associations are confined to single specialised purposes.[12] Corporate fellowships are brought into existence solely for one stated purpose related to the law of property, solely for one specified spiritual or moral purpose; indeed today it is chiefly for specific purposes [654] that people group themselves together. The composition and organisation of each particular corporation is bound up with this specification of purposes; for example, fellowships based on property are exclusive and constructed according to the law of property, whereas a fellowship based on labour for economic purposes or a political association is non-exclusive and constructed on a personal basis, and so on.

This is further related to the precise delimitation of the amount of individuality which the individual gives up to the fellowship, or, to put it differently, the relationship between unity and plurality. Even for the state there is an attempt, articulated in the demand for so-called basic rights, to express in a precise formula which sides of the individual personality could be independent even of the supreme universality [*höchste Allgemeinheit*], and which individual rights should be inviolable. It is even more expressly stated how much individuality a person should relinquish to other compulsory groups. In the area of association by free choice, it is possible to belong to one group of fellows or another with one's individuality as one wishes, sometimes with a precisely proportionate sum of personal rights and obligations, sometimes with a precisely defined share of capital, without the individual having to forego his own personality. If the individual as citizen helps form a state, province, district, and local community, and perhaps a range of special groups to look after the poor, or a school, or to maintain roadways, dikes and waterways; if as fellow-believer he helps form a church, or if, as a member of a specific vocational group, he helps form a corporation [*Innung*]; if, as a personally active member, he helps form any number of political, social, charitable or recreational groups, or again as a shareholder he helps to form however many business companies at home or abroad – in all of this in terms of law his individuality is so little used up that the possibility of helping to call new fellowships being being, for these or other purposes in life, appears quite limitless. Thus, while the corporation system ultimately fetters the individual, the modern association is compatible with the greatest conceivable personal freedom.

But, at the same time, there emerged in place of the fixed order of medieval fellowships encircling one another, a system of groups of varying importance intersecting one another at many points: hence the class [*ständisch*] foundation was overcome, and the danger of a new separation based on class was avoided. The old system of corporations united the *fellows* as closely as possible, in order to distinguish the fellow*ships* all the more clearly from one another; the modern association forces the fellows to unite only so far as is requisite for one quite specific purpose, so as finally to construct one collective unity out of single groups interlocking with one another in a hundred different ways. Here there is no longer any division according to class [*Klasse*] or estate [*Stand*].

The modern association, therefore, although it started in the towns, does not exclude the rural population but draws the whole nation into its circle. Lastly, the modern system of fellowship [655] is exempt also from the danger of raising the particular above the universal, and thus ultimately of creating states within the state. It is opposed by a strong unitary state which had developed before it. Furthermore, it has the tendency to prevent state centralism without weakening the idea of the state, achieved after centuries. For it recognises the latter's value, and willingly finds the measure and limit of its own sphere over against this powerful phenomenon. Up to now the real effectiveness of the new concept of association, which did not question the unitary state and free individuality resulting from the idea of sovereignty, but encompassed these in higher forms, emerged chiefly in two ways. First, it had a modifying effect on those groups whose existence was independent of their members' will. By aiming to provide these with an inner life conditioned and determined by the collective will, and an organisational structure to facilitate this – that is, the form of the fellowship – it has produced a series of radical transformations in public law which in many cases has breathed a new life into the old lifeless bodies.

Above all it has begun to relocate the state itself within the people. For, through a representative constitution, public control of the administration, the participation of the people in law-making and the restoration of traditional [*volksthümlich*] criminal adjudication, it has given expression to the idea that the state is nothing other than the organised people. It has built up the state under sovereign leadership but on the basis of a fellowship of citizens.

The reorganisation of lesser public associations too, along the lines of independent communities of fellowship, has in certain respects been begun by taking at least the first steps towards the autonomy, self-management and comradely [*genossenschaftlich*] organisation of communes, districts and provinces, of special commune-like associations, and of other corporations based on public law. In the church too the concept of the institution has already been forced to give some ground to the notion of religious fellowships.

Secondly, the concept of association has produced effects in its own right by its free activity, by calling into being a great number of free fellowships of the most varied kinds, for all conceivable ends. In a relatively very short time, the system of free groups has become a great power in private as in public law, in associations based on capital as well as on labour, in morality, social life and economics. An endlessly lively, independent common life pulses in these groups of comrades [*Genossen-verbände*]; a sense of community and self-functioning is generated. As small universalities over their members, they none the less willingly submitted to being members of a greater universality. Today the life of the nation and of individuals has already been enriched and strengthened [656] by this in ways which can scarcely be comprehended.

The effectiveness of the concept of association appears all the more considerable if one considers how little time it has yet had in which to develop freely. Its beginnings must be fixed in the eighteenth century. But while in England and the Netherlands (where there was almost unbroken continuity with the medieval system of corporations) it was already flourishing in much splendour, in Germany it was still confined to a few pitiful structures, and these based chiefly on private law. With the resurgence of the might of the German people brought forth by the oppression of foreign rule, the stirrings of the new idea gained power. But, until 1848, in the majority of German states it was often opposed by authority; and, even if not, as with enterprises of capital, societies for intellectual interests etc., in this period the association manifested only limited creative power. Its full efficacy . . . belongs only to the last twenty years, when restrictions from above declined, and from below the ancient power of German association awoke to an almost miraculous vigour.

Now that we have sketched in general terms the nature and history of the privileged corporation, of sovereignty, and of the modern idea of association, our task in what follows will be to consider the formation of the system of fellowship under the influence of these three principles . . . An examination of the history of the concept and dogma of the moral personality of the *universitas* will be reserved for [657] [volume] 2. As for the transformation of old fellowships and the generation of new ones under the influence of the modern concept of association, there can as yet in the nature of things be no question of a legal history of this development. For the present, one can only describe the connections of these more recent forms with their predecessors, and sketch their legal content in outline; here too the thorough examination of the juristic construct which both have in common and the overall legal and moral nature of the modern fellowship must be reserved for [volume] 2 . . .

Chapter XII

Rural communities 1525–1806 [55]

Fellowship in local community: the fate of the ancient rural communal fellowship

[657] The rural community of the old law, at once political and economic, had been little influenced or strengthened by the union movement.[1] For centuries it had been engaged in a struggle with forces hostile to it, and it was the first and most complete victim of the effects of sovereignty working on it from without, and of simultaneous disintegration from within. During this process of destruction, the economic aspect of the old two-sided commune was preserved only in isolated cases, when it was continued in a special corporation or an aggregate of private rights. The political aspect of the communal fellowship, however, became the starting-point for a new construct: although it proceeded at first almost exclusively from above, building up the rural commune as a state institution [*Anstalt*] with a juristic personality without, or almost without, elements of fellow-ship, nevertheless in our time it forms the foundation for the start of a reconstruction of a community based both on the state and on the fellow-ship ...

[658] *The destruction of the old fellowship of the Mark*

The external forces working towards the downfall of the community of the *Mark* can be summed up in the idea of sovereignty [*Obrigkeit*], under-pinned here (as ever) by foreign law, politics, philosophy and economics. The onslaughts of sovereign power, increasing steadily from the sixteenth century onwards, on the peasantry's fellowship rights, amounted to an uninterrupted continuation of ancient battles which landlords, stewards and the public power itself had waged against the peasantry's personal freedom and property, and hence also against their fellowship-based constitution. After the powers of lordship under the old law had all been assembled into a single concept [*Begriff*], then the destruction, rather than the restriction, of the *Mark* community became its aim. Till then, the relationship of each local community to its lord – and therefore the boundary between fellowship and lordship – had been determined by the special rights based on contracts and customs of individual communities. Now the nature of sovereignty began to dictate principles which were equally valid for the whole *Land*, negating the idea of fellowship not just in individual cases but *in principle*. The historical events which formed the starting point for sovereignty's attacks upon the community's organism, conducted on each occasion with increased vigour, were the failure of the Peasants' Revolt, the Thirty Years War and the spread of ideas which had broken forth during the French Revolution ... The property basis, without which the old fellowship was inconceivable, had been threatened of old by the twin tendencies to transform lands into the sole property of a lord, and to split them up into separate properties divided among the fellows ...

[662] Ordinances about common land [*Allmende*], pasture, and roadways, and even decrees and statutes about cultivation were enacted. Finally the entire administrative structure [*Polizei*] of the *Mark* fellowship was absorbed by that of the sovereign power. Thus the fellowship lost both its constitutional basis and its primary sphere of autonomous control.

The second tendency, towards the dissolution of the collective property into separate rights, was even more damaging to the old *Mark* community... [663] Communal property ... was everywhere distinguished from the property destined for the economic purposes of the individual members of the community... The former was regarded [664] as the purely politically managed property of a person existing outwith the citizens – a wholly alien Right-subject. It was to be managed entirely by the state ... the fellows' property, on the other hand, was conceived of quite differently. Where the view of communal property based on public law gained complete victory over the view of the citizen's property based on private law, the latter was regarded simply as the normal joint property of those who had rights to it. More widely disseminated was the theory according to which the property should belong to the local community but individuals should be conceded real private rights in it as if in property belonging to a third party ... Finally, in more recent times there has been a desire to generalise the concept of 'civil usufruct', i.e. the claims to common property which appeared simply to depend upon political rights of citizenship, whereby the existence of individual rights to common land as such is contested, and collective property [*Gesammteigenthum*] is declared to be the purely public property of the local community as a juristic person.

All of these views ... alike dismembered collective property as a concept, and so facilitated its disintegration in practice. [665] ... In cases where the property was assigned to the local community and the individual given private rights to it, a majority decision was sufficient for the lands to be divided, so long as, according to the principles of expropriation, compensation was awarded for the lost rights of exploitation ... If joint ownership was accepted, then anyone so entitled could demand that the lands be divided, or at least that his share should be separated out, provided that this did not affect the continuation of the community for other interested parties...

With the continuing disintegration of collective property, the *old* fellowship lost the basis of its structure and the chief arena for its activities; it lost the principle which gave it existence. However, even if the downfall of the community in its old form as an economic community had been thus brought about (as in the towns centuries before), the rural community too could have continued an independent existence as a fellowship in a new and changed form, regarding its functions in *public* law, had the process of destruction not then simultaneously turned towards the *personal association* of fellows and its importance as an independent political body [666] for mutual defence, justice, administration and supervision [*Polizei*]. Here too it was the idea of sovereignty which first consolidated the various endeavours of the lords, who since time immemorial had combated the independence of the fellowships, into a principled negation of fellowship.

The executive of the fellowships above all was increasingly replaced by a public official, or even made into one; or, finally, demoted from a position alongside such an official to an inferior position ... Whether the leadership of the community was at first confirmed (by the authorities) ..., whether the various offices at the head of a *Mark* community, group of peasants or village had become heritable, or again were connected with the possession of certain pieces of land – in one way or another the leadership of local communities was being made dependent, and this dependence was steadily increasing. With this change in circumstances, however, the concept and nature of office in the local community was also changed. It became a direct or indirect public office, the source of which was no longer the plenary authority of the community, but consisted rather in a transfer of the functions of authority on the part of the sovereign territorial power, which exclusively possessed all public power. The nomination or authorisation of the community officials by the territorial lord, or in his name, their swearing-in by the sovereign power, the fact that they conducted their office in the name of a higher power rather than of the community, their responsibility to and accountability before the sovereign power, their guidance by directives from the sovereign power, their standing as the lowest officials of state – all this now followed as the necessary consequence of the concept of the community office.

At the same time the importance of the community as a judicial fellowship [667] declined. The *Mark* courts, already divested of their old character due to the transformation of the higher district authority into a court which held sway over the whole area [*Marksgerichtsherrschaft*], finally (with few exceptions) became lower courts held in the name of the territorial lord. Instead of the fellows, qualified judges passed judgment. The penalties and fines from these courts flowed into the treasury of the territorial lord, and recourse was allowed from them to the higher territorial court. The courts of the overlords, stewards and other lordship-based courts were completely divested of their fellowship elements, and transformed, in part into upper and lower courts of the territorial lord, in part into patrimonial courts of a new kind based on the judicial authority of the landowner. These were increasingly treated as courts belonging indirectly to the state. The free courts of the villages and peasantry were more and more restricted in their competence, and finally entirely swallowed up by the courts of the territorial lord; or else tolerated as wholly inferior agencies of authority, deriving their full power not from the local community but from the court authorities, and therefore subject to cases being reheard, to inspection by the authority, and to appeals to higher courts.

That a fellowship could make law also seemed incompatible with the new idea of the state. For this reason, in most territories, the autonomy of communities was, from the sixteenth century onwards, increasingly restricted, and finally abolished ...

[669] The regulation of their own public law, too, began to be denied to the communities, since their organisation was regarded as emanating from the will of the state. Communal constitutions were constructed a priori to a ready-made model, in accordance with the conception of the communities as administrative districts of the state; they were introduced uniformly everywhere by means of general territorial legislation, without regard to local conditions. It seemed to jurists to be an irregularity that 'foolish' peasants should be able to create law: hence the principle (which had become increasingly well-defined in theory) that the creation of law

was an exclusive, inalienable attribute of sovereign power, and that neither custom nor agreement could set limits to the sovereign rights of the territorial lord, was here most rigorously applied in practice.

Even within the organisational basis prescribed for it, fellowship was no longer granted a free existence or self-administration. In the case of the communities' right to elect their own (executive) organs, their authority in supervisory and penal matters, their independent rights of execution and seizure etc., this follows from what has been said. In the same way, the right to self-taxation ceased, being replaced by taxation on the part of the authorities, and conscription by the authorities for personal services required by the state, the land-owning authorities, or the local community. In almost all respects, any communal decision whatever of any consequence was subject to examination and confirmation by the sovereign power, and all significant legal acts by the community were subject to state intervention, as indeed is the case even today in many local community institutions. The administration of community assets was subjected to extensive inspection and intervention by the sovereign power ... In most communities, it was as a result of decrees by the sovereign power that a communal budget and a [670] communal treasury were first formed at all. The use of revenues for purely public ends was not simply laid down; it was to be supervised on behalf of the authorities, and therefore income and spending were frequently subject to prior examination and approval. Contracts and trials were forbidden without the participation of the sovereign. Reviews of the administration and rendering of accounts were instituted.

There was no lack of a juristic basis for these modifications aimed at the displacement of self-administration by administration on behalf of the sovereign power. The *public* affairs of local communities were, in the context of the new theory of state, regarded as local affairs: the community therefore was an administrative district of the state. The exorbitant restrictions on the communities in private law were also underpinned by doctrines regarding their purely imaginary legal personality, their consequent incapacity to will or act, but above all by doctrines of the supreme guardianship of the sovereign over all corporations. This derived from the principle '*universitas cum pupillo pari ambulat passu*' (corporation and minor walk in step).

If the fellowship was robbed of its status as an independent organism and of the greater part of its economic, political and legal meaning, the assembly of its members – since it was of no purpose – was bound to be discontinued forthwith, or to change its nature completely. In practice, in the large *Mark* communities, the assemnblies of members gradually ceased to operate; while in villages and among groups of peasants, the right to free assembly was withdrawn from the communities. [671] Assemblies were only convoked by the sovereign so that they could receive his commands and ordinances, pay taxes, perform services or come to a corporative decision in those few matters still regarded as communal. Such an assembly was, however, no longer the visible manifestation of a free fellowship.

Finally, when the fellowship as a whole had lost its old significance, its structure – and therefore the Right of the individuals within it – were put on a new footing. In many local communities, acceptance by and settlement in the community were at an early stage subject to approval by the authorities. Soon, the state alone determined who should count as a member of the community. At its own discretion it raised members with merely protection rights to the rank of full members, and established the basis and requirements for active as well as passive entitlement to community rights. Thus the personal rights of fellows became merely the political rights of residents, their sole source being the will of the state. This completed the disintegration of the old fellowship into a state institution in which an undefined number of state subjects was united and endowed with a juristic personality. If the French, and later the Swiss, Republic completely annulled the rights of community citizenship as rights distinct from those of state citizenship, this was only the final consequence of the same trend.

Internal changes

If the system of sovereignty worked to bring about the destruction of the old local community fellowships, internal changes were (as in all bodies during this period) simultaneously leading them towards the same destination. Since the Peasants' Revolt (1525) the rural population had increasingly lost their creative power, and since the Thirty Years War (1618–48) their sense of community. First, a rigid maintenance of traditional forms replaced independent law-making; but at last that vital sense of community, which would once have united rural fellows to the death and beyond, finally perished in an oppressed and embittered people's selfishness and desire for privilege, their need and ability for public life being extinguished. The office of community leader, from being an honour and a privilege, turned into a burdensome duty. The local community assemblies, and to an even greater extent the larger *Mark* assemblies, were often not attended when convoked, and if not convoked were not missed. [672] There are cases of *Mark* communities being taken to court in order to establish their property obligations. Even when so desired, judges from within the fellowship could no longer be found for the courts.

Of course these unfavourable times could not completely destroy the *inner* community life, the comradely togetherness [*genossenschaftlichen Zusammenhang*], the corporate spirit. In many areas, even at times of the greatest oppression, communities continued a vigorous *secret existence*, expressed in assemblies, secret agreements, banqueting, the exercise of authority and the execution of disobedient members. But, even if it had been more than an exception, this secret life would not have been able to compensate for the diminution of public life. The local communities seldom submitted without a struggle; often they confronted lordly officials with very violent opposition. But, as the cases in which such opposition was successful became less and less frequent, as the protection afforded by imperial courts, and occasionally territorial estates, became weaker and weaker, and complaints and law suits more and more hopeless, so the very courage and will for opposition were finally bound to diminish.

Under these circumstances, the local community fellowships were more and more compelled to take the path which declining public-law bodies tend in any age to take: they wound themselves up. Since in this way they placed their internal structure on the basis of the law of property, without however wishing to give up their significance in public law, they came close to being transformed into chartered corporations. In this case, while their downfall as political fellowships was all the more inevitable, there at least remained the possibility of conserving their elements based on private law ...

[Gierke next discusses 'the continuation of the old economic community in agrarian fellowships' and 'the decline of the economic community'.]

The emergence of the purely political rural community

[693] As we have seen, the formation of a purely political local community was inextricably linked with the decline of the old politico-economic fellowship of the local community, and with the absorption or isolation of its enduring economic element, either in a private community or in mere private rights. This political community gave continuity to the political element in the old fellowship, and was most clearly manifested [694] when it came to the attention of jurisprudence as a wider community in contrast to the restricted economic community still existing within it.

It was of the utmost importance for the *form* which this political community [*Gemeinde*] assumed that it owed its emergence far less to internal developments than to a creative force working from outside. Of course in the early days a political community was often constituted from within ... Some single fellowships of peasants and villagers had, by admitting cottars and jurors to the status of fellows, been transformed into political citizenries based on descent and admission. They had built up a true communal directorate and council, their own community assets, and a communal budget. They had thus raised their 'village', just like the medieval 'town', into an independent community (*Gemeinwesen*) with its own intrinsic collective political personality.

Such isolated phenomena, however, could not determine their development as a whole, which most definitely tended much more often to involve constituting the local community [*Ortsgemeinde*] through sovereign power. Admittedly, an internal transformation contributed here too ... [notably] the desire of the cottars and jurors, whose numbers had greatly increased since the Reformation, to acquire rights corresponding to the impositions and duties they shared, especially taxes on immigration and parish dues. They wanted to be allowed to participate, just as much as full members, in community affairs affecting them, including matters concerning the church, schooling, poor relief, new communal amenities, the community treasury and so on; consequently they wished to be allowed to vote on public affairs. But the really positive creative impulse always emanated exclusively from the sovereign power which, while using existing components, constructed the political community from without and gave it more independence. It was decrees of sovereign power which led to the establishment of the community's own assets, treasury and fiscal policy, which specified and controlled the use of these for public exigencies and enforced rendering of the accounts. Control of the church, schooling and poor relief, local law and order [*Polizei*] and domiciliary laws were regulated by the sovereign power; this created important new factors within the new community of local citizens. The participation of the sovereign's officials in the communities' administration brought this ever closer [695] to the administration of a section of state.

But it was above all the new ideas of law and the state which came down to the communities from outside and from above. Roman law was applied to them by external courts. Those ideas pertaining to politics, philosophy and economics which strove simultaneously to unify the state and to emancipate the individual, took their effect from outside. And when, at last, the final consequence of those ideas had been drawn, and full personal freedom and absolute possession of their land had been granted to the rural population, via legislation on landed estates and the peasantry – which began in the middle of the eighteenth century and is almost complete today – this was not the result of an internal movement within the rural communities, not something they had wrested for themselves, but was rather a deed of the sovereign. If the trend culminating in the ideas of the French Revolution, while dealing a mortal blow to the old state based on privilege and its system of corporations, was also hostile to any organism which laid claim to its own existence between the omnipotent state and the liberated individual, and therefore initially had only a negative impact on the local community as a fellowship, none the less it was *here* above all that it also revealed its positive creative power, by producing the elements from which in our time a new independent local community organism is slowly being built up.

It is because the political rural community emerged through the action of forces working fundamentally from outside that it is possible to explain why it was first created in a dependent and lifeless form, not as a community organism living on its own vitality, but as an institution quickened by the state; and why still to the present day it carries the marks of these origins. The regulations concerning rural communities enacted at the end of the last century and the beginning of this one, whether they were dictated by the Revolution or by administrative absolutism, all equally pay homage to the principle that the local community is a mechanism of administration which can be constructed at will, which must be established in as symmetrical a way as possible by means of a geographical division of the state territory, with a geographically defined number of state citizens: an institution established in this way can be granted rights only as a corporation and for reasons of expediency. The new awakening of community spirit [*Gemeingeist*], of course, soon reacted against such a perception, fortunately in reality never fully put into practice here [sc. in Germany]; [696] but even today it is by no means vanquished, least of all in respect of the rural communities.

It was particularly disadvantageous for the rural communities that the tendency towards communal freedom came chiefly from the towns, and was formulated and implemented by them. For, in consequence of this, the more recent community statutes have, in an exaggerated desire for uniformity, either made towns and country completely equal, and constructed village communities simply as smaller and incomplete replicas of town communities; or else, while giving town and rural communities the same status, they have made significant differences in their structure and organisation ... but above all in the lesser independence of the rural communities. This was particularly the case in the six eastern provinces of Prussia . . . Thus the system of the supervisory state [*Polizeistaat*], in which the rural communities are politically no more than administrative regions [*Polizeibezirke*] and corporations controlled by private law, still persisted throughout.

Since, moreover, in Prussia the constitution based on landholdings still exists alongside the community constitution, since independent landholdings are given the status of a local community – organised on purely authoritarian lines – there can be no question of the transformation of conditions among the rural communities in Prussia by the modern idea of comradely [*genossenschaftlich*] self-administration. The unsatisfactoriness of these conditions has, admittedly, been generally recognised; to modify them is the inescapable duty of the immediate future, all the more so, since in the new areas of the nation the rural communities are already considerably better placed, partly according to old laws (Nassau, Kurhessen, Hanover, Frankfurt), partly by virtue of the laws of 1867 (Schleswig-Holstein). In the same way, in most other German states the beginnings of a regeneration of the rural communities has already been made, in some states as early as the 1830s and in some since 1848, without their having in any way yet completely overcome the disadvantages of their origins in sovereign power.

In the meantime, before we go more fully into the form given to the local community by the legislation of this century, we must briefly touch on the fate of the municipal communities. For today there is no longer, in principle, any difference in law between rural and town communities; we must therefore treat the local community [*Ortsgemeinde*] as a single institution.

Chapter XIII

Towns and cities from 1525 to the present [56, 57]

The decline of the civic community [städtische Gemeinwesen]

[697] The comradely corporative community in the towns succumbed to the same internal forces as the system of rural fellowship.[1] In the new system of state and law [*Recht*] there was no place for a free communal constitution. Only two paths were open to the towns: one towards full independence, the other towards full dependence. Both led to the fall of the communities based on fellowship before the principle of sovereignty [*Obrigkeit*]. They must either themselves become territories ruled on the principles of sovereignty, in which only one corporation possessed supreme territorial power; or else they must submit as dependent communities to an alien territorial power, decline politically into the status of administrative state institutions and, in terms of private law, into chartered corporations – in which case the times demanded that their privileges be increasingly demolished. The seeds of such a great change were, in fact, evident as early as the fifteenth century; the great resurgence of the Reformation period once more interrupted the decline of German municipal freedom, only to hasten its final downfall; here as in all other respects the Thirty Years War was a destructive force. From then on the principle of sovereignty has slowly and steadily been penetrating the minutiae of civic administration. The revolutionary legislation drew the final consequences by promoting a few towns to full sovereignty, and destroying the others as political communities.

In its basic principles, this entire development offers broad analogies with the decline of the rural communities. There are, however, fundamental differences. First, the organisation of the towns was quite different from the rural constitution and required quite different procedures: it was not a case of destroying a collective property and a fellowship based on the old

134

law, and replacing it with a newly created political local community; but rather of transforming an existing political common life into the new kind of local community. This involved the absorption of the living collective personality, regarding its status in public law, by the principle of sovereignty, and its transformation into a [mere] juristic person. Second, the private-law role in rural areas of the common land [*Allmende*] and the right to usufruct thereon, was here transferred to the privileges emanating from the municipal monopoly in trade and manufacture, the privilege known as 'citizen's livelihood' [*bürgerliche Nahrung*].[2]

As regards the first *internal* transformation of the municipal community, its seeds can be detected from the beginning of the fifteenth century, in the evident stagnation of the public lives of townspeople, which in spite of the flourishing state of the towns is a hint of their later torpor. The powerful impetus which in all the towns had until then, in proportion to [698] the increasing prosperity of the lower classes and the broadening of civic self-consciousness [*Bürgersinns*] by endlessly new, youthful elements, kept legal innovation in a state of constant flux through the extension, violent or peaceful, of the circle of full, equally enfranchised citizens, came to a standstill. Even when the artificially restrained power of the people burst forth in highly justified outpourings, the extension of the regime's constitution [sc. of citizen rights] was achieved only in exceptional circumstances. The principle of sovereignty, which was increasingly shaping the internal structure of the towns, was already clearly gaining the upper hand. In many cases, indeed, the existing communal constitution, aristocratic or democratic, was being supplanted by an authoritarian constitution [*Obrigkeitsverfassung*], aristocratic or oligarchic.

This first became clear in the defeat of the craft gilds in many parts of Germany. Till then they had been victorious everywhere: they ruled most of the towns in South and Middle Germany, in Swabia, Franconia, Alsace, Bavaria and Thuringia; even where they had not been able completely to overthrow the patrician class, they had a share in the ruling council (as in Frankfurt and from 1378 in Nuremberg). On the Lower Rhine and in Westphalia their domination was almost total after the destruction of the last, most powerful bulwark of the opposition – the patrician class of Cologne (1396). Even in the North East, if not initially equal to other citizens, in many country towns they gained access to town government or a share in it (especially in the Brandenburg Marches, but partly also in Pomerania, Saxony, Lausitz, Silesia and even in Bohemia and Moravia). Now, in nearly all of the big Hanseatic trading centres in North Germany, the artisans found themselves excluded from the right to a share in government. In nearly all towns adhering to the law of Lübeck, [artisans] belonged to the citizenry, and took part in the true assemblies of the collectivity. Their senior members were consulted by the council as representatives of the community, and involved in the general affairs of the town – in particular in the amendment of statutes. None the less the real *government* of the town rested with a council which was filled by members of the mercantile patrician class; these refused entry to the otherwise qualified 'man in the street' who earned his living in trade.

Under these circumstances, there could not fail to be violent uprisings within the trades in order to gain access to the council. The revolutions which took place after the end of the fourteenth century, however, brought about no change, or only impermanent change. At best, they [699] provided the artisans with the right to participate in a civic committee peripheral to the inner council. The main reason for these defeats was the interference of the Hansa in the internal affairs of its members. The restoration, in around 1392, of the town council of Brunswick, previously overthrown by the craft gilds, and the suppression of the gild movement in Lübeck (the principal town of Northern Germany), which lasted from 1374 to 1416, were primarily the work of the Hanseatic Confederation. In the same way, it took part to a greater or lesser degree in the suppression of attempts to form new craft gilds, which cropped up from the fourteenth century onwards in all the North German coastal towns, in Bremen, Hamburg, Wismar, Stralsund, Greifswald, Stettin, the three great cities in the lands controlled by the Teutonic Order etc. The increasing might of the territorial lord was, it is true, already also asserting its influence to the detriment of the craft gilds (e.g. in Silesia, 1391).

If, as a result of this, only a few isolated cases of government by the craft gilds [700] could be sustained in North Germany, while a city-council aristocracy, with the participation in more important matters of elders from craft gilds or a committee of citizens, became the usual form of constitution, the most important result was that in the course of these movements the idea emerged with ever-increasing clarity that the council, governing not in the name of the citizens but in its own Right, was the true sovereign of the city. In relation to it, the citizens had the same status as subjects of a territorial lord. This principle, which emerges clearly in all the city council decrees of that time, especially in penal measures against revolt, was formally sanctioned for the area of the League in the Federal Decree of 1418 (declared to be the constitutional law of the Hansa). By means of this decree, which was to be posted on council chambers every-where on pain of exclusion from the Hanseatic Assembly, for every complete or partial deposition of an existing council by the citizens, the town concerned was threatened with exclusion from the Hansa; for every attempt to limit the council's official authority, the town's envoys were threatened with exclusion from the Hansa assembly; refusal to redress such wrongs involved the threat of expulsion from the Hansa. The gates of every town belonging to the Hansa were to be closed not only to rebels but also to accomplices who failed to inform the courts...; an unauthorised assembly of the citizens [*tohopesaten*] was to be punishable by death, and even joint complaints to the council by more than six people were proscribed. In this way, the existing council was everywhere declared to be, by virtue of its very existence, an inviolable and unalterable sovereign; and the collective will was declared to be *not* the source of sovereign Right.

A similar transformation occurred, none the less, where the incorporated trades had a greater or lesser share in the city government, as in Frankfurt, Ulm, Nuremberg, Augsburg; and indeed as early as the fifteenth century even in those towns in the West and South of Germany which were governed purely by the trade gilds. [701] Increasingly the principle of election ceded ground to the principle of co-option – or simply became an empty phrase. In place of short periods of office, council offices came to be held for life ... The effective members of the council were hardly ever any longer selected from outside a circle of specific patrician families. The council named itself, and regarded itself as, a sovereign power; councillors gave themselves the title of 'lords', and characterised the citizens as 'their citizens' which soon meant little more than 'subjects'. The self-management of the narrower political and trade bodies was more and more restricted. Paternalism, intrusive government and the system of supervision [*Polizei*] gained greater importance than ever in areas ruled by territorial lords; secretiveness took the place of public management of city business; and 'eternal secrecy' was given priority in the oath of all public office-holders.

This new system of city government was completed by the transfer of the full council's most important powers to countless commissions and committees of the council. Eventually these ruled as standing committees, often appointed for life and enlarged by co-option, conducted in the strictest secrecy; dealing with finance and defence, they might even be empowered with all real authority for 'government [*Regiment*]' as such. As early as the fifteenth century, in many towns founded precisely on a gild constitution they ruled as oligarchies.

However diverse were conditions in points of detail, the displacement of the principle of a citizenry ruling itself through its own organs by the principle of a council ruling on the basis of sovereignty had been settled everywhere by the end of the Middle Ages. In place of the old contrast between citizens with active rights and those with passive rights, the contrast between council and citizenry, in the sense of sovereign and subject, now gained prominence. Internal municipal conflicts now revolved less around the relationships of one citizen to another than around those of townspeople to their government.

The idea of the rule of the people [*Volksherrschaft*] came to prominence once more in glorious fashion [702] in the Reformation period, which produced new ideas just as much as it buried old ones. Because the new teaching was embraced almost without exception by the gilds and the people, while the council aristocracy sought to uphold the old faith, the victory of the Reformation was at first associated, almost without exception, with the establishment of popular civic government, and the maintenance of Roman Catholicism with the preservation of the old constitution. But a political reaction usually followed within a few years; and this, while accepting the consequences of the popular movement in church affairs, restored a constitution which was either aristocratic or oligarchic, but in any case based on sovereignty [*Obrigkeit*]. The defeats of the Hanseatic towns (which had at first enjoyed a great recovery under the newly established popular governments) in their northern enterprises, the execution of the Lübeck weavers and the associated reaction in the other maritime towns, the re-establishment of the temporarily crushed aristocracy in the Prussian, Rhineland and South German towns, the forcible abolition of the gild movement by the emperor in Ulm, Augsburg (1548) and elsewhere in Swabia ... the final dislodging of popular rule by oligarchies even in the larger and smaller Swiss towns, in Zürich, Basel and Bern, the suppression and indeed the character of the politico-religious fanatical Anabaptist sects in Thuringia and Münster – all of these put it beyond doubt that the Reformation was not to reintroduce civic self-administration along with religious self-determination, but would rather strengthen the principle of sovereignty itself to an extraordinary degree.

From then on, the sovereign council strengthened its position in the religious confusion of that century, thanks to the recognition of the secular power's right to implement religious reform, the authoritarian [*obrigkeit-lich*] system of church government, and the decline in public-spiritedness; with the end of the Thirty Years War (1648), even attempts to reintroduce a communal constitution – and the very idea of such a thing – disappeared. From then on, with the increasing ossification and atrophy of municipal constitutions, the council became an ordinary sovereign power, or else the increasingly docile instrument [703] of a higher authority. The influence of the citizenship on appointments to positions on the council almost completely lapsed. But this too was either a non-essential, illusory form of representation, only seldom consulted; or, since it was no longer freely elected but made up of officials and committees of the increasingly oligarchical craft gilds, or else nominated at will by the ruling council or, finally, chose its own members, it itself took on the character of an authoritarian body separate from, and closed to, the citizens. There was no question of official tenure connoting answerability or of the council being accountable to the citizens; this was demanded, at best, by the territorial overlord. The forms corresponded to the content; and civic pride, a sense of community and wider horizons were lost to both rulers and ruled ...

[Further signs of this process are found in Prussia, in juristic theories and in the influence of 'the French system of municipality'.]

The local community according to the communal ordinances of the nineteenth century[3]

[There is no longer much difference between the communities in the countryside and those in the cities. 'The local community is regarded as a state institution with a juristic personality as conceived under the absolutist system.'] [757] ... A comprehensive survey of German community ordinances of the nineteenth century reveals that progress has been slow, but that remarkable results have already been achieved in the development of the local community into a common life based on fellowship. But it also reveals that we must look first and foremost to the future for the creation of local communities as independent organic bodies, and hence for true communal freedom, together with lasting harmony between community and state – in other words (if the watchword of the Austrian communal ordinance of 1849, which declared that the free community is the basis for a free state, is correct) for the foundation of all freedom in the state. Legislation is not capable of creating communities: only [758] the people's re-awakened sense of fellowship can and will fill these most limited of public bodies with a spirit full of vigour. And it will still take a long time before this process, already developing in the towns, can re-emerge in the countryside from the ruins of the old fellowship-based common life and community spirit.

But, if community life, like all things organic, can grow unaided from within, the role of legislation is to prepare the ground for this growth, to remove constricting limitations and to show it its place within the higher organism. To a greater extent than ever before, it must leave the path into which it was pushed by the influence of Roman ideas. Addiction to a machine-like apparatus, regulation of detail, schematisation and enforced uniformity have ruined many laws which were liberal in intent. The difference between town and country communities cannot be abolished by decrees. Economic conditions necessitate that each should be structured differently ... The rural community is capable of fully realising far fewer of the higher purposes of community independently within its own sphere, and therefore has need of a far greater dependence on higher associations.

But it should not be the state which steps in at once to limit the local community, but rather the nearest higher and more powerful intermediate association [*Zwischenverband*]: the local community must be able to unite with others to form collective communities [*Sammtgemeinden*], and it is essential that it becomes integrated into a free district community [*freie Kreisgemeinde*]. Within the particular types of community themselves, it is equally impossible to obliterate the differences between *Länder* and provinces, and even between individual local communities, without loss to them. For the rural communities in particular, in which historical development, circumstances of ownership, the nature of the land, racial characteristics and cultural and moral conditions determine such a multitude of ethical and legal differences, especially as to the distribution of rights in the community, complete standardisation would simply mean the annihilation of such organic life as still remains.

If, however, for these reasons legislation is sometimes formulated unequally for different regions and sometimes has to conform to local tradition and conditions, it must none the less everywhere be informed by a unified principle, which corresponds to a free, German and modern state. The point of departure this implies [759] cannot be specified by jurisprudence alone. Politics, economics, statistics and history must lay claim to a far greater share in the resolution of the emerging theoretical and practical questions. Jurisprudence is, however, due a far greater influence than it has hitherto brought to bear on the structuring of these circumstances. Above all, it cannot accept that considerations of expediency alone should be the determining factors when the highest and most important legal and moral questions [*Rechtsgedanken*] are at stake. On the basis of these considerations, it is to be hoped that in the immediate or distant future the imminent changes in the law of community [*Gemeinderecht*] may develop as follows.

First, on the basis of its intrinsic nature, it must be recognised that community is a *common life based on fellowship* [*genossenschaftliches Gemeinwesen*], that from below it is a universality, from above part of a higher universality, that over against individuals it is itself an individual. For the local community is as little capable of again becoming a medieval state within a state as it is of remaining a central-state institution whose juristic personality has been conferred by another. It has a right to its own original [*originär*] personality, created as little by the state as by the individual citizen, but as capable as is the individual citizen of asserting itself in law, restricting itself and being of service. In private law, this community personality is no more and no less than an individual (except where by the nature of the case its rights are more limited). In public law, this same community personality is, in one respect, a member of a higher organism, primarily of the state; in this regard its position corresponds to that of the individual citizen in his capacity as state citizen. On the other hand, for its members it is a universality, and as such the source of a *public legal Right* governing its particular sphere, the bearer of its own public power.

Here the analogy with the individual no longer suffices. For, since it is not a single being [*Einzelwesen*] but a communal being [*Gemeinwesen*], not only its outer life, as in the case of individuals, but also its *inner* life comes under the law. This results in a series of questions arising between state and community which cannot arise between state and citizen; even in respect of the inner life of the community, with regard to the creation as well as the activity of its organism, mediation is necessary between the rights of the state over its members and the rights of the community over itself. Here too the basis of all solutions must remain the recognition of the original personality of the community. This reveals first of all that the question, 'To what extent is it expedient to grant independence to a community?' should not be asked, but only the question, 'How far is it necessary, in the interests of higher universalities, to detract from the independence of the community?'

[760] It emerges, secondly, that the state ought not, as before, to be present within the organism of the community, but must step beyond it so that the community organism is *insulated* from the state. The state, which had previously been its patron, participated in its affairs and set limits on it, should now have only an external role in the activities of the community, supervising and prescribing its limits and helping it over difficulties. Finally, the third result is that the relationship of the state to the community is a legal and moral relationship [*Rechtsverhältnis*] and that therefore,

in common with all public law, it demands recognition as law (which had previously been denied to it and all public law). It therefore also demands protection in law, based on the right to go to court, rather than being subject to the decree of administrative authority.

Accordingly, the *composition* of the local community is determined by its dual substratum, as a group of citizens related to one another as fellows, and as a self-contained communal territory. Its detailed development takes many varied forms according to circumstances. In particular, free personality, as against ownership, is accentuated to a varying degree in the organisation of the community's citizens and members. As regards the relationship between community and state, however, here too the independence of the local community must be recognised in principle, and the basis of its bonding-together [*Verbundenseins*] be transferred to itself. Here too, therefore, it will be necessary to draw a distinction between the legal sphere [*Recht*] belonging to the state and the legal sphere belonging to the local community, and to bring about an accommodation between the two – a task which, given the confusion prevailing in previous legislation relating to residence, settlement, freedom of movement, and poor relief, will present great difficulties. The basis for this must be a recognition that both state and community have rights simultaneously within the scope of the community's territorial and personal domain; but that, if the district and number of persons in the community happen to correspond to the boundaries of an administrative region of the state and to a subdivision of the citizens of the state for political purposes (administration, the judicature, state control [*Staatspolizei*], defence, taxation, state elections etc.), they are not fundamentally or internally identical, but the correspondence is purely fortuitous and external.

From this there follows for individuals a sharper distinction between the powers and duties emanating from the right of state citizenship and the right of community citizenship. Direct state citizenship for all, and the direct territorial sovereignty of the state over its whole territory, mean that the state citizen *as such* has the right to live in any part of the territory of the state, to acquire holdings in land, to conduct a freely chosen trade and to establish a household; but for the state it means the power to remove these matters entirely from the influence of the local communities. The community can of course, in so far as the state does not demand that its own officials should be admitted to the community, call upon all residents to take their share in the burdens on the community. The community can also demand guarantees that anyone admitted into it does not become its responsibility as a pauper; [761] if its objections are justified, although it cannot deny admission, it can claim exemption from poor relief. On the other hand those circumstances of its territory and citizenship which relate directly to the local community, the structure and replenishment of that fellowship of citizens which is distinct from the sum total of members of the community, must all be given back to the more freely exercised self-determination of the community. When the course of law [*Rechtsweg*] is open to the community as well as to the individual, it is perfectly compatible with the independence of citizens for a community to have a *legally* [*gesetzlich*] decreed *duty*, given certain preconditions, to grant or deny rights of citizenship, and to have the complementary duty in certain circumstances to acquire the rights of citizenship. What is incompatible with it is the mere despotic [*polizeilich*] regulation [by the state] of rights of citizenship and ownership.

The *organisation* of the community will be transformed along the same lines. To the local community itself belongs its own organic structure. The community *as a whole* may indeed be an organ of the state: the organs of the community, however, cannot possibly simultaneously exercise the functions of state organs. In order to exercise supervision, the state in any event needs its own supervisory bodies; it may appoint special political authorities for any local administration which it either cannot or will not declare to be a matter for self-administration. But the prevailing system is untenable: it treats the community directorate [*Gemeindevorstand*], and in particular its leadership [*Spitze*], simultaneously as an agency [*Organ*] of local state control, and indeed even regards all their public authority as having been bestowed by the state ... If only there could once and for all be a resolve, at least within the sphere of the local community, to find the source of a public authority in the people! In any case, in the long term only one of two positions is possible: state government in the local community by state organs, or self-government by organs of the community.

The present ambiguous position of the local directorate, however, which combines the characteristics of independent headship of a community and dependent servant of central authority, obliging it to serve two masters, to take directives from both and represent the interests of each against the other, must of necessity come to an end. The duty to *support* the state government, to undertake *particular* state commissions in instances which are specified by law and to *promulgate* state decrees, is not precluded by a local directorate whose position derives purely from the community ...

[762] The *legal and moral significance* of the local community, regarding its private-law status and regarding its external status, will simply continue to develop; but regarding its status as a political and moral universality,

it will have to change fundamentally. At present, as a rule, all the local community's significance in public law holds good [only] as a sphere of activity conferred by the state upon it, or even merely upon its agencies. But, with the recognition of the local community as a common life based on fellowship [*genossenschaftliches Gemeinwesen*], it must be ascribed a legal and moral significance stemming from itself in public law as well. The community must beware of accepting the Trojan Horse of a state commission in matters of regional and state administration, since this puts a seal on its dependent status; and the state will have to guard against forcing the role of state servant upon the local community against its will. The community is bound only to undertake those functions deriving from positions of public trust which the individual too must undertake in community and state; it must not become a link in the official bureaucracy of the administrative service.

Conversely, we need a very meaningful expansion and liberation of the sphere of activity *proper* to the community and therefore *independent*. Above all, as a legal and moral fellowship, the community must regain self-determination regarding its internal organism, *autonomy*, too, in addition to self-administration. For 'self-determination under a foreign law is only half of freedom'. In its ordinances concerning the local community, therefore, the state should only prepare and define the position which the community is to take up, regulating its duties and establishing those fundamental elements of its organisation which are not subject to change. It must, on the other hand, allow sufficient room for local traditions and local statutes to develop their own law-making activity.

At the same time, the state must go one step further than hitherto; it must renounce its claim to be the sole source of objective, or at least of written law. It must not merely grant the local community the right to propose laws which become binding only when sanctioned by the state; it must recognise, albeit within narrow limits, the community's genuine right to make for itself laws, over which the state's power of inspection and sanction is confined to confirming that the community's sphere of activity has not been exceeded and no higher-order law or Right infringed. Instead of positively vetting the expediency of its content, [the state] should merely consider from a negative angle whether it collides with any other Right.

There will be no great return to local community *jurisdiction* alongside this law-making power. But the local community cannot altogether do without the judicial powers of a fellowship and the coercive power associated with [763] it (seizure, etc.); and the role of conciliator and arbitrator is well suited to the community's nature.

It does, on the other hand, need the greatest freedom in the sphere of its positive life-activity – the administration of its own affairs. For self-administration to become a reality, the state's co-administration must fade away. Mere *supervision* must take the place of *tutelage* (though the latter may continue in the most important matters). This supervision must of course be stricter than over individual citizens, whose inner life evades all control. The indispensable powers of the state against the local community are cognisance of all the proceedings of community life (since this is in the public domain), prevention of any overstepping of the lawful sphere of activity, compulsion to fulfil obligations to the state, arbitration on complaints ... and, in exceptional cases, active intervention in self-administration under legally stipulated preconditions, if an established law has been broken. These enable the state powerfully to represent both the community members and its own interest, against the local community body. But at present, since the validity of all important decisions and acts by the community is made dependent on the co-determination and co-operation of the state, and state intervention in its innermost affairs is regarded not as an exception but as a rule, the local community is now (as before) kept in the position of a minor.

But, if individuals have come of age, so too have communities. It is true that a community can misuse freedom more than an individual; but is freedom without the possibility of abuse freedom at all? Since it is true that today not only the bureaucratic spirit of the state, but also the lack of a fully matured sense of community, stand in the way of self-administration, can one believe that a community in bonds will ever learn to conduct itself freely and yet temperately? And can it be intended that the growth of a sense of independent citizenship and the capacity for self-administration should be fostered by depriving the community of a real decision in vital matters concerning its existence, and transferring these to the state ...? It has been suggested that by a special legal procedure, individual communities which had gone into decline could be placed under the special guardianship of the state, [764] on the ground of proven incapacity. Be that as it may, the legal presumption today is that the local community has come of age.

In terms of *content*, those affairs of the local community which properly fall into the category of self-administration encompass all aspects of human existence in as far as their realisation, or some part of it, does not call for a higher community. The maintenance of peace, order and security, and to this end the local community's preparedness for defence and its bearing of arms, care for both the material and spiritual welfare of its members, and to this end independent powers of supervision [*Polizeigewalt*],[4] the educational system, poor relief, roads, fire-fighting, and the control of morality – all of these are but particular aspects of an independent community's common life based on fellowship, directed to the commonalty of human ends.

As a means towards achieving its public aims ... the local community has its own assets and a public communal budget. Here too the local community still needs to be liberated from many bonds. It needs even more to stave off the danger threatening the community's freedom which comes from a perception (which has in many cases already found its way into law) that wishes to turn upside down the relationship between the life and the economy of the community – that is, to take away from the community its significance as a moral organism and to reduce it to the status of a grouping-together for proprietorial purposes. The most recent legislation, particularly in Prussia, has been seen to be moving precipitately in precisely this direction. To dissolve the local-community group based on fellowship, and replace it with a series of specially organised state groups for particular purposes, with public and moral authority represented by the state alone, and the civic community as such limited as far as possible to a *fiscal community*: such seem to be the goals of modern legislation.

One particular school of national economics does not seem to have been without influence on this trend. This, by a materialistic overevaluation of external goods, elevates the means to an end in itself; and, although initially it still allows the state its ethical significance, this school is of the opinion that it can therefore all the more easily claim that the local community is a mere economic institution.[5] [765] The logical extension of this is that the local community is divested of its political and moral nature and is falsely regarded as being based upon the principle of reciprocal obligations [*Leistung und Gegenleistung*], in a corruption of the old Germanic tenet of the correspondence between rights and duties. If this trend is ever victorious, then, even at its most liberated, the local community, thus alienated from its noblest task, will be of little worth for the political freedom of the people! Indeed perhaps an even more dangerous enemy of self-administration than bureaucracy and benevolent despotism would arise from within the people itself. For in such a community, instead of a far-seeing understanding of politics and a sense of community [*Gemeingeist*] which was willing to make sacrifices and put the general above the particular, an egoistic spirit of corporativeness based on private law could easily develop. Faced with this, the more far-seeing and highly principled state would now, as a hundred years ago, be inherently in the right even if it used despotic coercion as the representative of moral ideals.

[Commune-like groups for particular purposes include 'district communities without Right-subjectivity' and 'with corporation rights', church communities and also communities for schools, the poor and so on (chapter 58). There are local communities both within and beyond the *Ortsgemeinde* that were discussed in chapters 55–7: districts, provinces and so on. Gierke looks at Austria, Prussia and other German states (chapter 59).]

Chapter XIV

Parliamentary representation and the development of the modern state [60, 61]

The elements of fellowship within the state

[Gierke considers 'the territorial estate bodies (*Landsstände Korpora*) within the sovereign state', going back to the origins of the post-1525 system in the later Middle Ages. He examines their relationship to the territorial princes, 'their loss of comradely independence' and 'the downfall of their political significance'.[1]]

[814] Jurists acting in the interests of the courts were not at a loss for legal grounds by which they could extenuate breaches of explicit declarations and treaties. If the territorial lord was the sole possessor of sovereignty, then all other political rights within the territory were based on a concession by him; the estates were, therefore, 'privileged subjects' whose powers were vested in them by a concession from the territorial lord, as an act of favour, and consequently as privileges. Privileges were to be interpreted strictly: the rights of the territorial estates were exceptions which were not to be supported by conjecture in cases of doubt. If much could be achieved by interpretation and textual explication, lawyers soon took this much further, and taught that the territorial lord was not even always bound to unambiguous promises where these were incompatible with the welfare of the *Land*. For privileges ... could, they said, be revoked at any time for the sake of the common good. Other constitutional lawyers traced the rights of the estates back in such a way as to claim that they were extorted or obtained by false pretences; or they declared them to be obsolete, [815] or to have lapsed as a result of changed circumstances; or else they declared that they were invalid without the sanction of the emperor because they diminished the supreme territorial authority granted by the emperor as an inalienable right; or, finally, they applied the much-espoused principle that the successor was not bound to the govern-

mental ordinances of his predecessor; and used any other similar fictitious reasons which might be found. The final argument, however, always remained 'the public safety (*salus publica*)', which was supposed to derogate laws, freedoms, treaties, traditions and titles acquired by possession. In all of these cases, of course, the presupposition that the prince alone was entitled to decide what was demanded by the public good remained unproven. The statements of renowned constitutional lawyers contradicting such deductions fell on deaf ears.

[816] More than by all such juristic reasons, the princes were sustained and justified in their aspirations towards unrestricted power by inner necessity, by the fact that in any event, in the struggle with the estates, they were consciously or unconsciously representing the public good against private interests. Even if most had only the expansion of their own power within their sights, or were copying the example of Louis XIV, the nature of the affair indicated that they should oppose the estates as 'privileged subjects' on behalf of the interests of the unprivileged subjects, take the part of the peasantry against the nobility, and so become the representatives of progress while the estates fought for privilege. The new concept of a unified public Right was always on the side of the princes, while the estates could only produce on their side individual private rights.

For this reason, it was precisely the most forward-looking princes who were most hostile towards the territorial estates; with few exceptions these succumbed without any energetic resistance, or even without taking part in the struggle. And it was in the very state which was called from now on to be the representative of the German concept of the state, that the estates retreated into the most pitiful, shadowy existence. The Great Elector himself, with the founding of the state of Brandenburg-Prussia, simultaneously sounded the death knell of the system of estates. If he himself still encountered violent opposition, which in East Prussia – in the face of estates which were exceptionally vigorous and whose lively sense of community made them represent not only their own rights but those of the countryside and the peasantry – was only defeated by imprisonment and the scaffold, his successors, who pursued the same goal with unrelenting single-mindedness, did not have to fear any energetic resistance from the egotistical chartered corporations, and had not just [817] might but public opinion on their side. Frederick William I [of Prussia 1713–40] was already able to express the idea of the absolute state with the utmost clarity: 'we are lord and king and can do what we will', was his argument, 'I hold Souveraineté steady like a Rocher of Bronce', his goal.[2] He rejected as 'old matters long forgotten' the privileges cited in opposition to him (in

Jülich-Berg). Frederick II ['The Great': 1740–86] and Frederick William II [1786–97] continued this trend in both old provinces and newly acquired *Länder*; and, if they never explicitly annulled the setting-up of the estates, this in itself shows the extent to which they had sunk to a position where they were of no importance. The estates' institutions succumbed un-mourned and indeed almost unnoticed in most of the other *Länder* too; even against the regents' greatest acts of violence, voices of dissent could be heard only in isolated cases. The downfall, finally, of the German Empire simultaneously abolished the final restrictions from above on territorial independence, and formally annulled most constitutions based on the territorial estates; simply abolishing them by decree, not only in the secularised bishoprics, but also in the temporal *Länder*. [818] In those states which had become sovereign, the supremacy of the territorial lord [*landesherrliche Obrigkeit*], taken to its final conclusion, was elevated into a princely sovereignty entirely unrestricted from above or below. With this, however, it had at the same time reached its limits, and had to do battle with a new concept gradually emerging from deep within the people.

We can see clearly that this new idea, the idea of popular representation, was in fact not a continuation of the old principle which had been at work in the territorial estates, but a quite different, independent principle, by considering how the relationship of the territorial estates to the *Land* had changed. From being the fully enfranchised citizens of a territorial com-munity [*Landesgemeinde*] based on fellowship, they had become privileged subjects united in a *corpus* [body]. The idea that those who were specially favoured amongst subjects might represent to the ruler the interests of all the ruled had not been entirely extinguished. But in relatively few *Länder* were the estates conscious of such a calling, and in even fewer did they put this task higher than their immediate and actual goal, which was the maintenance and augmentation of 'their special rights, freedoms and privileges'. So long as their members and estates were free of taxation, the right to approve taxation was of little importance to the nobility; the establishment of standing armies and bureaucratic absolutism meant little as long as their members were assured preferential promotion as officers and state officials; the distancing of legislative power meant little as long as it affected only the common people and not the right of privilege. The municipal corporations, sunk in deep decline, and even such spiritual institutions as were still represented, scarcely thought otherwise. Even in those few *Länder* which ruled and represented the lesser and more exten-sive communities (e.g. the *Oberämter* in Württemberg) thought similarly. Most diets of territorial estates were therefore no less estranged from the people than from the prince; they stood as a third party alongside the two others. Indeed, the rural population had long since been accustomed to find in the prince a representative against the estates, rather than representatives against the prince in the estates. Even the most zealous proponents of the rights of the territorial estates call to our attention facts which not only demonstrate the selfishness, greed for privilege, pitifulness and cowardice of the declining corporations, [819] but prove at the same time that they had entirely lost sight of the idea of representing a *Land* or a people.

A corporation which was decaying internally, for which, as far as the prince was concerned there only remained, in Moser's words, the *gloria obsequii*,[3] and which, as a privileged *corpus*, was alienated from the people, could not be rejuvenated in order to represent the people. All attempts made with this in mind were doomed to fail, since new ideas could not come from the putrefying remains of a dying body, but only directly from the re-awakened public spirit of the people. Endeavours to establish external and internal historical continuity between the old territorial estates and the new popular representation were, furthermore, in truth unhistorical.

It is a characteristic feature of German history that here continuity of this sort has never bound the old to the new, as it has in part in England. Most of our great institutions have lived out their days in a one-sided deformity instead of filling themselves with the content of a new era . . . , and the newly awakening ideas, instead of transforming the old, have created new forms for themselves. So developments in Germany are not, as in England, like the consistent structure of a building which has always been extended according to requirements; instead, the old buildings, often misshapen and in a state of decay, frequently tumbled down to their very foundations. In the new buildings the rubble of the old was useful at best as building blocks. German unity was not to emerge directly from the Empire, nor the idea of the state from the emperor, nor sovereign administration from duties based on feudalism and service, nor modern association from the medieval system of incorporated trades, even though the same powers of the spirit of the people were at work in such kindred phenomena [820]. In the same way, the modern representative system did not spring from the estate-based constitution but, like the latter, directly from the spirit of the people, struggling for self-determination and struggling to create a form fitting for the age. The link which has frequently been established between these is purely external; its purpose is at best to conceal the break between old and new, at worst to produce an inherent contradiction between form and content – the seeds of dangerous conflict.

All the same, the influence which the presence of remnants of the constitution of the territorial estates exercised on the emergence and formation of the principle of representation in Germany cannot be underestimated. It would be folly to deny or belittle the share in the expansion and form of this principle which was exercised by the spirits of foreign peoples which had such a powerful influence on Germany; above all by the French Revolution on the one hand, and by British Parliamentarianism, on the other. It was the continued existence of the territorial estates, however, which gave a more clearly defined direction to the ideas stimulated by these models, the ultimate source of which was always the popular consciousness of the Germans [*das deutsche Volksbewusstsein*].

It was in this context that, as early as the mid-eighteenth century, the great teachers of constitutional law, who contributed as much to the revival of the dead public spirit as they did to scholarship, came forward as champions of the territorial estates against absolutism. Led by historical research to the conclusion that the territorial estates did not, as the court constitutional lawyers would have one believe, come into being recently through the favour of the prince but were coeval with territorial independence, that in the German constitution unrestricted rule was unheard of before that time, and that in all respects 'freedom is older than serfdom', they were able to vindicate independent and inviolable rights for the territorial estates *vis-à-vis* the prince. J.J. Moser,[4] above all, whose ideas were taken up by Pütter, the younger Moser, Strube, Möser, Häberlin and others,[5] was deeply critical of doctrines which maintained that the rights of the estates were revocable privileges and concessions, that all restrictions on territorial supremacy [*Landeshoheit*] were invalid, that the public good was the highest law and the prince the sole representative and guardian of the public good.

In the face of a theory which attempted to destroy the concept of public Right at its source, and to replace it with the concept [821] of an interventionist administrative structure [*polizeilich-administrative Ordnung*], they argued for the Germanic principle that the relationship between sovereign and subject was fixed, limited on both sides, and was a relationship in law [*Rechtsverhältnis*] based on rights and obligations guaranteed by the territorial constitution. They too, in accordance with the spirit of the times, saw the essence of the state as divided in two, as composed of sovereign and subject. But from this they deduced, not the absolute rule of the head over members, but rather the participation of the subjects in the state. 'The head alone is not the state and the blood supply does not exist for the head alone but for the whole body', taught Moser. The territorial estates were, therefore, 'subjects, both as individuals and *in corpore* [as a body] and therefore not co-regents or sharers in government, but equally they are not slaves', but 'the born advisers of the council; indeed everywhere they are encountered they are more than mere advisers', since 'in all territorial constitutions certain cases of importance in the government of the territory pertaining to its weal and woe are expressly laid down in which the *joint consent* [*Miteinwilligung*] of the estates is required when the ruler is to be able to do or omit this or the other' (J.J. Moser). The prevailing contractual theory of the origin of the state was also interpreted along these lines.

But these constitutional theorists not only demanded for the territorial estates a standing different from that which was actually accorded them simply in relation to the *princes*, but attempted to put their relationship to the *people* too on a different basis. The principle, repeatedly and insistently articulated by Moser, and then often reiterated, that the territorial estates represented the entire *Land*, was bound, however, to remain forever a theoretical requirement, a pious hope. Men like Moser gave to the estates plenty of exhortations for unity, for a sense of community, that the best interests of the community be considered [822] before their own interests; and then boldly championed the whole *Land* and each individual. But, with the best will in the world, the estates' whole organisational structure as privileged corporations would have made them incapable of achieving the status intended for them as 'representatives of the whole beloved fatherland' (as Häberlin would have it). Even in our century, the manifold attempts to revive constitutions based on the territorial estates without modifications which destroy their very essence, have demonstrated the impossibility of reconciling the estates' principle of representation as their own right with the principle of the representative state. If, however, the immediate goal of regenerating the corporations of territorial estates proved unattainable, efforts towards achieving this did contribute directly and substantially to the consolidation and deepening of the people's conviction of the necessity of popular participation in the system of the state, by means of popular representation; and thereby to the final realisation of the representative state.

The relationship of the modern German concept of state to the idea of
fellowship

Only a few remnants of the old principle of the territorial estates persist today in Germany. Apart from those states in which the estate constitution still exists, like Mecklenburg and Lauenburg ..., it has chiefly continued to bring its influence to bear in a more or less modified form only in the organisation of the Prussian and Saxon district, in regional and provincial associations, and in the constitution of a few chivalric corporations. It is therefore of significance for the nature of the larger communes and public corporations, but not for the nature of the state as such. It is true that now, and to a much greater extent in the first half of our century, the continuing concept of the estates modifies, and has modified, the representative system in a series of new territorial constitutions. But the actual concept of state was not and no longer will be determined by the uncleared rubble of old ideas, but by the sole principle of universal popular representation, a principle which is not invalidated but simply constrained and shaped by the remains of the old.

The principle of universal popular representation was the expression of the gradual transformation of the universal and equal status of *subject*, produced by absolutism, into universal and equal *citizenship* of a state. The state was being decomposed into an exclusively active, unitary sovereign, embodied in the person of the prince, and an exclusively passive, multiple [823] collection of subjects, brought together in a merely collective idea of 'the people'. Already at the beginning of our century this was taken to its most extreme consequences in the states of the Rhineland League; but they were bound very soon to accept, at least by sham concessions, the idea that the universal status of subject must grow into universal state citizenship. For, although the mock constitutions conceded by them on the French model gave only the *appearance* of popular political participation and mostly existed only on paper, the admission was there that it was untenable in principle for citizens merely to have obligations without corresponding civil rights [*bürgerliches Recht*].

With the resurgence of the spirit of the German people, the demand that the state be given back to the people grew stronger. Such desires and promises of course harked back more or less consciously to the old estate-based constitution, from whose revival in a modified form salvation was expected. The few constitutions which before long came into being in the South-West attempted to avoid an open breach with the old principles. But, whereas in other states the estates in practice continued to exist or were reactivated, these new constitutions all rested on a different basic conception: for in them the territorial diet always appears not as the organ of a distinct corporation of the various estates but rather represents in every respect the whole people as the aggregate of state citizens. Even more was the principle of basing constitutions on the estates abandoned in constitutions promulgated after the impetus of the new movement after 1830; after 1848 there was a complete and open break with this tradition. In constitutions introduced or revised since then, despite the diverse directions in which they were moving, no trace can be found of the old corporation of territorial estates, [824] even where the division into estates was retained during the development of popular representation. Rather, the idea of universal citizenship represented by the territorial parliament gained total victory.

The differences between modern popular representation and the corporations of estates of the Middle Ages and later are self-evident. In itself, modern popular representation gives neither full citizenship of the territorial community, nor a privileged corporation; it is no longer a corporation at all, but simply a public committee [*Kollegium*]. In relation to the people it is neither any longer a fellowship with its own full independent rights [*selbstberechtigte Vollgenossenschaft*] nor an aggregate of those possessing their own status [*Standschaft*], but a political committee, which in its totality exercises the political powers to which the totality of all independent citizens is entitled. In relation to the prince, it is neither a territorial community sharing the state with him, nor a corporation endowed with an aggregate of political rights, but a co-organ [*Mitorgan*] of the state.

This lack of its own status as a fellowship means that modern popular representation has an entirely different legal status to that of the old territorial assemblies. Membership in it does not depend on whether one belongs to a particular fellowship or corporation; rather, participation in it is a public function, linked by law to specific conditions. In principle, therefore, there is no difference between the elected representatives and those who are nominated or appointed, apparently in their own right, on a hereditary or property basis (especially in the first chamber). Election, nomination or personal characteristics are only the channels which lead to appointment to the office of representative of the people. The real source of the powers and duties associated with the office is neither a commission nor an inherent right, but the [825] constitution alone.

An important consequence of this, differentiating it from the estates, is that under the modern system each member represents the whole people. Conversely, the individual is neither entitled nor obliged, primarily or under any circumstance, to safeguard his own interests or those of his electors or his nominator.[6] Even when the old assembly of estates was a true territorial community, the *individual* within it primarily represented himself alone, or those from whom he had his mandate; only the collectivity of estates represented all individuals and the *Land* together. But now, whether an individual is more aware of the interests, desires and grievances of his constituency and presents them in preference to others, is a purely practical matter: his *legal and moral* relation to them is no different from that of every other representative to his own, or to any other, constituency. Indeed it would be an infringement of his public duty if he put his own interests, or those of his electors or his estate, above those of the general good. This has very important consequences: the inadmissibility of an election or nomination in any form other than that precisely laid down in law, the prohibition of attaching any condition to a mandate, the lack of binding power in law of any instructions, the irrevocability of a mandate, the inability to call any of the representatives to account, the exclusion of any proxies, and so on. Similarly, by his vote, the individual representative does not, as before, bind primarily himself and his mandators, and only secondarily, as a member of the territorial corporation, help bind the *Land*. Rather, the collective decision of itself binds the collectivity of the people and with it each individual. The individual member of the territorial parliament is no longer anything of himself and for himself, but is everything only as a member of the committee and for the sake of the collectivity.[7] Even popular representation as a whole is nothing for its own sake, but is everything as part of a higher universality. It entirely lacks its own collective personality, which the old territorial assembly had.

Only in respect of its collegial structure (the order of business, the examination and adjudication of its members' credentials, the election of its leaders and officials, the formation and designation of divisions and committees) does the modern representative body have powers of autonomy, self-jurisdiction (discipline) and self-management; these powers are by no means corporative in nature, but purely collegial, being based not on an internal corporative constitution but on the constitution of the state, which convokes a committee as the unified organ of the state. If today we still speak of a [826] representative 'corporation', this is an inexact use of language: a house of representatives is no more a distinct corporation than is a collegial judicial or governmental body, or a collective executive within a commune or society. (Indeed, it would be easier to ascribe collective personality to a court or magistracy, which is permanent, than to a committee which at times, e.g. after its dissolution, has no existence at all.) Hence the totality of representatives can manifest itself as a unit only in forms prescribed by the constitution of the state; otherwise it is not a legal unit but an aggregate of individuals.

Thus the medieval right of self-assembly has lapsed; the right of self-assembly retained in a few constitutions is of a wholly different nature, being exercisable in precisely defined instances. Further, the right to free association has lapsed, as has the right, based upon it, autonomously to develop its own organism and also the corporative power to judge and sentence members. Finally, the right independently to organise committees at will has lapsed: instead, even in those constitutions which provide for standing committees or specialised select committees, these are merely specially regulated organs of *state*, not *corporative* agencies based on the collective will of the representatives.

If, however, the representative committee [*Kollegium*] is not of itself a fellowship or independent organism, it is not some kind of agency [*Organ*] of a particular territorial community, or of a particular organism of the 'people', within the state either. Thus, in its relation to the state or prince, it is neither a Right-subject in itself, nor even the representative of a specific Right-subject; it is quite exclusively an organ of state instituted for precisely defined functions. Hence the right to grant taxation, in the sense of a concession given on behalf of oneself and others, has disappeared; there is now only a constitutionally regulated co-operation in the state's legislation on taxes. Gone is the possibility of having a territorial treasury separate from the state treasury, specific territorial assets and a territorial budget, or of a *Land* being able to raise and administer its own taxes; only the co-establishment and supervision of a unified state budget remains. Gone is the old right of armed resistance, and the legal possibility of a separate army raised by one estate ... Wars, [827] negotiations and disputes based on international or private law, conditional acts of homage, reciprocal bonds and privileges, those treaties once so common between prince and territorial assembly – such things are no more legally thinkable. For the prince and the *Land* are no longer two individual Right-subjects alongside one another; rather, prince and *Land*-representatives are joint representatives and joint organs of a unitary state. Their accords, therefore, are law, and their negotiations and disputes are the internal movements and upheavals of the organism of state. Least of all are independent legal transactions by the estates with extra-governmental [*ausserstaatlich*] powers, so frequent in the Middle Ages, thinkable today.

Territorial representation [today] lacks its own Right-subjectivity and is simply a state organ. In contrast, therefore, to the earlier undefined competence of territorial estates, which meant they were excluded from hardly any act of government and were frequently true co-regents, before sinking to the level of merely exercising their own privileges, *modern* constitutions have defined the function, within the organism of state, of popular representation with the greatest possible precision. Despite great dissimilarities in points of detail, they have been assigned everywhere a dual function; they themselves alone are the controlling organ of state, and together with the prince they are the law-giving organ of state. In so far as they will and act within their prescribed sphere, the state wills and acts through them; if they exceed it, they are an aggregate of individuals who will or act. In no circumstances does a collective personality distinct from the state, whether of the estates, or of the *Land* or of the people, will and act through them.

The ending of a separate *Land*–estates fellowship completes the unity of the state. The old duality of the state, for the conquest of which we are indebted to absolutism, has not returned with the new representative constitution. Conceptually, there is now only one, indivisible, simple state personality, not composed of the distinct personalities of territorial lord and territorial community, but manifest in both only as in its agencies. This unity has of course not yet been fully recognised by the legal consciousness [*Rechtsbewusstsein*] of the people; it has not even made its mark among scholars. The fact that the people have long been used to seeing the state as something above themselves frequently leads to the view that the prince and people are separate Right-subjects. Such a conception corresponds as much to our earlier circumstances as does most Latin peoples' concept of the state. This is true, whether it continues to posit the state solely in the princes, in the sense of princely sovereignty, and only concedes dependent participation to the people; or whether, conversely, it institutes popular sovereignty along French lines, only immediately to transfer the exercise of sovereignty to a representative of the state standing outside the people; or whether, finally, it favours the system of shared sovereignty. Such a view is in any case irreconcilable with today's Germanic concept of the state.

[828] If it were true, as many teachers of constitutional law hold, that under representative monarchy 'the people' is a personality distinct from the state, manifested through popular representation and through that alone, over against which the true personality of the state is embodied in the separate personality of the prince, then representative monarchy would be a step backwards from the state unity already achieved. But, in fact, if the idea of the constitutional state [*Verfassungsstaat*] is implemented, the prince as prince no more has a personality distinct from the state, with individual entitlements and duties, than the people have a personality outwith the state: he is quite simply an organ, a manifestation of the personality of the state. Of course at the same time he has an individual

personality in private law; but this is not the basis or content of his position as head of state. He is no longer prince in his own right, but prince by means of the law [*Recht*] of the state. He is called to this office not by hereditary Right but by the law [*Gesetz*], the constitution, on account of his descent from a specific lineage in a defined order of succession. The basis of his lordship is not subjective but objective Right. For this reason the extent of his obligations and powers, in as far as he is prince, are defined by the constitution alone; if he were to exercise functions other than those state functions conferred on him – for example, the administration of justice or legislation on his own – then it would not be the state acting through him, nor would he be acting as the prince but rather as an individual. On the other hand, in so far as he wills and acts within his constitutionally defined functions, he wills and acts neither as an individual personality, nor on behalf of the state; rather, the state wills and acts in and through him.

[829] If the sole and indivisible personality of the state is manifested in the prince and popular representation, this does not exhaust the number of direct organs of the state. On the contrary, one must also recognise among these first, the collectivity of independent citizens, and, secondly, the law-courts. The collectivity of independent citizens is of course restricted to the single function of electing the representative agencies; but for this important act they appear in primary assemblies – their visible manifestation – as a constitutionally defined organ of the state. The courts, whether nominated or elected, are likewise called to the fundamental part of their activity – the administration of justice – not by the special commission of another state agency, but directly by the legal organism of the state itself. In so far, therefore, as they administer justice [*Recht*], it is the state itself, not another agency of the state, which acts in them. This has not yet, of course, been fully recognised; but the requirement that they should, in a constitutional state, be independent, irremovable and unaccountable, together with the introduction of juries, rests on this assumption.

While the personality of the state, then, lives directly in four different organs – in the prince as its sole external representative and its internal administrative and executive organ, in the representation of the people as the supervisory organ representing plurality against singularity, in both together as the joint law-creating organ, in the courts as the organs which administer justice, and in the primary assemblies as the electing organs[8] – all other officials and functionaries of the state are simply *indirect* state organs. For they are all in the first instance the organs of a state agency, and only represent the state indirectly. The entire organism of [830] the state administrative officials, in particular, is in the first instance solely the instrument of the prince. The constitution of the representative monarchy only makes a necessary exception for the ministry, since, by transferring to it responsibility of which the prince is to be relieved – with the peculiar duty this entails of acting in the name of another while being responsible for these actions as if they were its own, in respect of the enforceability of its duties as regent – the constitution endows the ministry with the status of a necessary and independent complement of the supreme organ of the state. While in other respects the nature of the authorities which exercise power is, therefore, not fundamental to the concept of a constitutional monarch, the presence of a ministry in accordance with the constitution is essential to that concept; in reality it is not the prince alone who is the highest organ of the constitutional state, but a prince who has immunity complemented by a ministry which is answerable for its actions.

The essence of the modern German idea of the state is based, therefore, on the identity of state and people. The state is the people in organised form. As a state, the people, which manifests itself in the quite specific articulation of its spiritual, moral, economic, and even physical life as a historically developed essential unity, attains a collective personality in the legal and moral [*rechtlich*] sphere as well. Therefore, in the area of Right the invisible state-unity is the soul, the citizenry, associated and organised in a specific way, is the body, but the constitution is the organism of the people, which fits together the atoms of the body to make a unified, living personality. Admittedly, if this concept of the state has not been universally accepted by academics, it has been realised to an even lesser extent in real political life, nor even been fully and clearly grasped by the legal consciousness of the people as the goal towards which they should aspire. However, in all these matters a start has been made along the path which will lead to victory in the future. Theory will transfer the idea of state in its entirety back to the idea of the people. The habit of the interventionist state [*Polizeistaat*] – that Roman import of a state distinct from the people, for which the people, not the visible body but the mere sum of individuals, are simply its opposite number and the object of its attentions – will disappear from political life. The displacement of the organism by the machine will also disappear. As a spiritual and moral entity, the people will feel at one with the state and overcome the last remnants of a view which has its roots in the saddest centuries of German history, in which the German people had lost their identity in the sphere of public life [831] and handed over their living collective personality to an abstract concept of the state which hovered in the empty space above its head, poured forth from heaven or some other such place on to the sovereign powers, large and small.

Implicit in the demand for unity of state and people, is the further demand for the unity of state and legal justice [*Recht*]. In contrast to the ancient and Roman state, and also to the interventionist state [*Polizeistaat*] briefly implemented amongst us, the modern Germanic state is to be a state based on legal justice [*Rechtsstaat*]. This is not to say that the ancient Germanic conditions, in which the state was absorbed by Right, when it only existed for the sake of Right and consequently stood under the law [*Recht*], will ever return; but equally the state must not be above the law or itself absorb the law. Rather, the state is to be based on justice [*Recht*], since its organism itself is legal justice; since, in other words, public law [*öffentliches Recht*] is recognised and defended as being truly law. The constitutional state [*Verfassungsstaat*] can only move freely inside the sphere of its positive life within the constitution; and the law can only move freely in respect of individual details. The state, in so far as it comes into contact with any other sphere of existence, of an individual, a smaller universality or one of its members, is bound by legal justice. Conversely, public law – that is, the legal justice which regulates the relations between the state as a universality and the lesser universalities or the individual citizens as members of that highest universality, and therefore determines the organism of the state – is bound by the state. Since, therefore, in public law freedom retreats in the face of necessity, the state must, conversely, recognise legal justice as an insurmountable barrier to its freedom of movement.

Administration, therefore, which forms the content of the positive life of the state, finds in legal justice its boundary. It is true that, for both the state and the individual, the definition of their positive [sphere of] activity follows from considerations of expediency. But it is equally true that neither the state nor the individual may infringe legal justice for considerations of expediency: for legal justice reconciles differing interests and, in the last analysis, the general interests and the interests of individuals. The principle '*salus publica suprema lex esto*' (let public safety be the supreme law) is, therefore, turned on its head in the constitutional state [*Rechtsstaat*]. The public good is, of course, the positive content of the state's function; but statute [*Gesetz*] draws the boundaries between the pursuit of the *public* good and of *particular* goods. If the law [*Recht*] becomes inadequate for the needs of the state, it must [832] be changed by constitutional means through the *legislative* agencies. If the law is in doubt or in dispute, then the judicial agencies, the courts, must declare what the law is. The idea of the constitutional state culminates in the demand, still nearly everywhere denied, for the protection of public law through the courts by means of positive statutes.

The reconciliation of a fellowship-based foundation and an authority-based summit in the state of today

Let us, finally, ask how the modern idea of the state, which aims to replace the authoritarian state with the unity of state and people, and the administrative state with the constitutional state, is related to the idea of *fellowship*. We find that, although the alterations which have occurred or begun to occur, in the internal and external nature of the state, have originated in the idea of fellowship, that idea does not claim to determine the modern idea of the state exclusively, nor to be identical with it; rather, it is contained in it only as part of it. When Bähr, in his work on the constitutional state,[9] claims to regard the state in all its manifestations simply as the supreme, most comprehensive 'fellowship', this is based on a wider linguistic usage, since by fellowship he understands every human association. Even with this modification, Bähr's principle is correct only in so far as the state can be conceived of and organised in the form of an association (*Verein**); it is incorrect in so far as it relates to any historical manifestations of the state. For many nations the state has been, and is, far more an *institution* [*Anstalt*] than an *association*. Even the German state, at the time when public life was dead, was anything but a civic society [*bürgerliche Gesellschaft*]; rather, it was an institution (*Institution*] standing utterly above and beyond society, a personality transcending the people. If the modern trend, in harmony with the basic Germanic view which it has rejuvenated, endeavours to turn the state, in theory and in practice, back into a civic society, and to create a state personality immanent within the people, then in the spirit of this aspiration, the modern German state is indeed, as *Bähr* argues, nothing other than the supreme, most comprehensive human association.

Divested of its mystical character and traced back to the natural process of growth (instead of supernatural origins), such a state is not generically different from the lesser public-law associations contained within it – the communities and corporations. Its relation to them is only that of the more complete to the less complete stage of development. [833] It is the product of the same power which we still see on a small scale daily, constructing universalities of a more limited kind over particularities. It is, therefore, homologous with the communities and fellowships. The multitude of consequences which follow from this one difference are of course overwhelming: the state, as the highest universality, has no more universalities above it, and is sovereign, so that, while all other groups are still determined by something external and are ultimately regulated by something outside themselves, the state is wholly determined by itself alone and contains its own regulating principle within itself. However, the philosophy which deduces from this that the state has an absolute, unique political personality, while allowing to all the smaller universalities only at most a fragment of political personality, derived from the state personality, is incompatible with the modern idea of the state.

But even if the state actually, according to our contemporary idea of it, stands for the supreme and most universal association, it still does not follow that it is a pure fellowship, or nothing but a fellowship. Even if one were willing to define the idea of fellowship so widely as to include an association whose existence is based on necessity and whose form alone lies in the domain of free will, an association (furthermore) for which a territory as well as a plurality of persons is an essential prerequisite, then even the *organisation* of the state, as it has historically developed, has only half of a fellowship-like nature. For, granted that the idea of a fellowship-like association of the folk collectivity – that is, a fellowship of citizens in which the fully and equally enfranchised independent citizens are collectively the active citizens – forms the *foundation* of the modern constitutional state, none the less its *summit* [*Spitze*] has emerged from lordship (transformed into princely sovereignty). Indeed, to organise the state on a constitutional basis is to attempt to fuse the elements of lordship and fellowship together into a harmonious unity. The modern idea of the state, therefore, embodies the reconciliation of the ancient idea of fellowship and the ancient idea of lordship. Both of these have validity within their own sphere; but the hostile opposition of the two is to find its resolution in a higher unity.

The representative constitutional state, therefore, is neither a pure fellowship, like the earliest patriarchal state, nor a pure lordship, like the feudal state; nor again is it purely a community based on fellowship, like the medieval town, a dual entity made up of an independent lordship and an independent fellowship, like the medieval territorial state, a purely sovereignty-based system, like the modern states of territorial lords. It is, rather, a community which organically brings together the foundation of fellowship (the fellowship of citizens) and the sovereign peak (the monarchy), uniting them not as an aggregate but as a new living unity.

Chapter XV

The Empire 1525–1806 [62]

[Transformation of the Empire which during the period 1525–1806 becomes 'in its totality a corporation' and loses its 'state-like qualities'. 'Attempts to lay new foundations in our century ...']

[841] The great spectacle of the political rebirth of the German nation has been reserved for our day. The foundation stone of the building, which must and will take on the form at once of the German Empire and of a united and free German people's state [*Volksstaat*], and erect itself as the first state on earth, has been laid. There are two forces whose combination has brought about such an unhoped-for event, and will complete what has been begun. One force was the powerful [842] initiative of the strongest, most centralised and most far-reaching state-unity on German soil [Prussia]. The other force, however, without which the very idea of a national state would never have arisen, was the newly awakened power of the people. This built from below, and by means of fellowship-like association [*Vereinigung*], strove upwards from brisk individual activity towards the highest universality. Two ideas, which through the millennia of our history had wrestled in deadly combat, alternatively conquering and one-sidedly dominating, were finally working towards the same goal, finally creating the beginnings of a state in which there will be room for both, and in which both can unite in harmony.

The ancient opposition of unity and freedom, which in lordship and fellowship we have watched tearing German life apart from the very beginning – the opposition between the unity producing and determining plurality, and plurality producing and determining unity, the opposition between order and arbitrariness – this opposition will, we hope, finally be overcome by the constitutionally organised German collective state [*Gesammtstaat*]. As yet, of course, only an incomplete beginning has been made, as yet neither unity nor freedom has its due sphere assured to it, still less has either received full justice [*Recht*]; there is thus still an element of the provisional, the non-organic, clinging to the joint structures. But the path along which future progress will be made is clear to see.

Unity will have to expand extensively to full national unity, but concentrate itself over against its members intensively in full state unity. The legal and moral nature of the present German state edifice is hard to define because elements of a league of states, a federal state and a unitary state are mixed up in it; but the direction of its future development cannot possibly be towards a league of states or a federal state, but only towards a unified empire. It is difficult to envisage a true fellowship of states [*Staatengenossenschaft*] among monarchical states; but among states one of which exceeds in greatness the sum of all the others, it is impossible. The only possibility is a true unitary state, in which a centralised summit and a fellowship-like foundation, consisting of the collectivity of imperial citizens, unite to form a single overall organism [*Gesammtorganismus*] of the state.

In such an empire the individual states (if they are not to adopt a non-organic arrangement) can only retain the status of territorial communities [*Gemeinwesen*], midway between local community [*Gemeinde*] and state. They may still be differentiated from provincial or district communities by more extensive autonomy, their own self-jurisdiction and self-administration, and their own monarchic organisation, along with the peculiarities these bring with them: but these differences cannot bring with them any diversity in principle in their relative position within the empire. If the united German state is to become a reality, they must cease being states within a state. Of course it is only their nature as *full sovereign* states which they have [843] to relinquish, not their nature as states as such. For not only are they to remain associations homogeneous with the state, existing for themselves, only restricted in the interests of central unity; but even the provinces, districts, right down to the local community are to become such associations in the form of community fellowships.

If the realisation of the *unified* state demands far more substantial restrictions on individual states, conversely far more substantial independence for the lesser and greater communities is indispensable for the realisation of the *free* state. Here, too, the role of mediator between unity and freedom falls to the idea of fellowship; only organisms in between individual and state, full of life, endowed with their own political and individual personality, are in a position to ground on a sure and unshakable basis, by fitting themselves into the imperial organism composed of the central imperial power and the fellowship of imperial citizens, the united and free German collective state.

Political fellowships based on the law of nations

Above a collective nation-state, whether this describes itself as a league of states, a federal state or a unified empire with independent communal members, it is possible to envisage a state fellowship for particular purposes. There is at present such a state in the form of the German Customs Union [*Zollverein*],[1] which in its present form, however, is only an intermediate step towards a true state association of the entire German people. Beyond this, unions of independent states for common purposes have up to now existed only in the sense of contractual relationships based on international law [*Völkerrecht*], not as unions of states or peoples which have achieved an independent collective personality over their component parts. Even the apparently organised unions of several states, which exist for example for railways and the postal and telegraph systems, cannot be regarded as corporations under existing law. They are merely contractual relationships.

For up to now international law has not recognised the legal possibility of an independent collective entity above sovereign states. For international law, states are in every respect simply absolute individuals, in no respect are they members of a higher universality. International law as a whole has the character only of private law; it is lacking in all the concepts, structures and guarantees which are the prerequisites of the existence of public law. At the same time, it should not be denied that here too in our century the beginnings of an association-movement are becoming evident. In the near or distant future this will lead to a fellowship-based association of states and peoples, and finally to an organised universality over individual peoples which will have to be acknowledged in law as a collective personality.

[Gierke now considers 'fellowship in the church'. First, in the period 1525–1806, he considers institution-based and fellowship-based conceptions 'of the church as such', both Catholic and Protestant; the relationship of church and state; 'the development of new religious fellowships', although 'there is no right' to form these even in edicts of toleration; and 'spiritual fellowships' and their renewal, in both Protestant and Catholic churches, including 'the Society of Jesus as the high point of the Roman Catholic idea of association'. Second, for the period after 1806, he considers again 'the church as such', its relationship to the state, 'the development of new religious societies', and 'the recognition of freedom of religious association', and 'spiritual fellowships' (chapter 63).

Gierke next turns, in the final section of the whole volume, to what he calls 'the free fellowships', again covering both 1525–1806 and 1806 onwards. He divides these into 'the system of fellowship for mental, moral and social universalities' absorbed by the state, retaining for themselves only 'a private character': this goes for brotherhoods, gilds, nobles' associations and universities. New developments include 'limits on the right of association' (chapters 64–5). Eventually, he turns to free economic fellowships (chapters 66–70).]

Chapter XVI

Fellowships under benevolent despotism, 1525–1806; modern free associations 1806 onwards [64, 65]

The system of fellowships for mental [geistig], moral and social purposes;
the system of association under the authoritarian state: ...
Fellowship groups for social purposes

[879] *Social* comrade groups [*Genossenverbände*] aiming at associative fraternisation could, in so far as they aspired to be groups of a merely private nature, develop at any time, and in fact frequently came into being in aristocratic and bourgeois circles (divided up by status and profession). To the extent that they gave themselves a legal and moral organisation ... and as legal entities wished to possess a community house or other assets, they, like other societies, naturally required state recognition. Besides this, they did not escape mistrustful supervision by the sovereign power now any more than at other times during the period of absolutist government; quite often they were prohibited on suspicion of having secret political or religious tendencies.

The natural means of protection against supervisory restrictions is secrecy: lack of freedom and secrecy are always very closely connected. For this reason, secret associations always went hand in hand with the restrictions on societies. For Germany, as for neighbouring countries, this was at once proof of the lack of public law and of the newly awakening public spirit. From the beginning of the [eighteenth] century, though primarily in the second half, secret societies were formed in great numbers; this hid their existence when they were persecuted, and, even when this was not the case, hid their content from non-members, and established secrecy as one of the main obligations of the associates. Although these associations often proceeded from unclear or mystical philosophies and had fantastic aims, they were none the less in agreement in attempting to realise the idea of moral fellowship, of social brotherhood, in anticipation

168

of the great significance which the idea of fellowship was soon once more to acquire.

[880] Their significance for the deepening of the idea of fellowship cannot, therefore, be underestimated. The Freemasons [*Freimaurerbund*]¹ above all functioned along these lines. Although they had some connection with the great German brotherhood of stone-masons, they received their definitive constitution in England at the beginning of the eighteenth century, and spread from there into all countries. Adopted and protected by some German governments, especially Prussia (although it was banned by the pope), the great league was able to pursue its high purpose all the more unimpeded, within a series of more or less closely associated local societies. In this purpose, the moral and social idea of fraternity taken from the old craft brotherhoods, was enriched by the new ideal of humanity. Even when masonic secrecy, originally chiefly connected with a ritual developed from artisan and religious traditions, was increasingly extended over the whole character of the association, and the development of a system of various grades of authority and initiation wiped out the original form of a league of equally enfranchised brothers under a freely elected leadership – the great fellowship still worked beneficially for the [881] revival of brotherly community spirit, the indispensable basis of every association.

Of far less significance were the countless other secret brotherhoods, secret societies and leagues which emerged with the most varied organisations and the most varied of goals in the eighteenth century, and, sometimes favoured or tolerated by the governments of the time, but more often proscribed and persecuted, proclaimed the newly awoken spirit of association. From the time of political upheaval onwards, these secret societies often included political tendencies among their organisation's goals, or were suspected of so doing. Thus, from the French Revolution until our own day, secret societies have, in many nations, especially the Latin ones but also among the Slavs and Celts, played an important role in all political and social movements and upheavals. In Germany, however, they lived more in fear of the governments... The Germanic spirit of fellowship and the Latin [882] spirit of conspiracy are not only not identical, they are mutually exclusive. For the success of secret societies is based on a capacity for fanatical subjugation under an invisible unity, and for rigid centralisation, whereas the productive Germanic formation of fellowship requires an independent sense of community and the capacity for self-administration.

The modern system of free association for political, religious, mental, moral and social purposes[2]

Only the future will be in a position to define more precisely the role which the modern system of free association [*freie Vereinswesen*], grown in a short while from small beginnings into a world power, has played, in Germany and elsewhere, in the mighty progress of present-day culture in the spheres of political, intellectual and social life. It is already clear that it is a significant one.

The task of voluntary association in our century has been and is different from that of the medieval system of union. For if, on the one hand, the content and extent of its activities have been expanded by an incalculable enrichment of public, intellectual and moral interests, on the other hand its sphere of activity has been more closely restricted and its coercive power over the individual is less intense. This is because modern associations exist not, as medieval unions did, in a disorganised, stateless society, but in a powerful state and in the midst of many links in a chain of lesser and greater compulsory public associations [*öffentliche Zwangsverbände*]. It is also because the individual is incomparably more independent than before in relation not only to the state but also to the fellowship of his choice. Yet association retains a vast area, even within the boundaries laid down between established organisations and individual freedom, for purposes ideally suited to it; here it can and does produce, by its own creative powers, vigorous new structures.

The vigorous, unfettered building of associations is not only useful but indispensable if the individual and the collectivity are to have their lives shaped into a harmonious whole. [883] For the individual, it counteracts the danger of isolation, fragmentation [*Atomismus*]; at the same time it is a powerful confederate and effective balance for the free state: a confederate, because it educates the citizen into a sense of community, an understanding of public affairs and of self-government in a wealth of lesser and very simple communities; a corrective, because the vigorous power which, with ceaselessly rejuvenated strength, binds the uncommitted elements of the people's spirit into unity, organises what is as yet unorganised, and, having perfected and overseen earlier organisations, thrusts them aside in its rush for progress – that power alone can save the existing organism of the people from atrophy and final collapse.[3]

The modern system of association has, like all new phenomena, first had to win its place, by difficult struggles, in constitution and law. Not without reason did the sovereign state see in this its most dangerous enemy; even the constitutional state regarded it at first with suspicion. Old fetters, which made impossible the free development of association, were maintained as long as possible. Among these fetters was, then as today, the civil-law theory of corporations [*civilistische⁴ Korporationstheorie*] which, because it related primarily to the law of property, could make life difficult for associations which possessed property only as a means towards ideal ends, but could not have such a decisive significance for them as for the properly economic fellowships. Rather, the really effective means which made more substantial development of associations impossible, or at least held it back, was the sovereign state's tenet, based on constitutional law, criminal law and state interventionism, which both denied to subjects the right to form associations – and the right to assembly underlying this – and only permitted assemblies and associations after a concession from the sovereign.

[884] In England the spirit of association had already, in the last century, awoken in a very vigorous form and with a direct effect since [*c.*1750] on all public matters. With little difficulty it had overcome the many attempts to ban it by means of interventionist [*polizeilich*] restrictions, and thereafter free 'meetings' and 'associations' in all departments of political, religious, intellectual and social life have been elevated to the status of national institutions. In France, after the Revolution, this spirit, by completely unfettering association, had most dangerously abused it in the clubs of the capital and the provinces. The right of association was destroyed by the *code pénal*⁵ which prohibited any political or non-political association of more than twenty persons without the approval of the government; with a slight interruption it still remains in ruins today.

In Germany, on the other hand, the system of free association has [885] only ventured very gradually from the sphere of private associations for scholarly and social interests, or for interests based on status or profession, into the realm of public life. It has also only very slowly gained a secure position for itself in theory, and, after many setbacks, in practice too. It was the pressure of foreign dominion [sc. 1806–13] which first awakened a public spirit of association in enduring form and produced associations with a substantial content. It was, above all, the Prussian *Tugendbund* [League of Virtue] which helped to prepare the national uprising. Limited, by a statute authorised by the king, to moral and scientific purposes, in reality it intended to revive the public spirit and patriotism. ... Although at the insistence of the French it was declared dissolved by the king, its effectiveness did not end there. In the same way, similar associations were active in the nationalist cause in other parts of

Germany, although secretly to start with. The old prohibitions on association remained everywhere in force, but, for as long as the awakening public spirit was needed, they were hardly applied.

When, however, after victory had been gained over the foreigner, the aroused public consciousness turned to domestic affairs and tried to make the system of association productive here too; when the association movement communicated itself to ever greater spheres, in particular producing youth leagues among students along the lines of the men's leagues, which then extended their influence in the *Burschenschaft* [students' association] – then the struggle of governments everywhere against the right of association began, as a consequence of the reaction which set in after the Restoration. Old laws prohibiting all associations not [886] administratively authorised or, on account of their secrecy, able to escape state control [*polizeiliche Kontrolle*], together with laws against all forms of political association, were renewed and intensified. Federal and *Land* governments enacted special decrees against the associations of students and journeymen-artisans. When the movement produced in Germany by the July Revolution [in France 1830] gained ground none the less, and produced new associations, then all associations with political inclinations were unconditionally proscribed for the whole of Germany by the infamous federal decree of 5 July 1832. All public meetings required previous government approval; even then, all political talk or discussion, any speech-making or passing of resolutions, was forbidden on pain of severe punishment. Except where the introduction of representative constitutions gave rise to exceptions, this remained valid law in nearly all German states until 1848. Even then, only in a few states was a different view of the matter helped on its way to victory through regulation by decree [*gesetzliche Regelung*]. The denial of an independent [887] right to form associations did not, naturally, exclude a more or less tolerant policy on the part of individual governments, and towards associations which exclusively pursued ends in the public interest or otherwise acceptable to the government. It did not even exclude protection of associations by sovereign power, although this admittedly was usually associated with paternalism [*Bevormundung*]. But it did bring about a situation where not only could no system of political associations develop at all – or only clandestinely – but also one in which the apolitical associations were deprived of their full vigour because of the pressure of administrative [*polizeilich*] approval, obligations and intervention.

No prohibition, however, could prevent the *idea* of association from spreading, intensifying, and extending from educated circles to take hold among increasingly large sections of the population. This process was even reflected in the world of learning. Most writers on public affairs [*Publicisten*], agreeing with current legislation, denied the independent right of association on the basis of jurisprudence, constitutional law, policy [*Polizei*] and the criminal code; they held that, for each association (unlike company contracts in private law), state approval was mandatory ... and regarded participation in an unauthorised association as a criminal offence. Yet despite all this, increasingly important voices were [888] loudly urging that such principles were in no way demonstrably valid as common law [*gemeines Recht*], far less philosophically justifiable. These maintained, rather, that the right of association *in itself* belonged, in the nature of the modern state, to every citizen, independently of special permission; that penal measures, even against clandestine associations, had to be justified on grounds of inadmissible methods or purposes, or of their being perpetuated after express prohibition; and that a merely repressive system and state supervision regulated by law should take the place of preventive measures and interventionist paternalism.

The year 1848 first saw the introduction in practice of the free right of association and assembly, and the partial abolition of the old restrictions by provisional decrees ... Thereafter, these views, today only seldom contested in theory, were officially sanctioned in the eighth article of the German fundamental rights, [889] and transferred into the German Imperial Constitution (sections 161, 162).[6] This article granted to each German the right to form associations, without permitting any restriction through preventive measures; but it granted the right to assemble peacefully and unarmed without prior permission, with the sole proviso that open-air meetings of the populace could be prohibited in cases of imminent danger to public order and safety. The constitutions of the individual states did, of course, add a reference to laws to be enacted separately, and reserved the right to regulate more closely the exercise of the right of association, to ban unauthorised open-air meetings (this ban has already been enacted), and to restrict or provisionally to ban political associations. But they recognised in principle the citizens' right to association and to assembly. The laws made shortly afterwards in the individual states on the right of association and assembly held fast to this view, however much they might enact decrees restricting the exercise of these rights. Only in Austria were all political associations completely forbidden once again (1852), and made dependent on administrative approval ...

[892] Finally, one should note that, regarding particular types of persons and activities, special restrictions on the right to association and

assembly are still valid everywhere ... Special restrictions applied to the military, to state officials, students and schoolchildren. The most important such provisions are the so-called anti-combination laws [*Koalitions-verbote*], which under pain of punishment prohibited employees, and generally employers too, from forming associations which aimed to achieve [893] concessions or negotiations through a general strike (or through layoffs or lockouts) ...

A great number of more or less independent associations did, none the less, spring up all over Germany even before 1848. Some of these were persecuted by the state, some were tolerated, some approved and authorised, some even formally accepted into the system of public institutions. After 1848, however, a many-sided, much-ramified system of associations was elevated to the status of a chief actor [*Hauptorgan*] in public life. In terms of their content, these associations can be divided up into different groups primarily according to their aims, or their chief aims; for the tendency of the modern association-system to promote single, more precisely defined goals is particularly pronounced in them. It should, however, be noted that a combination of several aims and tendencies is frequently found even today. Indeed, there are still associations in existence (and there were even more at the time when the association-system was developing), which attempt to satisfy as many aspects of human social need as possible. On the other hand, if the grouping of people within associations today is determined *primarily* by the aims of the association, and *legally* associations are generally no longer restricted to specific types of person [*Personenklassen*], there are nevertheless many exceptions to this rule. What is more, *in practice* the splitting-up of types of status [*Stand*], profession or social group exercises a considerable influence even today in determining and structuring each association.

Differentiation according to purposes

First, *political* associations, that is those whose purposes consist in directly influencing public affairs, form the most important group. They can be divided further into *associations for political education* and *associations for political agitation*. The former give enlightenment and instruction in public affairs, either to their members alone, or to outsiders as well: thus they aim to have an effect on both the intellectual and the moral aspects of public thinking. The latter aim to have an effect on [894] the external life of the state, the church, communes or other public bodies, be it a lasting involvement in one particular area or the realisation of particular goals in respect of legislation, administration or the political involvement of the people (elections). Although in England such associations [sc. for political agitation] have been widespread in all forms, and particularly effective as an irresistible form of agitation in every reform movement from the middle of the last century,[7], in Germany (if we disregard the political aspects of the League of Virtue, the students' societies, clandestine groups, and a few local societies), political associations first played a significant role in the revolutionary year of 1848. The constitutional and democratic associations of that period were followed at the time of the reaction by loyal alliances [*Treubünde*], patriotic unions and more local and short-lived groupings summoned up in every locality by the political questions of the day.

From 1859 onwards the association movement again assumed a more general character. All over Germany, the National Association developed its ability to work for the creation of a German state; associations of elected representatives and a General Assembly of Representatives worked towards the same end. The German Reform Society [*Reformverein*] and many local associations loyal to Greater Germany [*Grossdeutschland*] represented the opposite aims. The Schleswig-Holstein crisis and the desire for a German navy also gave rise to the formation of pan-German associations. In addition, many forms of political association were constituted in every single *Land*, province and town. Factional associations [*Parteivereine*] attempted [895] to organise political parties or bring about the implementation of specific political programmes; many electoral and reform societies were formed for more transient goals. Permanent local societies and, in the larger towns, countless district associations, attempted to keep the public spirit alive and spread political knowledge by means of periodic meetings, regular debates on current topics, lectures, libraries and educational institutes. Everything here is still very much in a state of flux: but it is impossible not to recognise that here too, as happened long ago in England and America, the system of political association is developing into an integral part of political [*staatlich*] life.

A second group is formed by the *religious* associations. Religious fellowships, and the spiritual societies organically bound up with a church, have been discussed above. The modern spirit of association, particularly in the period from 1814–48, has already produced in large numbers free associations for specific religious purposes. The following groups can be distinguished, according to their aims:

(1) groups which act directly in the cause of *religion*, either (a) primarily among their members (devotional societies, religious educational societies

and reading circles, Catholic associations for pilgrimages, etc.), or (b) externally, aiming to provide religious instruction, distribute Bibles and religious tracts or pictures, devoted to mission work at home or abroad. [896] Others are involved in one specific religious or confessional school of thought, like the Gustav Adolph Society, the Protestant and Catholic leagues, societies, itinerant meetings, assemblies, associations of preachers and societies of theologians, the Germany Protestant Association, etc.

(2) There are associations which have an *ecclesiastical* rather than a simply religious aim, such as societies for reforming the church's constitution, administration, external life or status as a whole. Such associations generally assume the character of quasi-*political* religious associations.

(3) Then there are associations devoted ... to pious or charitable aims while maintaining the religious character of their association (religious fellowships for education and instruction, for moral improvement, for the care of the sick, and for charitable work) ...

[898] Countless groups [*Vereine*] are active in the fields of *commerce, trades, industry and communications*. Some of these attempt to promote one specific branch of economic life by means of encouragement and stimulation, joint institutions and conferences. Some aim to represent the interests of a branch of trade or commerce externally; others to provide for the intellectual or technical instruction and advanced training of their members, or of non-members. The commercial association [*Verein*] founded in 1819 by Lisst belongs to this type, as do the lesser and more extensive groups which were active in expanding the system of free trade and the national union of the German Trade Congress (which developed from the trades' corporations, chambers of commerce and commercial associations). The countless trade and industrial associations, etc., had a similar effect on trades legislation, while general trade and polytechnic societies came into being alongside them for advanced technical training in trades. For individual branches of trade, specialised associations [*Vereine*] were formed alongside the trades' corporations [*Innungen*], more so in their absence. These were inclined to produce more extensive, and where possible pan-German, associations with local and provincial branches ... Special associations were active in the sphere of mining (e.g. the miners' and metal-workers' associations in Silesia, the Union for Mining Interests on the Rhine, the Union of Iron Workers in the Customs Union, etc.); elsewhere too, free unions of particular categories of industrialists and manufacturers can be found. Finally, within the field of communications, unions for the railways, post, telegraph, shipping, etc., make possible the unified regulation of communications as a whole by means of operating cartels...

[899] Associations for *physical education* came into being in many guises, as unions of marksmen, [900] gymnastic clubs and periodically in the Youth Defence Leagues; these too proclaimed the tendency of the modern German association-system towards more comprehensive joint organisations – where possible on a national basis.

There are also *language associations*, which work towards the purification of the German language, the preservation of a local dialect or similar ends.

Associations for the protection of *persons or property* no longer have the same significance as in the days of the old protective gilds, since the state has essentially taken over these duties. But even now there are still instances of associations for *legal protection* (particularly abroad). Fire brigades, unions for the care of public health, associations of coastguards, associations for the protection of emigrants etc., can all be counted as protection associations.

A very important category of modern groups [*Vereine*] consists of those groups which *represent the interests* of a class [*Stand*], professional group or sex. Many of the groups already mentioned, such as those for academics, artists and artistes, for commerce, trade, industry and agriculture regarded it as their duty – alongside the promotion of a specific branch of economic or intellectual life – to represent also the interests of the professional groups dedicated to these fields. In other associations this is the sole or primary aim. Such associations can be classed as political groups if they are seeking to bring about, by political means, a change in the social position of the classes they represent; but, in so far as they work solely through joint activities within the power of private individuals, by contracts in private law, by informing their members, public opinion and the authorities, or by similar methods, they are apolitical in nature. The representation of mutual interests can either be directed solely towards one other specific group of individuals, as in the case of the German Stage Union in relation to actors, and of several associations of employees *vis-à-vis* the employers (and vice versa); or it can be directed towards all of the rest of society, and towards the state itself. To this group belong, for example, associations of lawyers, writers, the press, teachers, etc.; likewise the 'Associations for the protection of the interests of land-ownership' which have come into being in recent times; and, further, the associations for the protection of women and 'for the promotion of the earning capacity of the female sex'.[8]

Last of all, the unions of employees [*Arbeitervereine*], which aim to improve the conditions of the working classes [*Klassen*] and to represent labour against capital, are of particular importance. Since 1848 they have emerged into public life in Germany in varying forms and to varying degrees. [901] Although the 'Central Association for the Welfare of the Working Classes', founded in 1848, consisted for the most part of the unemployed, even at that time a 'General Congress for Craftsmen and Trades' was formed, which aimed towards establishing an overall organisation with subsidiary and branch associations. These attempts have subsequently been renewed on several occasions; from 1863 onwards a General German Workers' Union has come into being alongside many divergent local associations. Many associations of this sort pursue goals simultaneously in education (for example the 'General Association for Workers' Education' in Vienna, from 1867 onwards), or exist both for these aims and for the purpose of providing support (like the associations of tradesmen in all the larger German cities).

The associations active in the area of *ethics and morality* can be divided into those which aim to have an impact on the outside world and those which relate exclusively or primarily to their members. Among those directed towards the outside world, there are some associations active for the preservation of good morals or the abolition of bad habits, and even for elevating the moral tone of society as a whole or of individual groups. Those active in special areas are, for example, the Association for the Prevention of Cruelty to Animals, the Temperance Societies, and so on.[9] More general aims are pursued by associations for the Family and the Nation, groups for the dissemination of the principles of morality, and all the educational associations already mentioned. These seek to promote moral alongside intellectual development. Associations for the institution and maintenance of institutes for the care of small children, kindergartens, etc. belong to this group. Lastly come the countless associations for the restoration of a corrupted or endangered area of morality, like the associations for bringing up neglected children, inns of refuge for poor young women, or those deserted or abandoned to run wild, associations for the prevention of child begging, the succour of citizens, and the moral and social reform of former prisoners.

As for the relations of members to one another, these groups, although primarily constituted for different purposes, for the most part continued the ancient [902] custom: they set up a common social life [*sociale Gemeinschaft*] among group comrades. This was manifested in the social gatherings held after the formal meetings and in regular or special group celebrations; but they also to some extent became the basis for higher moral duties. Alongside these, an incalculable number of groups pursued exclusively or primarily social ends: the *Gesellschaften*, salon societies, recreational groups, men's clubs, soldier's clubs, unions of fellow-countrymen etc., etc. In some of these, membership tended to be exclusive to certain social groups and classes (the nobility, citizens, local dignitaries, servants, journeymen, etc.); some were more open. Other groupings of a similar kind endeavoured to transcend mere sociability by pursuing the old fundamental notion of brotherhood, aimed at a closer moral fellowship. Lodges of Freemasons, for example, students' associations, remnants of the old fraternities of journeymen and associations of youths, can all be described as moral and social associations of this type, as can modern unions of tradesmen [*Handwerkervereine*], and those for the advanced education of workers, etc.

Lastly, since the re-awakening of the spirit of association, countless independent *charitable associations* have been formed, alongside the remaining or newly established public and private institutions for charitable purposes. These support or complement the activities of state, commune or corporation. ... Sometimes, they function in a provisional form as auxiliary agencies in emergencies; as associations for the establishment of specific institutions; to provide the leadership for gatherings for specific purposes; to provide care for the sick and wounded in time of war, etc. At other times, they seek to organise poor relief, care of the sick and relief agencies ... on a permanent basis: for example, associations for the relief and care of the poor, for the sick, for crèches, for invalids, for indigent new mothers, for the medical care of the children of poor parents, for providing the poor with wood in winter, savings associations for the less well-off, housing associations for building family dwellings for those with no means, for the establishment of public wash-houses and baths, etc.[10] In more recent times the form of a public company has been used for these. [903] In Berlin (1848) and Stettin (1853) and elsewhere, so-called 'mutual building societies' [*gemeinnützige Baugesellschaften*] have been formed which pay 4 per cent or 5 per cent interest on the share capital and in return construct buildings containing a number of apartments, which they then rent cheaply to people of no means. The intention is to allow the title of the apartment to pass to the tenant, but to transfer ownership of the whole piece of ground after thirty years to the collectivity of tenants, the so-called tenants' fellowship [*Mietsgenossenschaft*]. At this point, however, we leave the area of personal association, on the one hand, and of pure charity on the other, and take a step into the realm of the *economic association*, to be discussed below.

The place of modern group organisation in the history of fellowship: its
relation to the gild constitution

Such a variety of aims corresponds to an extraordinary multiplicity in the *composition* and *organisation* of the free associations. The modern association system [*Vereinswesen*] is assured of developing more fully and more independently than the medieval system, precisely because the versatility of form in the modern system enables it to suite equally well the most general and the most specific purposes, and to be rigidly immutable as well as capable of extreme freedom of movement. The medieval system of association, in spite of its wealth of forms, was comparatively poor in the number of shapes it took because it was dominated by the forms of league and gild. Equally, the modern system of association tends to put certain basic principles of organisation into practice in the same way everywhere. In respect of associations lacking any economic aspect, there is an unmistakable link with the old gild constitution, and with its formation and development.

The *membership* of all these associations, whether composed of individuals or of collective personalities (communities, public corporations, economic corporate bodies or other associations) – for example, the postal, telegraph and railway companies, the Burial Fund Union of the German Railway Companies, the Trades Congress, the Union of German Fellowships and many collective organisations, etc. – or of institutions and foundations, or indeed of several of these types of persons, is both conditioned and determined, just as in the earliest gilds, by the twin factors of *personality* and *free-will*. The only way of becoming a member is a free declaration of intent to join, on the one hand, and admission by the association, or the agencies it specifies for this purpose, on the other. However, in a few of its branches the modern system of association has adopted such a free, [904] loose form, that some associations declare in advance that they will recognise as a member anyone who enters his name on a list, pays a contribution, or lets it be known in any other pre-determined way that he intends to be active in pursuing the aims of the association. In general, the modern system of association is opposed to any form of exclusiveness... This is not to say that very diverse conditions of membership are not often laid down, depending on the aim of the association; nor that, while some associations simply demand acceptance of an obligation to pay a certain contribution or undertake certain personal duties, others demand evidence of certain qualifications pertaining to class, profession, family, religion, society, education, or again mental or physical attributes ...

Even when the association is based on a combination of real and personal rights, and still more when it is established purely on the basis of obligatory contributions, it is a general rule that all members have equal rights and duties in all affairs of the association, and particularly equal voting rights. Even where dues are unequal, not at members' discretion but by being graduated according to an association's compulsory scale of taxation, it is normal for fellows' rights within the association not to differ on the basis of a higher or lower contribution. If distinctions and different classes of membership do appear, they are almost always based on *personal* characteristics (age, worthiness, reputation, length of membership, etc.). Equally ... both the rights and duties of the association's members towards one another, and the rights and duties of the individual to the association, are purely personal in nature. In matters of detail there is of course incalculable variety according to the articles of the association. The relationship of the association to its members, the degree to which the individual is absorbed by the association, and the rights which he receives in return, are extraordinarily varied. There is hardly any longer in practice, and certainly not in law, any question of such a strong power subjecting the individual to the united association as that possessed by the old gild system. A large number of associations, however, although their constitutions are of course not enforceable in law, have the intention of forming a union encompassing almost all their members' life, temporarily or permanently. [905] In others, a limited number of personal obligations, the fulfilment of which is secured by penalties and the association's courts, are established along with a corresponding number of rights, notably participation in the events and privileges of the association. In still others, the members' duties consist only of their obligation to pay dues, and their rights only of the right to participate in a possible future meeting, which does not necessarily have to be convened. In completely independent associations, not invested by public authority with additional significance, the individual can break off his relationship with the association at any time by leaving, and the association its with the individual by excluding him.

Intermediate stages between assembly and association

The *organisation* of associations structured in this way, as determined by the freely chosen articles of the association, and subsequently developed by the association's autonomy, is so variously constituted according to their needs and purpose that perhaps every conceivable constitution is represented in one association or another. In all cases the *organs* of the association are its assembly and a directorate, consisting of one person or else collegial. In addition, there are frequently committees or representatives of the association which represent the collectivity to the directorate; and paid or unpaid association officials in very varied positions, and of varying importance, to see to technical matters, administer assets, represent the association to outsiders, and so on. The legislative, judicial, administrative, decision-making, executive and supervisory functions of the executive's life are divided very unequally between these organs ... Sometimes the emphasis is on the directorate or on a committee, which perhaps founded the association and directs it without even calling a meeting of its members; sometimes the collectivity of the association sees to all its affairs itself. It frequently happens that a meeting constitutes itself as an association, and then immediately transfers its authority to a permanent committee, which elects its own members, and which is only entitled, not obliged, to convoke a new assembly when need arises. Many assemblies which were originally completely independent, such as most periodic assemblies of academics, which had no fixed meeting place, the assembly of lawyers, the Trades Congress, the Congress for Political Economy, church assemblies, meetings of delegates and political parties etc., do not even adopt a formal structure, but only institute a committee, whose duties are to convoke the next assembly and execute other business; it may also occasionally act in the meantime in the name of the assembly in promotion of its material interests ...

[906] The growing significance which the system of free association has won for itself in our day in the sphere of politics, the intellect and social life, corresponds to an increase in the use by the state itself of organisations resembling associations ... If we disregard the compulsory state organisations and the compulsory formation of associations, we must emphasise, first, the greater tendency of the authorities to form collegiate structures. This produces everywhere colleges, commissions, deputations, committees, representative bodies and so on; sometimes, it produces an organisation resembling an association, for example associations for literary specialists, colleges of medicine, the economic colleges of the *Länder*, and other technical deputations, as well as those boards of trustees and commissions established to administer individual institutions. On the other hand, there is a frequent tendency to regard certain classes of people, connected by their office, profession or interests, as natural fellowships and to constitute agencies for them in this capacity; these are then generally elected with the participation of all union members: [907] for example

the setting up of the chambers, or councils, of commerce and trade ... The state organisation of chambers of advocates, or of honorary councils elected by the lawyers within any Prussian appeal court district, which are vested with disciplinary powers, are based on the same perception of a natural corporation of professional fellows.

Chapter XVII

Free fellowships for economic purposes from 1525 to the present [66, 67, 68]

The system of free fellowships[1] for economic purposes: the various types of economic organisms

[907] All of the larger economic organisms [of the later Middle Ages and early modern period] were *fellowship-based in nature* ... Although the economies of individual landowners, tradesmen or merchants were structured on the basis of lordship, in themselves they represented only a manorial or domestic economic structure, while for all more general economic purposes which extended into public life they were members of a local community, gild, incorporated trade or some other such professional fellowship. The emergence of the territorial state initially produced no change in this situation. Although a unified state fiscal policy was developed, it did not at first extend any further than the immediate requirements of the state, and in the sixteenth century there was still little talk of the state organising the territorial economy on a basis of principle. The lord of the *Land* was a great husbandman of his domain; he was only distinguished from the lord of an estate by the extent of his economic power.

The territorial state was not a unified economic organism as was the rural community, town or incorporated trade. Hence no true economic *institutions* [*Anstalten*] existed alongside the economic associations [*Verbände*]. The lack of state institutions is self-explanatory. Communal or private institutions for the promotion of the economy did not exist because each fellowship or economic [908] association satisfied the economic needs of its members by its internal arrangements, as the commune did for its citizens. If charitable church institutions and pious foundations did in a sense have the character of economic institutions, alleviating an economic need of the community, their primary purpose was spiritual or charitable, and only indirectly did they fulfil the purposes of the general economy [*Volkswirtschaft*]. Further, there was an inner correspondence between the economic structure of the people [sc. nation: *Volk*] and their articulation overall [*Gesammtgliederung*]: neither fellowships nor lordship groups existed solely for economic purposes, even less for specific economic purposes ...

Where a new unitary economic organisation existed over the members, it was at the same time a political, religious, military, moral and social group; even in its economic features, it was not confined to any one of the aspects of economic association which today are separate, but pursued every aspect of an economic grouping. Consequently, economic fellowships were usually based on groups comprising both persons and property. Fellowships originating in a purely personal grouping [*Verbindung*] based themselves more and more on the law of property, by acquiring joint assets in the form of land, movable capital or an exploitable privilege ... Where a community of capital [*kapitalistische Gemeinschaft*] had been established first, and a fellowship had emerged from it, the latter always tended to produce a personal association alongside the association based on the law of property. Hence there was no chance of a fellowship emerging which (as in the case of the public limited company [*Aktiengesellschaft*]) was determined and conditioned by and existed solely to serve the community of capital; rather, a personal economic union came into being which also aimed to produce a community of peace, justice [*Recht*], life and morality. The result was that all fellowships with any special economic significance contained, in their basis and organisation, a [909] mixture of personal or public elements, and of material or private law-elements.

Similarly, along with this organism of fellowship went the pursuit of the whole variety of economic purposes. It was at one and the same time an economic co-operative [*Wirtschaftsgenossenschaft*] and a co-operative economy [*Genossenschaftswirtschaft*]: as an economic co-operative and an economic universality, it aims to provide protection, support and furtherance for the individual economic groups contained within it, but is itself economically active only so far as the fellowship-purpose demands it. As a co-operative economy, the collectivity as such is economically active, organises itself on this basis, and regards the separate particular economies subsumed by it only as factors within a unitary, common economy. Both of these elements were contained, undivided and indivisible, in the old associations of fellows. As an association for economic control [*Wirtschaftspolizei*] and the support of economic activity, as an insurance and credit union and frequently (to put it in modern terms) a raw-materials, warehousing and consumer co-operative, each craft gild was also a productive trading company [*Gesellschaft*]. Each *Mark* community combined the characteristics of a rural productive association with those of an association for protection and support for the aims of individual economic groups. And so everywhere the collectivity's care for the economic life of its members was combined with the partial absorption of the separate economic groups into an independent, communal, economic structure – except in the cases where, as in the monasteries and in many fraternal communities, the separate economic groups were *entirely* swallowed up by a communist collective economic structure.

With the changes in conditions generally since the sixteenth century, the structure of economic organisms, too, gradually had to change completely. They are now faced with new changes in our century. The internal disintegration of all associations mid-way between the state and the individual, whether based on fellowship or on lordship, the absorption of their public-law elements by the state and their restriction to the sphere of private law was bound to result, in the economic sphere, in the state monopolising the role of economic universality: apart from the state, there were now only private economic structures. In accordance with its task, the state elevated itself to the position of supreme economic organism; but, since it intended to be not merely the supreme, but the only, universality in all spheres, every other collective economic structure was to be absorbed within the state economy as a contingent and dependent branch of it. Apart from a much-ramified state economy, there were to be only individual economic organisations. The direct or indirect state institution for economic ends, with which of course a more or less corporative constitution could be combined, became the dominant form of economic organisation; while the independent [910] association of fellows for economic purposes increasingly disappeared. Free association, in the dual form of the association of capital [*Kapitalsvereinigung*] and personal fellowship, has only recently re-emerged to oppose economic centralisation and fragmentation on the basis of single economic organisations. It is once more winning an important independent niche between the state and the individual for associative economic groups [*Gesellschaftswirtschaften*].

First, then, the medieval economic associations faced gradual disintegration. Local communities, gilds, incorporated trades, brotherhoods of journeymen, and all other corporations which had an economic aspect, became state institutions not only in their political, supervisory [*Polizei*], and moral aspects, but also in the protection and promotion of economic activity. At best, they retained their own significance as communities which owned and exploited assets or profitable privileges. The lordship-based economic groups were undermined in the same way. So far as they retained the status of public organisms, their leader (e.g. the lord of the estate) became a minor state official; for the rest, the relationship between the head and members (domestic workers, apprentices, journeymen, day labourers, etc.) turned into one based purely on obligation and private law.

The state undertook the duties of an economic universality either directly through its official agencies, or through institutions established by it for the protection, control [*Polizei*], and promotion of economic activity. When these institutions could not be set up by using older associations drawn into the state economic structure, it set up new institutions for specific purposes, or allowed communities and corporations to be established under state supervision. In this way institutions [*Anstalten*] for commerce, banks and credit banks, stock exchanges, loan companies, insurance institutions, widows' and retirement funds, saving banks, the compulsory savings schemes for miners and trades journeymen, agricultural institutes for the development of land etc., came into being as direct or indirect institutions of the state. Beyond this, the state itself entered into a number of profit-making branches of the economy, as landlord, merchant, industrialist and manufacturer, and founded a large number of state trading institutions, some of which were monopolies. Indeed, the first larger trading companies to develop were taken into its service so that these too were characterised as state institutions with a company structure. But, both for the organisation of economic activity and for trade, the state increasingly had to call upon *free association*, which was awakening to renewed strength. This is why, from as early as the eighteenth century, fellowship is given a prominent place alongside institution in the structure of a number of newly founded economic bodies.

The independent economic association of individuals, on the other hand, could only maintain a position within this system as a strengthened *private* economic structure. Initially there was nothing to prevent [911] such a view, either in the case of associations of equals in which individuals were only collectively bound together in a relation of partnership [*Societät*] or communion, or in the association of the merchant, manufacturer or estate-owner with his servants and labourers. But this did not correspond to their actual circumstances, since, with the mighty resurgence of the modern economy, new comprehensive economic organisms emerged, purely on the basis of the law of property, in two forms: as a lordship or else as a fellowship based on capital.

The lordship of capital [*Kapitalsherrschaft*] created a new form of lordship group, based on capital, in the relationship between the entrepreneur and the employees. Although this is in fact an independent organism, just as capable of extending into public as into private law, present-day law in principle gives it the significance only of an aggregate of private rights operating between the One and the Many [sc. the individual and the group]. Legislation has, to be sure, never put this principle into effect under specific circumstances, or else it has already abandoned it. This does not require further demonstration for those landed lordship groups which still have the status of a local community. But when, for example, factories and manufacturing enterprises [*Etablissements*] get political representation in local or regional assemblies, when they are taxed as units, when overall regulation of relations between employees and employers is introduced by the state; or again when (as under the new industrial legislation in Saxony, Thuringia, Brunswick, Baden and Württemberg) it becomes legally obligatory in concentrations of more than twenty employees in a communal workshop for a set of rules for manufacturing and service industries to be enacted and published;[2] when the state makes it obligatory for individual factories to set up a relief fund in which the master and the workers have proportional shares – all of this implies the legal doctrine that these groups, too, are organic units with *public* significance.

After many less than satisfactory preliminary stages of development, *fellowships of capital* found a perfect form in the limited company [*Aktiengesellschaft*]. It never escaped the state's attention that this was no longer simply an extension of individual economic units by means of a partnership or common ownership [*Sachgemeinschaft*](as many jurists claimed for so long), but signalled the creation of a new economic organism. For the state did not merely, in so far as the purpose of the association lay within the public sphere, ... act by way of concession, inspection, or co-management; but, from the very beginning, regardless of the association's aims, the state asserted its power to supervise the internal life of the society and (following [912] the prevailing theory of corporations) its right to approve their existence and organisation ... The property-based fellowship is the first case of an independent economic organism developing out of the free association of separate economic undertakings, and acquiring a recognised, if not completely free, status.

The personal fellowship for economic purposes has also already, under the influence of the modern idea of association, begun to build new structures alongside the state, private institutions and capitalist groups, by means of the free union of atomised forces. Initially, it relied on the state, was under the state's direction and guardianship, and so existed in conjunction with state institutions. It can, in a similar way, be combined with a capitalist group. More recently, however, it begins to emerge with greater freedom and independence. In terms of content, too, it is reaching higher and higher stages of development: from being a means of mutualising risks and loans it has progressed towards putting individual aspects of economic activity under collective control, in theory at least, by collectivising labour in the producers' associations.

It was vitally important for the internal development of forms of economic association that contradictions inherent in both their basis and their aims during the Middle Ages were successfully separated. After the waning of their formative power and of the union impulse, which by means of a ceaseless flow of new structures had maintained the momentum of medieval occupational organisation, and so had safeguarded the harmony between different classes [*Stände*] and their sub-divisions, between collective and individual interests within groups, between ownership and labour – after that, the continued mixture of opposing elements was bound to lead to sharp contradictions between form and content. Both the individual within the union, and the union within the higher universality sought to make their influence decisive; yet they wished to retain those more far-reaching powers which underpinned the common organism, in the form of privileges. Thus, in an economic context too, fellowships sought to conduct economic individualism with corporate backing [*korporative Individualwirtschaft*] on a privatised basis, and none the less to continue to enjoy economic privileges awarded to them as economic organisms and as branches of the national economy. But, here as everywhere, universality found a powerful – soon a too-powerful – representative against the chartered corporations in the state, which was increasingly taking over the overall organisation of the national economy, leaving to private unions only collective activity for profit [*Erwerbsthätigkeit*]. In this way the ground was prepared for the internal, and to some extent external, separation of the property-based and personal elements in the fellowships ...

[913] New economic organisations, which were forming themselves, or being formed by the state, were from the first founded *either* on a property-based corporation *or* on a personal fellowship; as a rule their aims were so precise and specific that the old mixture of dissimilar elements disap-

peared of its own accord. Modern economic association has not relinquished this advance ...

As regards their *basis*, the property fellowship and the personal fellowship for economic purposes are opposites. In the former, the fellowship is determined and conditioned by its collective assets: in the latter, the fellowship takes precedence and a community based on property exists only in so far as the nature and the aims of the fellowship require it, and in the form which they demand. Here it is an aggregate of personal forces (ultimately labour itself) which associates itself [*sich associirt*]; property only comes into consideration as a personal force (hence only as an obligation to pay dues). In the former, on the contrary, it is property itself (especially capital) which comes together [*sich vereinigt*]; personality only becomes relevant within the association through a piece of property and according to its size.

As regards their *aims*, one must distinguish between a fellowship aiming at common economic activity and one promoting individual economic activity. [914] ... The aims of the latter can be combined with political, religious, moral and social aims, ... so that in one respect even today the local community and the state can be characterised as economic fellowships of *this* type. Fellowships for such specific purposes can be organised on a compulsory or voluntary basis; and in fact in recent times an enormous number have been founded for such purposes. These are to be contrasted, on the other hand, with fellowships which are only a means to the end of some common economic activity, to which other aims are, at the most, subordinate and ... are therefore unimportant for its legal constitution. These fellowships, generally in the form of trading companies but also sometimes as societies for capital investment, make the conduct of an economic activity, based on its assets or the forces of the members, the direct positive content of its group activity. All compulsory fellowships (above all the state and commune, but also compulsory commercial associations) have ceased to be common economic enterprises of this kind. The purpose of an economic company can, therefore, only be achieved through *free* association, whether of capital ... or of labour ...

There remains only a discussion of the history of independent fellowships intended exclusively or predominantly for economic purposes, or of the fellowship-based elements in such compulsory associations. Here we must remember that, apart from their legal aspects, all these formations have a series of other aspects to do with other areas of life, and that these are usually incomparably more important. We must also remember that, even in the legal sphere, the only circumstances of interest here are the fact that they are fellowships, how this manifests itself, or whether they contain elements of fellowship; this by no means allows an exhaustive investigation of their substance, indeed it is often only of slight importance for their overall role … For example, in the case of a limited company (A) for banking or loans and another limited company (B) for the management of a spinning mill [915], the only circumstance which concerns us here is the one that they both have in common – of being a limited company … And if, with regard to the insurance system, insurance companies which issue shares and those which are based on mutual agreement simply appear to be sub-species of the same type of institution, none the less with regard to the question which is alone of relevance here – which principle of society is dominant? – both are less closely related to the other than the one is to a mining union and the other to a co-operative society. From this point of view we have yet to discuss: first, the trades fellowships of the older kind, then the property-based fellowships, and finally the personal fellowships for the purposes of economic activity and profit, with regard to their legal and historical features.

The fate of the old trades fellowships: the system of craft gilds[3]

In our description of the medieval system of craft gilds, which [916] were the source of the magnificent developments in German trade and even art, we have been able to observe, especially in the fifteenth and early sixteenth centuries, the seeds of gradual decay. From now on, with the transformation of the German system of fellowship as a whole, the internal disintegration of the craft gild into a privileged *corpus*, and its simultaneous demotion by outside forces to the role of state institution endowed with a juristic personality, progressed unabated. The history of the craft gilds' deep and tragic decline, the ruins which tower from their era into ours, are far better known and more accessible than the former glory of the craft-gild organisation. Here we have only to indicate the associated transformation of *legal* perceptions as to the nature of a trades corporation.

The internal changes in the gild, which began in the fifteenth and were completed in the seventeenth and eighteenth centuries, were affected by the 'gild spirit [*Zunftgeist*]' which was supplanting the old sense of fellowship, and at that time was so rampant among tradesmen that the expression could be used to denote the tendency of an entire age. Under the influence of this spirit, the tradesman's innate perception of the nature of his associations underwent a metamorphosis. Instead of the free union of those engaged in the same trade, the basis and aim of the gild became the right, formed into a 'privilege' and if possible a 'monopoly', to engage in a specific type of trade. Whereas the nature of the gild as an independent moral fellowship had previously regulated the nature of the artisan's trade, the existence and structure of the gild was now conditioned and determined in the smallest detail by the profitable common trading right. The notion of public office gave way to that of privilege based on private law; compulsory gild membership, from being a means of compelling those engaged in the same type of trade to join the fellowship, became a means of excluding those who were not members of the gild from practising the trade. For its members, the gild itself, from being a miniature community, became a private-law institution for the utilisation and exploitation of the shared privilege.

The other aspect of this development [917] was the moral content of the gild and the transformation of the old comradely virtues of the class [*Stand*] into the corresponding vices. The sense of community was transformed into a spirit of exclusivity; the aspiration to power, honour and high repute, into egotistical greed for profit; the old craftsman's pride into petty vanity; love of honour into blustering ambition (which often served only as a means of covering selfishness); reverence for custom into empty lust for ceremony; the exclusion of the unworthy into narrow-minded exclusiveness; the sense of brotherliness and equality into a fear of competition and professional jealousy; and a lively awareness of public life into the separatism of a corporation constantly harping on its monopoly ...

[Trade fellowships such as craft gilds became 'privileged corporations', membership became 'a private right'. The absolutist states treated craft gilds 'as institutions of state policy [*Polizeianstalten*] with a [merely fictional] Roman juristic personality' under 'the system of concession'; the gilds lost their autonomy. Merchant corporations also turned into 'authorised unions for the protection of business interests'.]

The fellowship-based organisations in modern commercial law[4]

[949] If the right to work in a trade, once a public office, had become a privilege based on private law under the system of privileged corporations, ... in our century, after a long period of struggle, the new idea of *freedom to practise a trade* has been victorious. This regards the right to engage in a trade of any kind as a free civil right. Even without legislation, the wholly altered economic circumstances were bound to riddle the old industrial structure full of holes in all its aspects. An independent structure of free economic organisms came into being, alongside the gild-structured trades,

[950] thanks to the release of commerce from state control and a connection with industry, the development of large-scale trade, capital projects and factories, and to the emergence of a great number of new branches of industry not organised on a gild basis. In the long term the law was so much the less able to withhold recognition of the new principle. Freedom to practise a trade had been realised first of all in France thanks to the Revolution, transferred thence to the German territories occupied by France, and implemented by Prussia in 1810–11. Admittedly, after the Restoration, it was not only denied to all other German states, but, in several *Länder* in which it had already been put into practice, even succumbed once more to a reaction which was half political, half gild-inspired ...

The nature of the craft-gild, in the form given it under the system of privileged corporations, was destroyed beyond recall. Not only had the gilds' vitality been sapped by the withdrawal of their economic aspects; the rigidly structured old corporations had become even more untenable due to the altered commercial conditions. It is clear that the modern development of occupational freedom, even where it does not directly attack the corporative features of the gild system, still aims in the final instance to dismember the old organisation of trade into disjointed atoms. Alongside this tendency to break up the old, can be felt the powerful stirrings of the new movement – free association – which will mould the loose atoms into new freer, higher organisms. However, for the transitional period which we are now living through, legislation was justified in seeking to conserve at least in part the elements of fellowship in the old associations ...

[952] The corporate system was the subject of legislative experiments. Regarding the old trades corporations, trade regulations followed a three-fold system.

1. Some laws annulled them or forced them to break up. This was the case on the left bank of the Rhine, the Kingdom of Westphalia and the Grand-Duchy of Berg, as well as in Nassau in 1819, in accordance with the procedure adopted in France – where the legislation of 14 July 1791 not only annulled the existing gilds but prohibited all future associations of workers engaged in the same trade, the introduction of membership lists, society funds and administrative bodies. Of the more recent trade legislation, that of Württemberg, Baden and the latest Bavarian legislation also followed this path. In these cases the gild assets are as a rule treated as public property.

2. Other legislation annulled only the special privileges of existing trades corporations, and otherwise left it to their own discretion whether they wanted to continue as private fellowships for the furtherance of

mutual trade interests, or to dissolve their association. This system, which in England, [953] with the gradual progress towards occupational freedom, came to be put into effect by the transformation of the gilds into *free companies*, was tacitly accepted by Prussian legislation before 1845, and then again by the ordinances on the conduct of existing trades in Hanover, Kurhessen, Hessen-Homburg and Schleswig-Holstein. Absolutely no special conditions were laid down concerning the legal status of the gilds. None the less this leaves room for doubt as to whether the gilds did lose their legal character. Trades corporations, on the contrary, were expressly declared to be free fellowships by the trade ordinances of Oldenburg, Bremen, Hamburg and Lübeck; they were granted their existing assets as private property, and could therefore keep them and continue in existence, or else bring about their own dissolution by a majority vote and divide the assets. In all cases each individual was granted the free right to leave the organisation.

3. Most legislation, however, attempted to preserve the old trades corporations as associations in public law ... Where a complete system of publicly authorised trade corporations is put in place of the old system of craft gilds, those corporations which continue to exist must comply with the framework of the new legislative organisation. If they have the character of compulsory associations, as in Austria and Bavaria until 1868, then the old craft gilds are officially changed into the new form. If, as in Saxony and Brunswick, a certain kind of voluntary fellowship is vested with authority in commerce, or, as in the states of Thuringia, they alone have corporative rights, then the older corporations are allowed to choose between dissolution or a revision of their statutes along the lines of the new [954] public trade corporations. In Prussia, too, the older incorporated trades were allowed to choose between being broken up, or revising their statutes in accordance with the regulations enacted for the new incorporated trades. But the decision voluntarily to break up the corporation was dependent on a two-thirds majority and the approval of the government. Moreover, the government was awarded the right to dissolve unilaterally any corporation which refused to accept the statutes as officially revised and instituted by the government, and also to annul existing corporations, or to integrate several into one on the advice of the trades council, on the basis of overwhelming considerations of the good of the community. Since, in this case, the incorporated trades always retained their public character, their assets, too, were generally treated as public property ...

[Gierke then considers 'the Prussian system of publicly authorised and dependent corporations with trading rights', and 'chambers of industry and of commerce'.

He now turns to 'the origin and full development of the property fellowship' (chapter 69), which 'culminates in the joint-stock company [*Aktienverein*]'. Can property fellowship be found in the territorial communes, the 'collective hand [*Gesammthand*]', in fellowships based on use of a common mill, and so forth? He considers 'fellowships [co-operatives] in the law governing salt-mines', and 'business societies'.

Finally he comes to the *joint-stock company*. He considers first its earlier history in Italy, Holland and England, for example amongst merchant companies. He notes 'the multiplication of joint-stock companies in England' and English legislation since 1720. He examines 'continental and especially French developments', 'the perfection of the capitalist nature [of the joint-stock company], the triumph of its independence from the state', the *Code Napoléon*, and recent French legislation of 1863 and 1867; and then 'developments in Germany', from 'the state-institution character of the old joint-stock societies' to 'the passing of initiative and formative influence, in practice, to self-associating capitalists'. He considers 'the joint-stock company of the most recent German legislation as a property fellowship', 'modern theories of *societas* and *universitas*' and 'the modified juristic person'.]

Chapter XVIII

Economic fellowships based on property: the joint-stock company [*Aktienverein*] and domination by capital [69, 70]

The development of the joint-stock company[1]

... [1008] This structure could never escape the basic type of the Roman *universitas*; the institutional element remained and, instead of being conceived of as a whole which lived in its members, the union was broken up into an external unity alien to it in the form of a person artificially ascribed to it, and a plurality with no legal identity. The need to escape such an alternative gave rise to attempts either to extend the concept of society [*Societät*] so that the company could still be legally valid as a unity – the so-called formal or collective unity; or else to modify the Roman concept of the juristic person through the company [*Gesellschaft*] principle.

To the much-abused theory of fellowship, however, [1009] is owed the distinction of first distancing itself from such artificiality, and conceiving the limited company as an independent creation of German law, not fitting into the strait-jacket of received Roman concepts. This theory was, admittedly, untenable when it was claimed that the fellowship was an intermediary between corporation [*Körperschaft*] and society [*Gesellschaft*]. Such an intermediary can exist historically, but not juristically. However, the founder of the theory, Beseler, has already expressly recognised that the joint-stock company is a *corporation*; it is, however, a 'corporative *fellowship*', a corporation not built on the basis of Roman law nor dominated by the principle of *universitas*, but based on German law and structured according to the principle of fellowship.

However, all these theories only took into consideration one aspect of the joint-stock company – the association of persons; they made the relationship between unity and plurality basic to the juristic model. The specific difference between this form of association and other fellowships

– the special relationship between the persons' unity and the united capital
– was either not considered or even expressly declared unimportant.

Here was reason enough to give rise to a series of different theories
which, conversely, gave one-sided emphasis to the formative influence
exercised by capital. This happened in two ways. Either the sum of assets
itself was made the embodiment of the institution; in this case emphasis
was put on its structure, and a modified community of property
[*communio*] or a society based on real rights was established ... Alternatively, the independent legal personality of the union was kept, but instead
of the combination of persons, the sum of assets was made its basis, so that
the personality of the union was changed into that of a foundation or
institute, and the corporation [1010] into a 'trading institution' ... In this
way the capitalist theory, to which we undeniably owe the prominence of
a new form of union (although its emergence was inevitable), was pushed
to the forefront through a complete negation of the elements of fellowship.

In the meantime, undismayed by all the contradictory theories, the
joint-stock company has continued to develop its own legal life in a
manner suited to its nature; it has become more and more clearly formulated as a complete property fellowship. Of course neither scholarship
nor the law had any creative role in this: but they were forced to recognise
what the autonomy of associating groups had created, first of all as a
special norm in concrete cases, and finally as a universal right manifest in
special ways in a particular case.

The *company articles*, through which particular fellowships of capital
gave and give themselves their law [*Recht*] are, therefore, the most important sources of information as to the nature of the new institutions, and
above all as to their status among fellowships and in the system of justice
as a whole. And, if one looks to law not for a dead pattern but for a living
organism, this source of information remains important even where
general laws have been passed for all companies or for individual classes
of them. For all legislation [*Gesetze*] regulates only the external norms
[*Recht*] of the joint-stock company in a complete and unconditional way.
For their inner norms, while legislation may establish particular overriding limits, it only regulates their positive workings in a subsidiary and
incomplete way. Hence a joint-stock company, unlike a community,
cannot exist at all without articles. The law itself not only makes the
existence of articles of association, bound to certain forms, a condition of
the company's existence, but positively requires a minimum content. And
there is more! It is in the nature of things that the law [*Gesetz*], while it is
a subsidiary factor in regulating the norms [*Recht*] of the fellowship,

chooses out of all possible conditions those which restrict and bind the individual least; [1011] that the articles of the association, on the other hand (the intention of which is to produce an organism capable of life and movement with the possibility of further development) must regularly constitute norms, stronger than generally recognised in law, for the unity of the company over against the plurality; that many conditions are thus laid down in law, only to be changed in the overwhelming majority of the articles of association; and that consequently anyone who tried to determine the nature of the overall phenomenon of the institution solely from the subsidiary common law without taking the articles of the association into consideration, would arrive at a completely false picture...

The pure joint-stock company [Aktienverein] ... as fellowship

[1019] However, all this represents only one aspect of the association. The joint-stock company is of course a property fellowship but it still remains a *fellowship*. Capital, which has been set aside for a specific purpose, self-contained, is in itself lifeless and motionless. It can be imbued with vitality and direction solely and exclusively by a personality. Such a personality can be an individual, several individuals bound by a contract, the state, a local community or any volitional personal collective organism; or again an institutional personality ... It is of course true that the members of the association are members with only a part of their *property* personality, but still with a part of their *personality*! But, if the elements from which the whole is constructed [1020] are partial personalities, and if, because it is organised, the whole is internally and externally an independent entity distinct from the sum total of its parts, then this entity, too, is a personality. And, if this collective personality draws its vitality only from its members, but is in no way alien to its members, and exists rather for their sake alone, reverting to its constituent parts when it ceases to be, then this is no corporation based on Roman law, but one based on German law constructed not on the principle of the *universitas* but as a fellowship.

Thus the very *existence* of a joint-stock company is by no means determined by the original capital sums alone, but in addition by a personal *collective will*. Collective will brings the corporation into existence by a constitutive act (which has been falsely construed as a contract and is still called 'company contract' [*Gesellschaftsvertrag*] in the trade statute book) and in the *articles*. Collective will gives it its constitution, its law of existence; and, within the bounds of this constitution, it is a collective will which in the first instance controls any changes in, and the final dissolution of, the organism. Creative collective will manifests itself as the collective will of a *plurality* [*Gesammtvielheitswille*], and finds expression in civil [*bürgerlich*] autonomy; on the other hand, the collective will acting according to a constitution is the collective will of a *single* entity [*Gesammteinheitswille*] and sets *corporative* autonomy in motion: both, however, are capable of autonomous decision-making, creating objective Right. The character of these acts of volition is, naturally, not altered by the fact that, in the interests of constitutional law, modern legislation requires that they should be authenticated and published in a specific way, in particular that they should be entered in the public register; that, before it has fulfilled these formalities, it will not accept the existence (or change) of character in the fellowship as an independent body in law ...

[The composition is an association of persons, so that, in relation to the association, membership is neither a free private right nor purely a property right.]

[1023] It is the *organisation* of the joint-stock company which, above all, makes it into a fellowship. In itself, the fact that its elements are bound together produces only an aggregate. But this aggregate as such would *not* be able to exist like an open or limited partnership [*Kommanditgesellschaft*] in itself; for only partial personalities are contained within it, while in order to live it requires a complete personality. It would simply remain a chance legal community [*Rechtsgemeinschaft*] of several members with capital, if the binding together of these elements did not take the form of an *organisation* from which a living whole emerges out of the collectivity of partial personalities – a complete personality acting through its organs. These organs' formation and sphere of influence is determined in its essentials by law, and in matters of detail by the *constitution* of the fellowship. The capitalist nature of the whole is always in evidence; and, in so far as the entire organisation refers back to the collectivity of shareholders as its ultimate representative, the association is in fact manifested solely as organised capital.

Yet it is characteristic that, the more they are called on to represent the unity and positive activity of the association, the more personality predominates over capital in the individual organs. The general meeting itself no longer merely represents shares in capital, but demonstrates the individuality of the members. It still, however, manifests itself here as a non-essential, in which individuality coincides with the colourless characteristic of possessing shares. [1024] The element of chance is only overcome by the fact that it can be assumed that, in the overall result, the greater number of other voters will wipe out the single instances of a deviant vote provided by a quota of capital. This guarantee is, admittedly, inadequate for most articles of association and many laws: by special provisions for the conditions and exercise of the right to vote, they attempt to secure both the representation of the impersonal interests of capital against arbitrary individual acts, lack of perceptiveness or unworthiness, and also to safeguard the status of individual members' resolutions as being resolutions of the fellowship, against the might of capital.

Personality achieves even greater importance in committees set up by the general meeting, especially in the supervisory board [*Aufsichtsrath*] (usually appointed and thereafter entrusted by law with special functions). Status as a shareholder is still, of course, required; frequently, the possession of multiple shares, or other special qualifications in share-ownership, are demanded. Yet the choice is made by election from among those who are qualified, and not (for example) by who has the greatest holdings.

Finally, the capital-based element disappears completely within the executive board [*Vorstand*]. It is possible to appoint non-shareholders to positions on the board, and if often the articles (and, in France, the law itself) demand the possession of shares, this remains of secondary importance in the election (or other form of appointment) as compared with personality. It does not serve as the basis of the office, but simply as a guarantee that business will be conducted honestly and in company interests.

Apart from this distinctive tension between the capitalist and personal bases for appointment to the organ of the association, the organism of the joint-stock company is no different from other organisms based on fellowship. The modern spirit of association, for which here the law prescribes as unalterable (in the interests of trade) only certain basic guidelines, others being subsidiary, and for which it tends to draw stricter boundaries regarding only external representation, has created an incalculable wealth of many differing forms for the joint-stock company. These forms are not, however, peculiar to the limited company; similar types can be found in all modern associations and fellowships. They are indeed nothing but offshoots, branches and a continued development of the Germanic gild constitution [*Gildeverfassung*].

Here, as in all voluntary fellowships in German law, the chief agency is the assembly of fully-enfranchised members. This meets at general and extraordinary meetings, convoked and directed according to the constitution by the management board, which has an obligation to call meetings at the request of a certain number of members. In doubtful cases, this assembly passes resolutions by a majority of duly invited members present; only in special cases, for example [1025] a change in nature or acceptance of a loan, are decisions taken with a larger majority. According to many companies' articles, the presence (in special or all cases) of a specific number of shareholders, or of representatives of a specific quota of the total capital, is required for the meeting to take binding resolutions. The general assembly may be severely limited in scope; but it can never be done away with. It is, usually, the organ which makes the laws [*Recht*], decides on all questions concerning the company's existence or change of character; it also conducts elections, supervises and is the final decision-making authority.

Apart from the assembly, only a management board is essential to the company. This can be very diversely formed, constructed and organised. It is found sometimes as an individual director; sometimes as a collective directorate; sometimes as a bench, with a unified or collective leadership or executive more or less sharply distinguishable from the rest of the board. But it is invariably the organ which administers and represents the fellowship; and which in practice generally arranges the actual direction of common association business, the convocation and ordering of assemblies, book-keeping and account-keeping; and, in the case of dissolution, sees to liquidation ...

[1026] The joint-stock company has in every respect the legal status [*rechtliche Bedeutung*] of a fellowship personality, possessing, within the life-sphere prescribed for it constitutionally and limited by law [*Gesetz*], an independent capacity to do justice, to will and to act. In relation to its members, therefore, the association does not exercise merely private rights, but general corporate rights [*Körperschaftsrecht*]: autonomy, a specific area of jurisdiction,[2] ... and fellowship self-management. The most important branch of the last is administration of assets, conducted according to the fellowship's particular fiscal policy. The questions of how the rights of the plurality are related to those of the single entity, of how the close association of unity and plurality (characteristic of the German fellowship) produces, in the case of the limited company, distinctive effects on property law, can only be dealt with more fully in volume 2.

Regarding third parties, the joint-stock company [1027] is on the same footing as any other corporate personality, in that the character it assumes as merchant when conducting business affairs does not affect its legal status. In relation to the state, finally, the limited company is likewise subject to the general legal principles of corporations ... It is already, in many respects, better placed than other fellowships, but it shares (with all corporations which do not directly mesh with the state organism) the demand for complete abolition of the remnants of the authoritarian system; for the establishment in its place (through an extension of the public sphere [*Öffentlichkeit*]) of strict civil-law liability for all infringements of the law, or of the commercial code of honour; and for judicially determined penalties for offences against order or the criminal law. The joint-stock company cannot, on the other hand, withdraw itself from the general state supremacy over corporations, nor from the supervision of its internal workings entailed thereby. If it sometimes demands a complete removal of controls, on the ground that it is only a *private* corporation, this is based on a misguided perception of the nature of a private corporation. If, by this expression, the joint-stock company is trying to give notice that it is primarily or exclusively subject to private law, then this is true only regarding its external affairs. Its inner organism, as will emerge later, is not, any more than that of any other corporation, based on private law, but rather on the law of fellowship, and as such extends into the public sphere of justice.[3]

It stands to reason that the wider relationship into which the association enters by means of the particular object of its undertaking is in no way connected with the relationship of the limited company *as such* to third parties and to the state. As the manager of a factory or an employer of assistants and workers, for example, the joint-stock company is subject to exactly the same law as the individual. Equally, the special relationships which the association has by state privilege (e.g. issuing bank-notes, the right of expropriation), by a particular franchise (e.g. for a trade) or from the nature of the effect of its undertaking on the public good (as with all institutions for communications, banking, credit and insurance) – all these do not belong to the law of fellowship, but to the sphere of justice pertaining to administration, trade, insurance, railways, etc. Hence individual entrepreneurs, other types of society and institutes are, in these respects, in principle equal [1028] to the limited company. But it is easy to see how in reality the state's right of supervision over the association *qua* bank, railway or insurance institution, and over the same association *qua* a body of property claiming for itself an independent legal personality – deriving as these do from quite different legal bases – could on many occasions merge.

Lastly, if we ask what *actual* significance, in the life of the nation as a whole, is attributable to this fully developed modern property fellowship, this is to be found in the increased potential productivity of capital. This is true in two senses: first, in so far as the way is opened for smaller amounts of capital to take proportional shares in large enterprises; second, in so far as limited companies alone can make possible the existence of modern enterprises which require that large-scale capital should function as a single entity. The miracles wrought by the association based on capital in the area of large manufacturing enterprises, which far exceed the capabilities of a single individual, are clear to see. The limited companies have, above all, become an indispensable means of facilitating the development and exploitation of transport routes and means of communication (railways, telegraphs, canals, shipping), of trade in credit and all branches of insurance. They have also been formed and expanded for many branches of large-scale trade and industry; in the mining, steel and iron industries they are almost beginning to displace the older associations of mining entrepreneurs; they exist in large numbers for spinning and weaving mills; they are engaged in trade in real estate; they provide towns with lighting, mains water and sewerage services; they concern themselves with mutual building enterprises, are engaged in deep-sea and fresh-water fisheries, construct steam mills, institutes for mechanical engineering, chemical factories and larger industrial establishments of all kinds.

In all these cases, it is the commercial purpose which brought the association into being: while it only furthers the common good by indirect means, the possibility of a capital-based fellowship which serves the common good in a disinterested way for its own sake is proved by the existence of countless non-profit-making limited companies for museums, theatres, exhibitions, public baths, charitable institutions, etc. If most limited companies have pecuniary significance only for their members, nevertheless clubs, reading circles and so on, show that it is possible [1029] to make this form of association directly serve members' personal needs as well.

In considering the institution as a whole, however, these methods of using it pale into insignificance besides its use as a capitalist trading company. If the economic nature of the joint-stock company is that of an 'impersonal economic body existing for itself' which comes into being through the grouping-together of capitalists 'plus the annulment [*Aufhebung*] of the individualistic determination of the will of society [*Gesellschaftswillens*]';[4] if in the whole structure the fellowship of persons appears to be merely the consequence and extension of the organism of capital; if directing intelligence and creative labour alike are both paid servants, and capital alone the master [*Herr*] of the association – then the overall direction of this institution is bound to be speculative–capitalist. Beneficial and necessary as the form of the joint-stock company is as a link in the chain of economic organisms, if it alone ruled it would lead to the despotism of capital.

It is therefore a happy circumstance that this danger is counteracted by the endlessly rich structure of modern economic life. In reality, the significance of entrepreneurial individualism in relation to large-bulk capital is safeguarded, first, by the fact that, for a great number of industrial and commercial undertakings, the form of individual, or personal-company, enterprise is used – indeed exclusively used. These, if they have the same capital means available, are superior to undertakings by limited companies because of the unity, intelligence and personal involvement of their management. The state, furthermore, endeavours to protect the common good from exploitation for profit by capitalist bodies of superior power, with a *de facto* monopoly, not so much by indirect supervision, but rather by setting up competing disinterested state or communal institutions for the same purposes: state railways, public banking and loan institutes, public insurance and welfare institutions, etc. Finally, so that the element of selfishness does not vanquish the moral impulse in the economic sphere as well, so that the noble concept of association does not here too decline into mutual speculation for profit, and above all so as to reduce the danger, intensified by the limited companies, that the free human personality might waste away in areas without capital – the most powerful enabling factor working towards these ends is the *personal* fellowship for economic purposes. This has long since been operating vigorously alongside the property associations. In the recent past, it has created new structures which, by developing special forms of fellowship among the working classes, promise much for the future. It is these which we must now discuss.

The personal fellowship for economic purposes

[1030] The personal association [*Association*] for economic and trade purposes is as old as association itself. But, while at an earlier date it was only one aspect of associations encompassing the whole personality, modern developments have brought into being personal fellowships for single, specific, exclusively economic ends. While they in no way rob the state, local community and other public associations of their status as communal economic entities, they none the less relieve them of the most immediate and most direct level of economic provision.

In the authoritarian epoch, it was chiefly only public institutions that were established to promote specific aspects of the economy, while the association was restricted to individualistic forms of company [*Gesell-schaft*]. But, from the end of the seventeenth century, the fellowship-based association of groups of individuals was already often in evidence, working alongside the institution [*Anstalt*]. Hence some compulsory public economic groups with corporative constitutions, and some corporations which were officially authorised and chartered, but otherwise free, emerged alongside the institution. In our century, initiative and creative power have passed back to the people: the free personal fellowship, never entirely extinguished, has been developed into a great number of different branches, and given a form capable of fitting the most varied purposes.

On the other hand, of course, the scope of these fellowships has recently been once more restricted, in that the economic advantages they offer their members have at the same time become the object of profitable speculation by the businessmen. The private institutions thus developed are, in subjective terms, capitalist trading enterprises; only through what they do are they indirectly institutions serving a common good: in the main they are narrowing the effective scope of economic fellowship, namely to the propertied classes. Among the non-propertied classes, on the other hand, self-defence against the predominance of capital-based enterprises has recently led to an enrichment in the content and form of the system of fellowship, producing a system of entirely new personal fellowships for economic and trading purposes. This holds within it the beginnings of a development of fellowship which will be of inexhaustible richness and will have incalculable consequences ...

A *fellowship* only exists when an organism with its own collective personality, living in its own members, arises out of a voluntary act of association. Countless individual societies and communities for economic or trading purposes do not belong to this category, precisely because such a personality does not exist. [1031] In particular, the compulsory commercial societies [*obligatorische Handelsgesellschaften*], discussed above, are excluded from this concept although they are the last stage before the personal fellowship, and are already in many ways very close to it. Public institutions for economic purposes, on the other hand, often have their own personality; but this personality is only a part which has branched off from the personality of the state, local community or corporation from which the institution derives its existence and purpose. Here, however, as everywhere else, there are many intermediate organisations between the pure institution and the pure fellowship: for example, compulsory public groups [*öffentliche Zwangsverbände*], in which the will of the associates does not help determine the existence of the organism but does share in determining its activity; and authorised corporations [*autorisirten Körperschaften*], in which, conversely, the collective will is the primary determinant but the will of the state a necessary complement.[5] Between fellowships and private trading institutions there are, likewise, mixed organisms: such as those where the persons who are the object or means of trade are linked individually to a trading institution, or where an economic fellowship also contains a trading institution within it.

But the fellowships described here are also *personal fellowships*, in contrast to the *capital-based fellowships* culminating in the limited company: they are based on the bringing together of personal economic powers into a collective power. In view of this, it is immediately evident that, just as the association of capital would remain moribund without an element of personal fellowship, so the personal fellowship cannot develop an economic existence without accepting capital resources into its organism. It is possible to conceive of an intellectual or moral fellowship without capital; economic success is unthinkable without at least the indirect participation of capital (e.g. as a basis for credit). Therefore, each personal economic fellowship unites an objective community based on property law with a subjective personal one. It differs from the association of capital in that, whereas in the capital association the capital is the factor which determines and defines the nature of the association, in the personal economic fellowship the personal fellowship plays this role: in the former capital dominates, here it serves. Thus in the personal economic fellowship the persons are legally and morally bound as persons, not simply as representatives of shares in joint capital. Both conceptually and historically, the property-based fellowship is therefore a heightened form of the (specialised) community of things [*Sachgemeinschaft*]; only as the result and extension of this community does a subjective community come into being. Here, on the other hand, we are dealing with a heightening of the company contract [*Gesellschaftsvertrag*]: the association is held together by a bond ... developed from intensified *obligatio*, incorporating not property but persons; community of assets is manifest only as a result and extension of the community of persons.

This leads to a membership whose nature is quite different from that based on shares. This is not in itself [1032] a thing [*Sache*], nor is it principally determined and conditioned by a right based on property; rather, it is a highly personal right and as such cannot be traded as property. Hence the number of members is open-ended: the fellows' rights [*Genossenrecht*] as such cannot be divided, accumulated, inherited or transferred. They are acquired solely by means of personal admission, on the basis of an undertaking to carry out the duties of membership, and are correspondingly lost only by leaving or being expelled. In cases of doubt, the content of rights is the same for all, so that each fellow is called on to bear an equal share in the life of the association; any differences are brought about by the establishment of different classes of fellows, never by arbitrarily permitting the existence of greater or lesser rights. The equality of the fellows' rights is naturally not affected by the fact that the economic burdens and powers may, at an individual level, be very unequally distributed. Each fellow as such has an equal right to the economic advantages; but actual inequality arises from the circumstance that the economic needs and capabilities of individuals are variously determined, by a standard which has nothing in the first instance to do with the rights of fellows. Similarly, the rights of citizenship in a local community are equal in nature, and in purely personal terms; while in practice individuals' ability to pay taxes, individuals' needs and so forth, are the basis of unequal participation in the civic burdens and benefits. The *personal* nature of membership, then, corresponds to the organisation of the association as a whole, to its legal and moral significance for outsiders, and to its ultimate aim. The personal element comes to predominate everywhere; the economic fulfilment of the individual personality forms the content of the entire organism.

However, the more the personal fellowship is perfected and the more therefore it approaches joint production with the purpose of joint gain [*Gemeinproduktion ... Gemeinerwerbes*], the more inevitable it becomes that it weaves the capitalist element, without which it cannot survive, into its organism. It is of course possible to treat the capital purely as an object and not as a factor contributing to its development; but personal fellowship only becomes truly capable of existence when it produces an organic connection between the fellowship and fellowship-capital. In practice this takes place in very different ways among the different types of personal fellowship; but it generally happens in such a way that a capital share in the joint economic enterprise becomes an essential component linked to membership.

In this way the right of fellowship becomes a right like share-holding in a joint-stock company, in that representation of an association and a property right are essential components of it. But it remains diametrically opposed to share-ownership, in that here the property right is a dependent extension of the personal right. Therefore, as long as the association continues, it must conform wholly to the nature of the association. The nature of the shares, conversely, is essentially based on property right, and the personal element is drawn along in its wake. [1033] We find the purest realisation of the form outlined above – the absorption of capital into the organism of the personal fellowship – in the linking of the attribute of being a fellow and the so-called '*Geschäftsantheile* [business shares]' peculiar to the German trading and economic fellowships.

These modern fellowships are distinguished from the old gilds and economic communities they are called on to replace, which underwrite their members' entire personality, by the isolation and precision of their aims. The tasks they set themselves are quite specific economic ones: their aim is to complete the economic personality of their members in some specifically defined area. This does not of course in any way exclude there being a combination of various economic aims in the same association. And, because its ultimate aim is *the human personality*,[†] these fellowships, unlike the associations of capital, are also able in addition to accommodate direct provision for the fellows' intellectual and moral needs; just as, conversely, a great number of the associations discussed above, whose aims were primarily moral or social, endeavoured at the same time to promote their members' economic well-being. In fact, the more personality was manifestly the basis and goal of the fellowship, the more the fellowship shared a tendency to pursue moral and social aims. Here too, however, the modern tendency towards precise definition of aims comes to predominate over the earlier undefined universality.

The prescription of the aims is connected with the *defining of that portion of the personality*[†] which the fellowship demands its members should sacrifice. No modern association of fellows encompasses the totality of a human being, even in economic terms: the aspect of their economic personality which forms part of the association is strictly defined. There is, of course, an enormous gulf in this respect between particular types of fellowship: in some only mutual responsibility for a risk is demanded, in others the duty is to guarantee the fellows' specific economic obligations, and in yet others it is the mutual provision of economic needs. In all these cases, it is possible that the only sacrifice for the individual consists in specific contributions; while the producers' co-operative [*Produktivgenossenschaft*] can extend to demanding the full labour of its members. However, even in this last case, the individual retains an incomparably freer individuality outside the association than, for example, the old gild unions allowed to the gild members. Beyond this, the constitution of the fellowship can delimit the personal resources united therein in many and various ways. Levies or duties can be predetermined,

† Editor's italics

or made dependent on certain circumstances; in the latter case, they are either unlimited, or confined by an upper limit, or restricted by an objective characteristic (e.g. one's possessions).

The further question of what credit the personality of the fellowship is allowed *vis-à-vis* third parties is distinct [1034] from that of the nature of the partial economic personalities from which it is constructed. It is possible that the personality of the fellowship is its own sole guarantor, so that third parties can only have recourse to *it*, and cannot, either during the lifetime of the fellowship or after its dissolution, hold individuals liable. But it is also possible that, behind the personality of the fellowship, the individual fellows act as guarantors for a directly or indirectly determined amount; or that each is unconditionally responsible for the share which is his due; or that each in solidarity guarantees the entire amount with all of his assets, whether they are liable for it as personal debtors alongside the personality of the fellowship, or as guarantors for it. The moral-juristic personality of the fellowship as such is, naturally, not altered by the fact that, on the basis of its articles or laws, individuals can be fully and entirely responsible for it – least of all, of course, if such responsibility is only subsidiary. A feature of the personal economic fellowship is that, while the association of capital has an unfailing tendency to establish strictly limited liability, in its higher forms the personal fellowship inclines to stake personality wholly and entirely for the collectivity. The subsidiary joint liability of the modern German industrial and economic fellowships is but the final expression of a trend which, in contrast to the limited company (which gives capital a role as an independent entity in commerce), introduces instead, as a unitary entity into economic life, an organism composed of personal economic resources.

Depending on the nature of the associated resources and the purpose determined thereby, four main types, with various sub-divisions, can be distinguished as forms of the personal economic fellowship or co-operative.

(1) *Warranty fellowships* [*Garantiegenossenschaften*] (risk associations, insurance fellowships in the widest sense). These unite defensive resources against economic mishaps, and are sub-divided, depending on whether they give members a guarantee against material damage, or against economic disadvantage brought about by personal circumstances.

(2) *Financial fellowships* [*Geldverkehrgenossenschaften*], which form mutual companies based on the circulation (mutual banks) or acquisition (credit fellowships) or investment (savings fellowships) of capital for their

members. The credit fellowships can be further sub-divided into property and personal-loan associations.

(3) *Distributive fellowships*, which unite resources to provide for the continuing needs of individual economic concerns, thus distributing certain of the costs of the concerns among the collectivity. These aim either just to satisfy general human budgetary needs by means of a fellowship, for example the normal necessities of life (co-operative societies)[6] or the need for living accommodation (housing associations), or, conversely, they may unite a specific aspect of economic production [1035] (in industrial, mercantile or agrarian business), such as the procurement of materials (co-operatives [*Genossenschaften*] for raw materials), the means of production (co-operatives for tools, workplaces, pasturage and many similar things), or distribution (warehousing co-operatives, and so on).

(4) *Producers' fellowships* (labour co-operatives), in which the productive labour itself forms the association. These are the highest stage of development of personal economic fellowships. They are distinguishable from all the rest, first, by the fact that they completely or partially annul the independence of the individual economic concerns (which in the others remains intact); and, secondly, by the fact that, in so far as the economic activity has been raised above individual spheres and structured as co-operative production, they aim directly at *common*[†] gain, whereas other fellowships only indirectly increase the yield of the particular economic concerns they promote.

The practical significance of these various (and, in terms of their legal and moral content, closely related) fellowships is extraordinarily dissimilar, not only in the variety of their aims, but even more in the variety of types of individuals they encompass. The system of economic fellowships among those classes [*Klassen*] threatened in their economic independence by modern capitalist development presents a more or less sharp contrast with economic associations among other ranks [*Stände*] of society. Because, for the former, the system of fellowship is in immediate contact with the great social problems of the present day, it presents itself as a special phenomenon, a link in the chain of modern socio-political endeavours. Yet, here too it still remains simply a special manifestation of the same *idea of association*[†] [*Associationsidee*] which is determining the physiognomy of the latest developments in all areas: it is, therefore, a link in the chain of forms of fellowship.

The personal economic fellowship in all its ramifications may also not be entirely without a general significance, different from that of fellowship

---

[†] Editor's italics

in general. For everywhere it is called upon to bring *self-help* to bear against externally imposed institutions; and, because this self-help is co-operative [*genossenschaftlich*], it is also called upon to embody the *ethical* factor in the economic sphere of life, so often motivated by self-seeking alone. Over against the egoistical principle of capitalist speculation for profit, which remains predominant in the capital-based group and the collective company [*Kollektivgesellschaft*], it is the sense of economic *community* [*Gemeinsinn*] which calls forth, directs and sustains the personal fellowship. A sense of community, however, is at once the product and the producer of moral ideas. One can also conceive of the sense of community as a form of egoism, which has recognised that an individual subordinated to a greater whole as a member of an association wins back many times over everything [1036] he has lost as an individual. There remains, none the less, a qualitative difference between exclusive selfishness and an endeavour, motivated in the same way, which has as its consequence sacrifice for others and submission to a greater whole ...

The free fellowships based on mutuality have a two-fold value. They form a counter-balance to state patronage and speculation for profit, by pointing back on the one hand to self-help and, on the other, to a sense of community as the ultimate sources of economic well-being.

Incalculably more important and unique, however, is the significance of the personal economic fellowship in guaranteeing, or achieving, economic independence for the working classes. The *working* classes, in the sense intended here, are those social groups for whom personal labour is the decisive factor determining their economic existence. They are also called the *propertyless* (*besitzlose*) classes.[7] This does not mean that they are absolutely without property; for they too can command some material and immaterial properties. But they are *relatively* unpropertied, because their property is exhausted by their personal needs in life and work; and because they are confronted with other social groups for whom surplus material and immaterial property, though it may not exempt them from work, has an independent function in their economic life and is decisive for their overall economic status. The superior strength which ownership of capital, in particular, has achieved through the development of modern large-scale business, brings with it the fact that, in spite of increasing overall pros-perity, an increasingly large proportion of the people appear relatively propertyless. Consequently, not only all the masses of actual wage-labourers in factories, commerce and on the land, but increasingly the smaller independent tradesman and rural smallholder,[8] come into the category of the working classes.

The development of capitalist big business robs all of these classes of their economic personality, or threatens to deprive them of it. For the old economic organisms, in which collective existence was either equally distributed among all or in some way divided between head and members, became atrophied and developed into chains; these have finally burst apart into loose fragments. Out of these fragments, however, new economic organisms built themselves up into a dominant structure, ever increasing in power: for these, capital is the basis and master, labour only a dependent tool. These organisms are the capitalist business enterprises of all kinds – above all factories, but equally large-scale farms, large commercial institutions, etc. They all live solely within the capitalistic 'head', allied to intelligence: [1037] the labouring members are not living participants in the body but the object and tool of its activity. It makes little real difference that the law – from which they are admittedly forced to deviate often enough – does not regard such associations as organisms, breaking them up, rather, into a sum total of private-law relationships between one individual and another. For, in terms of actual success, the greater the extent of the enterprise and the more diverse its structure, the clearer it becomes that the capitalist firm is not the sum total of its component parts, but a whole, an organised unitary body.

In its inner nature, however, this unitary body is nothing but a *lordship group*, in which the representative of capital (the capital body as it were) is the absolute economic master. That same lordship group which, since time immemorial, has been struggling to gain victory over fellowship, is reproduced here; in a more limited form, on the one hand, because it does not extend beyond the sphere of economics and economic purposes; harsher and less restricted, on the other hand, because the [lordship]principle, which in former lordship groups was modified at an early stage by the emergence of dependent fellowships, is here implemented unconditionally. For, in the economic lordship associations of modern times, there are no links between the members themselves, no plurality with rights over against the unity, no constitution which could guarantee the collective will some influence, however modest, on the life of the whole. In it labour is without rights. Unconfined by Right, lordship becomes here in fact more steely and immutable than that of the manorial lord ever was. For, with the predominant importance of capital, the human, personal relationship between master and worker becomes ever smaller, the impersonal might of capital comes between them in an ever more divisive way, and finally the owner himself is ever more powerless, dragged into the service of his own capital.

Hence, economic personality no more belongs to the worker in capitalist enterprises than ecclesiastical personality does to a layman in the church hierarchy, or private-law personality to a serf in the legal fellowship of the nation. Of course, the worker lacks economic personality in the first instance only in a specific group, which he enters as a matter of free choice; it is conceivable that he was also an independent participant in other economic groups. But the choice concerns only the 'where' of subordination not the 'whether'; and by natural necessity the capitalist group aims to absorb the economic existence of its subordinate members utterly and completely. So the worker has nothing left of his economic personality outside the organism in which he finds himself; and, since his whole economic existence is utterly determined and conditioned by an alien power [*eine fremde Macht*], in whose life he is not granted the slightest active participation, he is devoid of economic rights of citizenship not only within the single group, but in the entire economy of the nation.

[1038] Of course this does not at all lessen his personality in private law, his political, ecclesiastical personality, his human personality *as such*; but in the long term, the lack of economic independence necessarily affects all other aspects of his existence. Capital is inevitably forced, under the influence of competition and of the drive immanent in it (as in all powers) to expand itself, to push the limits of its sphere of lordship further and further outwards. Only the resistance of the beings under threat sets a limit to this tendency. But the more the personality behind this resistance is deprived of its capacity for independent economic life, the weaker and less successful this resistance is bound to become. In the end, it is only life itself which is being fought for. Since the wrestle for existence [*Ringen um's Dasein*] absorbs the totality of all resources, the free human personality becomes more and more stunted till only its name and abstract Right remain.

If just individuals were threatened by this danger, the only question for the nation would be its moral obligation towards its members. But in truth it is the foundation of the nation's existence [*Volksexistenz*] itself which is being undermined. For the extent of economic lordship organisms is increasing incessantly, and their numbers decreasing relatively; the masses are ceaselessly swelling in numbers, and the power of individual dependent economic existences decreasing in relative terms. Under the pressure of unrestricted competition, the smaller and middle-sized economic concerns, unable to compete with the large concerns, are more and more disappearing; those which cannot raise themselves to the status of big business decline into wage labour. The disappearance of intermediaries further demonstrates the full extent of the danger: that the gulf between owners and the unpropertied will expand until it is immense. If no other elements were to intervene, it would necessarily come to a point where the nation became divided into the two opposing camps: the economic rulers and the economic ruled [*Herrschende ... Beherrschte*]. Transition from one to the other would be harder than to move from one caste to another in India. That would be the eve of the much-prophesied social revolution, the beginning of the end for the life of the people [*Volk*].

Chapter XIX

Economic fellowships based on personality: the producers' co-operative [*Producktivgenossenschaft*] [70 cont.]

Yet there is one power mighty enough to dispel such dangers, and it has already begun to accomplish its two-fold task of defence and creativity. This power is the economic association.[1] [1039] It and it alone can and will protect those fragmentary economic atoms still in existence from losing their independence; it and it alone can and will raise the status of the masses of those who today are only the object of an alien economic will to economic personality.

All the experiments and theories which in our century aspired towards a new form of organisation of labour agree on one single point, that the *association*[†] [*Association*] of these dislocated atoms is an indispensable means to achieve their goal. In fact it seems almost vulgar to suggest that the evils emanating from disintegration into loose atoms, powerless in themselves, were capable of being healed merely by being united into a higher *collective*[†] power [*Gesammtkraft*].[2] There were, none the less, from the very beginning two opposing lines of thought. One looked to the state for help, the other to the creative power of the people. The latter saw salvation in *free* association, the former wanted to achieve association by unified organisation from outside and above. Once more, as always in history, the most prominent representatives of the latter were the Latin peoples, while the formation of free fellowships fell to the Germanic nations.

The Roman tendency found its chief expression in the systems and experiments of the Communists and Socialists. Although their methods and aims diverged greatly, they all aimed to bring into play the highest universality, whether the existing state or one which was to be created in its place; so that another economic organisation, instead of the prevailing one, would pronounce decrees and execute policy from above. They had

[†] Editor's italics.

215

different ideas about the form and content of the new organisms. Some aimed towards the despotism of equality – in comparison with which Asiatic despotism would be freedom itself. Others demanded proportional regulation, which would make the bureaucracy of the *Polizeistaat* look like a total absence of government. The theory of national workshops, put into practice in France during 1848, came close to the transfer of militarism into the economic sphere. In the long term, even the milder suggestions of Lassalle for the establishment of producers' associations with regular and comprehensive support from the state,[3] give the power of initiative to the state, introduce [1040] uniformity, patronage and the rule of bureaucrats into economic life, and threaten to stunt the development of that great achievement of the modern world, individuality. What all such approaches have in common is that, in the final analysis, the personality (which they intend to preserve for, or bestow upon, the worker) is conferred not on the worker himself, but on some kind of appointed joint institution [*Gemeinanstalt*]. One need hardly mention that, in their more extreme forms, they sacrifice the individual's political, or even private-law personality along with his economic one; with this loss they threaten not simply one class, but the whole of society.

Only *free* association creates commonalties [*Gemeinheiten*] which preserve economic freedom. For only those organisms which emerge from the initiative and formative powers of their own members enhance the individual existence of their members, as well as the newly established communal life. It is as impossible to make a gift of independence in the economic sphere as it is in any other. Therefore, those classes which are threatened in their economic existence can obtain true and lasting independence only for themselves.

But while *self-help* excludes state initiatives and state structures, it is easily compatible with contributory *state aid*. A claim on state aid, indeed, is not the working classes' privilege but their right, given this particular form by their circumstances, a right which is available to all sections of the people over against the supreme universality. If the state is a moral being (and not an institution based on reciprocal services), it is its inalienable right and inescapable duty to intercede, in the last resort, for all its members, when individual resources, even when united with others, are not sufficient to achieve the purposes of human personality. States have, in fact, by no means been unmindful of this call, nor are they entirely lacking in awareness of the duties which will be incumbent on them in the future. State participation in the association-movement of society is primarily negative: it is a matter of sweeping away barriers (stemming from the system of *Polizei*) to free association, and of refraining from any intervention in fellowships' internal affairs. Since the universal right to form associations is almost always the decisive factor, the anti-combination laws still in force in most German states are an exceptional restriction on the working classes. Their days are numbered.

State participation is more positive so far as it is a matter of the *legal* [*gesetzlich*] regulation of economic organisms. Here it has a partly restrictive role: as in factory legislation, where it prohibits employment of young workers, restricts hours of work, bans certain forms of paying wages, enforces factory rules, and so on – all in order to protect the personality against capital organisms. But also, [1041] in the course of imposing restrictions and guarantees on newly forming fellowship-based economic organisms, it creates an assured moral and legal existence for them; or even (as to some extent in England) gives them a privileged position due to their general utility. But the state, and lesser associations, are in addition required to establish positive institutions for their advancement. These enhance economic freedom, either universally or primarily for specific classes. Some intervene at first only indirectly in economic life; educational, cultural and demonstration institutes do so by increasing intellectual, moral and technical resources; and all charitable institutions do so by the support they offer everyone in the worst cases of need. Others promote economic life directly, above all the savings banks, but also the public institutions for pensions, for care of the aged, for widows and insurance; public lending and credit funds, commercial institutes and so on. It has already been mentioned that in Germany most states have also endowed the smaller independent tradesman with the ambivalent gift of publicly authorised trades gilds; they have made the dependent workers the far more dubious gift of compulsory relief funds. Here as everywhere, the state's right and duty to give direct subsidiary relief must be upheld, whenever there are no other means to safeguard a public interest, or to rescue a section of citizens whose existence is threatened. Whether and how the state will deal with each individual case depends on the decision of the state as a moral community [*sittliches Gemeinwesen*], motivated by specific circumstances.

It need hardly be mentioned that, in addition to state aid, the help of the higher social classes has up to now had an important part to play in the social movement. Individuals and associations alike have created benevolent or charitable establishments for the intellectual, moral, social and material improvement of the working classes. Special 'Associations for the Well-being of the Working Classes' operate in many places. In associations of the class itself, the incentive, direction and instruction of outside parties has been much in evidence, as well as a certain degree of protection at the start. All these phenomena, apart from their success in individual cases, have the lasting value partly of complementing self-help, and partly of enabling it to develop more fully.

Capital itself has in recent times initiated the transformation of particular enterprises so as to give independent participation to the workforce: this move is quite different in character. Initially more the result of isolated cases of benevolence, such a form of organisation, which reconciles the workers' fellowship with the capitalist lordship-group, could be elevated to greater and more universal importance, if its implementation should ever become a necessity for the masters of the workforce, due to the competition and interest resulting from the pressure of countless producers' (1042) co-operatives.

The only creative force, meanwhile ... is the *free* association formed from within. This has in fact begun to emerge among the working classes in the major European countries, with the express purpose of improving the workers' economic status. In a short time it has achieved significant gains. We must consider, first, the many associations which only indirectly further the economic status of their members, being primarily aimed at increasing their intellectual, moral, social or political resources. Most important are the *educational fellowships* (unions of tradesmen, associations for further education, trade schools etc.) because, along with intellectual powers, they directly enhance the earning capacity of the fellows. Temperance societies, recreational associations, social brotherhoods and leagues also belong to this category. The workers' political associations (e.g. the campaigns for the introduction of a universal franchise) have also an indirect effect on economic conditions. Closest to the actual economic fellowships, however, are the associations for representation of the general interests of labour or of labourers, or alternatively of a specific branch of work or a specific group of workers. Such associations often acquire a directly economic character, when they include, among their aims, the desire to influence concrete economic conditions.

This is particularly true of associations designed to bring about common measures inducing employers to provide better working conditions. To this end wage labourers ('working men') themselves in England, in particular, have created in the labour unions ('trades unions') organisations of special power. These unions have developed from the 'trade societies' intended for mutual support and further education, and they still preserve their original aims. Their chief purpose, however, is the organisation of strikes and the introduction of arbitration or settlements with the employer. They have assembled significant funds by means of entry fees and contributions; by means of the organic linking of the individual unions with one another (from 1866 there has been a 'United Kingdom Alliance of Organised Trades'), the holding of general and specific congresses, and the establishment of central and local committees, they have shaped themselves into a unified power. Every strike must be announced to the union committee; its justification and likelihood of success are then examined by the society. If it is approved, support can be provided, if necessary, from the union's funds; but in any case all members of the union are banned from working for the relevant employer. It goes without saying that in principle only decisions taken by the committee are valid in this context. At the same time, it is well-known (from events in Sheffield in 1867)[1043] how individual unions have made much more far-reaching use of their powers against refractory workers, displaying both their mighty power and the dangers of corruption of these associations, imbuing the masses as they do with a unified will.[4]

On economic structures as such, some of these associations only have an indirect, some only a negative effect. Meanwhile, however, an association movement has begun which aims to create new economic organisms directly by the personal combination of those spheres whose independence is endangered. In England and France, this is usually called the 'co-operative' movement, and in Germany simply the 'fellowship' movement. It is progressing along the lines of the main types of economic fellowships distinguished above [pp. 209–10], step by step. Thus everywhere the first step takes the form of the warranty fellowship for single unspecified accidents (whose origins are in part older), and of welfare organisations to assist and support the working classes and to provide sickness and funeral expenses. The second step is the formation of credit and distribution fellowships. But the goal of this movement is the producers' fellowship, in which labour attains full rights of citizenship[5]...

[1047] In the nature of things, the economic fellowship movement, in common with the modern association generally, took root first of all and most vigorously among the urban population. But no less a future awaits it in the rural economy. Here too it is used in all its forms, modified by the peculiarities of rural economic conditions. Here too there are two distinct classes: the independent smallholder and the dependent wage-labourer. For the former, the role of the economic fellowship movement is to preserve their economic freedom, and for the latter to win that freedom. A promising beginning has already been made, in Germany as well as abroad, in implementing a system of rural fellowships for guarantees, for the procurement of capital, for distribution and even for joint production.[6] Just as in the towns almost the same epoch witnessed both the last struggles of the old incorporated trades system and the rebirth of the idea of fellowship in trade, so too in the countryside we see the final demolition of the age-old *Mark* community and the collapse of the only slightly more recent manorial association – along with the first stirrings of life for the *free* agrarian fellowship, called to the task of replacing them.

[1048] One need hardly mention what the system of free economic fellowship achieves, and is capable of achieving, in the areas in which it is active. The material advantages which flow from collectivity back to members often create the primary basis for full human development. But even greater than this is the growth human beings achieve as human beings through the fellowship. Its achievement can be summed up as the elevation of the worker to the status of citizen of an economic community [*Gemeinwesen*]. Participation in an economic organism, represented in its entirety by a voluntarily united collectivity of those striving towards the same goal, creates or saves some aspect (modest enough, maybe, at first) of economic personality for its members.

In the producers' fellowships, this is elevated even for the simple worker into the full personality of the entrepreneur. In contrast to the socialist communal entities, the individual retains his individuality. But, even in economic affairs, this individuality is not limitless and wholly self-determining; rather, it donates part of its being to the whole, as a member of which it can overcome the dangers in the existence of the isolated atom. The consciousness of gratitude for the elevation of one's own powers – through association with the equal powers of one's fellows – produces that sense of citizenship, at once proud and self-denying, which since time immemorial has been held to be the model of public virtue. A school for the whole of public and private life, the fellowship is before all else a school of morals.[7]

In saying this, we also express the importance which fellowships have, beyond their immediate fellows, for state, economy and society. They introduce worthy citizens into the state. In the economy, in the face of the lordship of dead property, they conquer the right of citizenship for labour – the right due to it as the manifestation of its living personality. They preserve society from the dangers threatening it in the social embitterment of the numerical majority of its members. Only fools are capable of believing that the association movement will ever banish from the world all economic dependence, or eradicate all social miseries. But it does not seem too bold to hope that it will bring to an end, or prevent, a situation in which economic dependence is the rule, and social misery the fate of the majority. Even if that did not happen, even if – and it has often been criticised for this – the system of fellowship only raised isolated privileged sections of the working classes to independence through their ability and good luck, it would still have accomplished what is greatest and most important. For it would have thereby averted the most dangerous ailment of a social organism: the drying-up of its sap. Peoples were always healthy, their illnesses curable, so long as they kept alive the ability to bring to the top the best of the unused elements among the people; the body of the people always ailed as the circulation [1049] of its blood was cut off by the exclusiveness of its rulers. Even if at first it is only a few who achieve independence through fellowship, even if the road is long and the goal uncertain, the sole knowledge that the possibility of such elevation in status does exist for the man who is dependent on his own labour, has an infinitely beneficial effect on the life of those who miss the path, or do not reach the goal.

[Gierke goes on to consider 'insurance fellowships', 'fellowships based on monetary exchange' such as banks and other institutions offering credit, and 'savings fellowships'. He next turns to 'distributive economic fellowships'; and last of all to producers' co-operatives.]

[1088] The personal fellowship for economic purposes is perfected in the *producers' fellowship*. Realised at first in small ways, in Germany chiefly only as a combination of a not very great number of craftsmen of the same trade,[8] and in these early stages organised [1089] in very different ways, producers' fellowships have so far hardly achieved any one clearly defined form. Their one common feature is that in them associated labour itself, whether on its own or alongside capital, becomes the embodiment [*Träger*] of a productive enterprise ...

[1090] Regarding the internal structure of the fellowship's organism ..., one may chiefly distinguish two separate systems. The first is based on the personal fellowship and draws an association [*Vereinigung*] of capital into its service. This was originally developed in England and largely retained there, is the principal system in France and the only one in Germany. The second, no less widespread in England, and recently sanctioned in France, is based on the fellowship of capital and modifies this along the lines of a personal combination of the workforce. Clearly the first system alone can, in a moral and legal sense, be described as a true fellowship of labour; but in terms of practical results the second can produce very similar structures.

The true labour fellowship is based on the idea that [1091] labour itself is the economic, legal and moral representative [*Träger*] of the enterprise. The worker as such, and he alone, is an active member of the body of the association. Membership of a producers' fellowship, therefore, is a purely personal right. The number of members is unlimited. New members can be denied admission because of a lack of work; but as a rule no worker who is admitted would not, after a trial period, be entitled and obliged, upon fulfilment of the statutory conditions, to acquire the rights of being a fellow [*Genossenrecht*]. Membership can only be acquired through an admission procedure, which is usually the preserve of the general assembly, and frequently requires unanimity;[9] it is lost through death, departure or expulsion. The rights of fellows are equal in content and above all give them equality in representing the life of the association – that is, equal franchise and equal eligibility.

Certainly, as in all economic fellowships, this personal basis is necessarily bound up with a union [*Verein*] of capital. Reasons of expediency demand, even more compellingly than in loan and distributors' fellowships, that an element of capital be admitted into the organism of the union. But here too, as in other personal fellowships, this remains a subordinate factor, its legal and moral status defined and determined by the personal union. Each fellow, therefore, must deposit assets at a specified rate, or make up the total in regular instalments. The fellows are compelled to increase their holdings, recorded in a special account, to a stipulated level, and thereafter are permitted to increase them to a (usually specified) maximum. This is done partly by deductions from wages, and partly by investment from profit. But the 'business shares' produced by this [1092] are not the basis of the fellows' rights but a consequence of them. Like the fellows' rights themselves, they cannot be transferred, mortgaged or alienated; and can only be withdrawn after a fellow leaves the fellowship or is expelled from it ... In addition to this, the union possesses a core of assets in a reserve fund, made up of deposits, contributions and investment of profit, on which neither those who leave voluntarily nor those expelled against their will have any claim.

These business shares do not determine the rights of fellows as such; but they can be decisive for determining the economic rewards of membership. This does not change the nature of the personal fellowship. This has indeed been the rule until now in German producers' fellowships. After payment has been made for the association's creditors, administrative costs, the reserve fund etc., profit and loss are distributed in proportion to the business shares; labour as such receives only the usual wage. In other producers' fellowships, however, such holdings were guaranteed only specific rates of interest, and profit was shared out on an equal basis or according to the value of the work undertaken. A third system, finally, pays interest on the assets, and wages on the labour, and then divides profit into a dividend on capital and a dividend on wages; here again in individual cases there are a great many different arrangements.[10]

In practical terms, all of these systems for distributing profit [1093] produce only secondary differences, so long as each fellow is also a worker, and each worker is drawn into the fellowship: they are completely inconsequential for the legal and moral [*rechtlich*] nature of the association as a labour fellowship. For the distinctive feature of this form of association is not the share which labour takes in the profit, but the role of the worker's personality as the embodiment of the fellowship of the enterprise. The distribution of profit is an internal question to which the autonomous fellowship, taking into consideration the relationship of labour and capital as contributors' towards the formation of capital, responds in as many different ways as does, for example, the open commercial company in its contract of association.

If capitalists who are not members are promised a capital dividend, or if workers who are not members are promised a wage dividend, this does not in any way change the essence of the labour fellowship. But a modification of the labour fellowship does follow if individual fellows participate in the enterprise *only* by virtue of holding business shares, and the duty or authorisation to work in person for the enterprise of the fellowship as such is not set down as *essential* to the rights of fellows. This is also the case when, conversely, workers are employed without a statutory right and duty gradually to acquire the property appropriate to a fellow. In neither case, however, is the character of the personal fellowship *annulled*. The presence of dependent [1094] workers does not affect the internal organisation of the others. And non-working fellows do not participate like shareholders, merely on the grounds of their property investment. Rather, they are included as persons in the enterprise group [*Unternehmerverband*]; so that their rights are non-transferable, and in doubtful cases, despite their greater holdings, they have simple voting rights and are personally liable.

As the highest form of personal economic fellowship, the producers' co-operative associates the personality most powerfully, thus elevating it to the utmost; similarly, the moral element [*das sittliche Moment*] in the personal fellowship becomes most effective in the producers' co-operative. Here (in direct contrast to the capitalist commercial company) the more definitively the labouring personality as such is the embodiment of the economic organisms, the more it seeks to use the organism to create a spiritual [*geistig*] and moral fellowship. It acts as a relief and support fellowship for fellows who are ill or unable to work and for their dependents; indeed, they often pay fellows who are ill full wages and sick pay as well. It makes provision for educational institutions, libraries, common recreation rooms and festivities. It not only exercises control of work but also a true moral control [*Sittenpolizei*], imposing the penalty of expulsion (or other punishment) not only for actions (or negligence) contrary to the economic interests of the society, but for any unworthy, dishonourable or immoral act. In relation to outsiders, finally, it acts as a moral community, but without corporative egotism.

The constitutions of producers' fellowships are as diverse as modern fellowships themselves. The distribution of power between the general assembly, the elected board of management and the supervisory committee is naturally very uneven, depending on the greater or lesser size of membership and the object of the enterprise ....[11]

[1096] We must mention, finally, the form of association which attempts to combine the capitalist lordship association and the labour fellowship. So far as it is simply a matter of paying labour with a proportion of the profit, the economic organism as such does not undergo change. Recently in England, however, a particular form of society has in fact emerged from this process under the name of 'industrial partnership'. By creating business shares for the workers, partly through deposits and partly by withholding proportions of the profit or of their wages, it makes the workers co-representatives of the enterprise. These business shares, therefore, lay the basis not only for a proportionate share in the profit of the business, but also (to a greater or lesser degree) for the right of supervision (to be exercised jointly by the participating workers or by a committee), or even for a degree of participation in management.[12] This form of association has been recognised and given legal and moral protection by legislation; and the liability, particularly of the partners, has been limited to their share of the business. Attempts have been made to imitate this in Germany, but up to now there has been no company form suited to the development of such an institution ...

[1097] Finally, regarding the status of the various personal economic fellowships in the legal system, only the most recent *English* Companies Act[13] is advanced enough to comprehend all of these. Every economic or trading fellowship with at least seven members can, if they observe the legal formalities, obtain the rights of corporations and protection of the law. The five types of corporative fellowship [indicated therein] give enough latitude for the most diverse forms on a capitalist, personal or mixed basis ...

[1100] [In France] a legal construct [*Rechtsgestattung*] very close to the personal economic fellowship is made possible. But, in direct contrast to English law (which takes the community of persons as its basis, and maintains this principle in the most important respects even in the capitalist corporation), [in France] the capitalist principle is established as the basis of all company law. The personal fellowship with a corporative constitution is regarded and treated as a mere modification of the association of capital.

In *Germany*, common law leaves the personal economic fellowship in a state of complete uncertainty. This has been brought about by Roman corporation and company law – the arena for countless controversies. The laws of the *Länder*, too, have only recently partially cleared the way for a [1101] revision of the whole law of fellowship, and in part created a specific law for defined types of fellowship. Thus, in so far as there is no universal legislation (as there is for warranty fellowships and for credit associations with personal liability), or in so far as a fellowship is unwilling to submit to the new purely optional legislation, the situation which derives from the principles of positive law regarding corporations and companies (and which was until recently universal) continues to hold good.

The fellowship has only two choices. First, it may constitute itself as a private company without a recognised personality in law, by meeting on the basis of the right to free association, and by structuring itself internally like a corporation, by means of a company contract with safeguards. In this case, even though it might with goodwill find a bearable *modus vivendi* in a limited sphere, it has to forego the possibility of taking its place in commerce as a recognised entity. Or alternatively – and for all larger mutual fellowships with a public role this alternative becomes in practice a necessity – it must obtain special state incorporation. In so doing it buys for itself an assured position in private law but loses independence, since the state naturally links the bestowal and retention of juristic personality (indispensable to the fellowship) to conditions which seem fair to the state. Moreover, even if we completely disregard the distribution or non-distribution of corporative rights, state approval and supervision is in many cases absolutely compulsory for many classes of mutual fellowship, for administrative reasons.

[1102] The lack of a universal legislative regulation corresponds to a gap in theory. The few comments which have been directed towards the mutual fellowship, usually primarily with regard to mutual insurance companies, seldom penetrate deeply into their essential being ... Regarding the relationship between unity and plurality, the controversy continues as to whether one should proceed from the concept of the Roman 'society', of the corporation, of a juristic personality of another kind, or of a fellowship based on German law. There is no less difference of opinion over the relationship between the fellowship and the community of property ...

[Gierke considers various types of commercial company available or conceivable in Germany, turning finally to the 'registered fellowship [*eingetragene Genossenschaft*]'.[14] What follows is in effect a commentary upon the law regulating such a body.[15] It is perhaps a lame conclusion to volume 1, but Gierke is clearly optimistic about its potential for fulfilling his ideal of *Genossenschaft*.]

[1106] As a completely free fellowship, a registered fellowship is the product of civic autonomy. It has, therefore, no need of state approval. It is given existence by a constitutive act, for whose proclamation there is a prescribed written form and for whose content certain immutable principles and a minimum state of completeness are prescribed. Otherwise it is left to devise its own structure at will. To be recognised by the law as a corporation, the fellowship has to be entered in a public register, organised basically in the same way as the trade company register. It must submit a list of members to a court of law, which displays this for public inspection; [1107] at the same time an extract from its statutes is published in the public press. But these formalities do not, like the entry in the register, determine the fellowship's status in law ... In the same way any change in the articles is subject to the fellowship's autonomy; but the effect in law of an amended resolution depends upon its being proclaimed in writing and entered in the register of fellowships. The fellowship can also pass a resolution terminating its existence; this too must be published and registered.

Reasons for dissolving the fellowship are the expiry of the specified time-limit, bankruptcy, or sentence by a court of law. Dissolution on the grounds of bankruptcy proves that a fellowship cannot exist as an economic union without assets. Yet the fact that neither its origin nor its continued existence is defined or determined by basic capital assets of a specified amount, demonstrates clearly how little it is regarded as a fellowship of capital. The victory of the constitutional state's conception over the corporation theory of the bureaucratic state is demonstrated by the fact that the fellowship cannot be dissolved by administrative fiat, but only by sentence in a court of law, at the instigation of the higher administrative authorities, if it is guilty of illegal acts or omissions which endanger the common good, or of exceeding its sphere of economic activity.

The characteristic features of the new form of association are most clearly evident in its composition and in the principles governing the conditions and contents of membership. Fellows' rights are acquired by the sole means of a declaration of intent to joint, and of admission according to the conditions which must be stated in the articles ... They can be lost by leaving (always permitted, if a fellow has announced his intention to do so); or by expulsion, which is under the control of the fellowship. At the same time, the fellowship is not only empowered to provide in the articles the guarantee necessary for its personal and moral character, but is even authorised by law to exclude a member on account of the loss of his civil rights. It is clear that fellows' rights in an association in which there is no limit on the number of members, are intrinsically incapable of assuming the character of property rights, so that they are neither transferable nor inheritable ... But the financial nature of the whole demands that a capitalist element be involved; hence the building up of a business share of a precise amount is obligatory upon each fellow. This business share, however, is not [1108] treated in law, like a share-holding, as the basis of the fellows' rights, but as a claim on the association, organically linked with the fellows' rights. While the fellows' rights exist, therefore, it is similar in nature to them. If, on the other hand, a fellow leaves or the fellowship is dissolved, [the business share] does not become a joint property share in the association's assets, but an individual title to a precise amount of property, clearly visible in the accounts of the fellowship ...

Regarding their *content* the fellows' rights are also primarily personal in nature. In cases of doubt, each fellow is accorded an equal share in the joint representation of the association's personality, and therefore one and only one vote in the affairs of the fellowship. Each fellow as such is called to take an equal share in the economic advantages; only actual differences in their participation in the business can ... be the basis for unequal economic success. The subsidiary legislative provision for the distribution of profit and loss according to the size of business shares gives legal expression to this concept. The personality of the fellows' rights emerges above all, however, in the joint liability of all members for the obligations of the fellowship, a liability which cannot be altered in the articles, and which encompasses all the fellowship's assets. This joint liability is based on the idea that each individual stakes his entire property-based personality for the fellowship. But, because the fellowship has an independent personality, this liability comes into force only as the security of the individual personalities for the collective personality [*Gesammtpersönlichkeit*] ...

[1109] The organisation of the fellowship is fundamentally left to the articles. However, in the same way as with the limited company, the basic features of the constitution are prescribed in subsidiary laws; in the public interest, certain compulsory regulations are added, particularly for external representation. The general assembly is constituted as a necessary agency for the exercise of all rights reserved for the collectivity. It is convoked by the management board or perhaps the supervisory council, which also publicises the purpose of the meeting, according to the terms of the articles; but it must always be convoked at the request [1110] of a tenth of the members (or some other number prescribed by the articles) ... Furthermore, as its second necessary organ, the fellowship is obliged to elect a management board from among the fellows. This board can be dismissed from within at any time, is confined to the limits of its mandate and is the responsible executive authority. In external relations, however, it is unconditionally authorised ... to represent the fellowship in courts of law and elsewhere; the fellowship is directly bound and empowered by its actions ... Finally, public duties are imposed on the boards by legislation: they must submit annually an organised register of members, keep the required accounts, publish an annual balance sheet, and avoid all actions not directed towards the purposes of their business.

The articles are empowered to place alongside the management board a supervisory council (committee or administrative council) elected by the fellows from their number. When commissioned, this exercises the lawful powers of a supervisory agency, convokes the general assembly, can suspend the fellowship's officials, and represents the fellowship in legal disputes or in contracts, alongside the board. The fellowship can appoint other authorised representatives and officials, and, in case of a law suit against the members of the supervisory council, can elect special deputies to represent them.

From all this it follows that the *legal and moral status* of the registered fellowship is that of a free voluntary corporation. Both externally and internally it acts as a collective personality, which expresses itself internally in its corporative organisation and in the complete separation of the fellowship's assets from those of the individual. Externally, it can acquire rights and obligations as a business, acquire property and other real rights to pieces of land, sue or be sued. In commerce, it has the rights and obligations of a merchant.

[1111] With regard to the state, finally, it is a free economic organism existing in its own right and not subject to any special bureaucratic controls. The public interest is safeguarded by the unconditional implementation of the principles of constitutional law, by joint liability of members of the board in civil law, by the threat of disciplinary penalties against the board, and by the possibility of a judicial dissolution of the fellowship . . .

[End of Volume 1]

THE GERMAN LAW OF FELLOWSHIP

VOLUME 2: THE HISTORY OF THE GERMAN
CONCEPT OF CORPORATION [*KÖRPERSCHAFT*]

Outline of contents[†]

Part I. Basic Concepts of the Old German Law

. . .

    Chapters 3–4. Right-subjectivity [*Rechtssubjektivität;** sc. laws and rights pertaining to persons]
    Chapters 5–6. Right-objectivity [sc. laws and rights pertaining to things]
    Chapter 7. The concept of law
Part II. Fellowship and Collective Right [*Gesammtrecht*]

. . .

    Chapter 9. Collective Right in fixed goods
    Chapter 10. Collective and particular Right in the *Mark*
    Chapter 11. Fellows' Right and use Right
    Chapter 12. Fellowship and collective ownership

. . .

    Chapter 15. Collective claims and obligations
    Chapter 16. Collective political Right
    Chapter 17. The concept of law and the old fellowship system
    Chapter 18. The capacity of the collective [*Gesammtheit*] to will and to act
Part III. Church and Empire as Legal Persons [*Rechtssubjekte*]

. . .

Part IV. The Personality of the City

. . .

    Chapter 30. The capacity of the city to will and to act
    Chapter 31. The náture of the personality of the city.
Part V. The Diffusion of the Concept of Corporation [*Körperschaft*]
    Chapter 32. Types of corporation
    Chapter 33. The concept of the state

[†] Abstracted from pp. x–lvi, where Gierke gives a detailed breakdown.

Preface

[page v] In 1868, when I published volume I of a work on *The German Law of Fellowship*, published under the title of *The Legal History of the German Fellowship*, I set out, in the preface and introduction, the plan of how the work was to be continued. With the publication of this present volume I am fulfilling, albeit late and only partially, the promise I made there. I have taken a long time to fulfil it not only because, as often seems to be the case, a work which had appeared to be complete in its conception only revealed the many difficulties which had been overlooked or underestimated during its actual execution, but also because many external interruptions intervened to prevent me from completing it, above all my participation in the Franco-Prussian War.

I am only partially completing the task, which I had set myself to achieve in full, because its extent and far-reaching implications became apparent only in the course of carrying out the research which follows here. This compelled me to devote the present weighty tome, originally intended as the final part of the whole work, to [these findings] alone. My original intention was that this volume should contain an examination of the legal and moral nature of German fellowship in two sections: the first was to examine 'the history of the concept of corporation' on its own, and the second was to analyse 'the current law of fellowship'. Now, however, this second volume has been filled up by what was intended only for the first section. And I have not even been able completely to master the history of the concept of corporation, [page vi] but have taken it only as far as the reception of foreign laws. I have called this volume, therefore, the history of the *German* concept of fellowship, to indicate from the outset that it does not yet include the history of the Romanist theory of the corporation. I intend to insert the latter as an introduction to the third volume, where, for internal reasons, it may serve a more useful purpose.

The rest of the third volume will deal with the theory of the current law of fellowship.[1]

Although the following history of the German concept of corporation forms a constituent part of my work on the German law of fellowship, I have none the less attempted to give it the form of an independent, self-contained study. This study relates to the first volume like a narrow tower built on a foundation surrounded by wide walls: in this penetrating analysis, however, I have at all points been able to avoid borrowing the supports for the present edifice from the next volume, something I was often forced to do in the first volume. I hope, therefore, that in this volume proof will be found for many ideas which were presented without backing; much that was only sketched there will be examined in greater detail, and much that was not fully resolved there will be more fully clarified. In this self-contained analysis none of the component parts necessary for its validity is missing.

I have discussed the subject and method of my investigation in greater detail in the introduction. The peculiar idea of writing the history of a *concept* demanded in part a peculiar method of research. I am fully aware that, in the nature of things, this task can only be accomplished imperfectly, and even less perfectly by me. I am none the less firmly convinced that the idea of such an analysis is in itself fruitful and that if the correct method is applied it guarantees a relatively high degree of accuracy in its findings. This conviction, that by the method on which I have embarked it was possible to find positive evidence for things which are generally purely the concern of subjective conjectures of dubious value, convinced me most of all to pursue the path I had embarked on to the end, without allowing myself to be distracted by considerations of any kind. The presence of characteristic concepts and philosophical perceptions in the legal consciousness of a particular people [page vii] and a specific epoch, is as certain as the fact that the identification of their true philosophic content is for the most part uncertain and variable. To undertake such a process, therefore, on a purely objective basis, by combining conclusions arrived at by deductive and inductive means, seemed to be an experiment which would repay the greatest possible expenditure of energy, if it were successful. In undertaking this experiment, it was essential not to be intimidated by the complexity and difficulty of the reasoning. In the crucial parts of the book I have often had to heap up the documentation; aspirations to elegance of presentation and ease of understanding often had to be subordinated to my aspiration to seek out the truth. Outsiders will be able to judge better than I the extent to which I am justified in the hope that this method has resulted in the main findings of my investigation bearing in themselves the nature of fully documented facts.

The history of the concept of corporation in its widest sense, and subsequently of its heightened form as the concept of state, is always the central pivot of my case. This concept, however, cannot be grasped in isolation: contrasting concepts had to be developed at the same time to reveal all the many series of concepts which interacted with it. The investigation thus led me far beyond the single legal concept at its centre. Just as at night a single clearly illuminated point sheds light on all its surroundings, so too identifying the changes undergone, in German legal consciousness, by the philosophic idea of unity in human groups, simultaneously gave rise to a series of surprising revelations about the changing content of that legal and moral consciousness as such. It is precisely this which gives the main guarantee that the results I have arrived at are correct and, since their significance extends far beyond my immediate goal, that the work involved in attaining them was worthwhile. I have, therefore, so far as possible, always followed the threads linking one concept to another, without of course being able to execute on related fields such thorough research as I have in the main area of my research. Moreover, if my main findings are presumed to be correct, findings related to the other phenomena [page viii] in the legal consciousness and life of our nation, which were conditioned and determined along with them, could be explained in a manner consonant with my own findings and clarified, just as my main area of research has been; and this fact seemed to be an important test for the conclusiveness of my reasoning.

With regard to the source material I have used, I must mention that I had already finished collecting it five years ago. It was unnecessary to supplement it with more than individual details from more recent publications because the assembled material always seemed more than sufficient to support the conclusions resting on it. In the main section of this volume the problem was less that of finding documentation for the relevant legal perception than that of recognising, in such an overwhelming mass of sedimentary material, the concept manifest in it.

Otto Gierke
Breslau, January 1873

Introduction

[1] The task the following investigation has set itself is to examine in greater detail the *history of the concept of corporation in Germany* on the basis established by the legal history of German fellowship [sc. by vol. I]. It aims, therefore, to trace the history of one single concept, that is the process of its development, or growth and change, as determined by the laws of cause and effect. This concept is a legal–moral concept [*Rechtsbegriff*] – or at least only this aspect of it is under consideration. It can be defined objectively [*aüsserlich*] as the philosophical definition of the independent legal existence of a single unity consisting of a number of legal entities. The intellectual process, however, which the emergence and transformation of this legal concept represents, should not be regarded as a number of more or less fully developed ideas, invented by individuals, but as the formative workings of a unified and continuous consciousness – namely, the legal and moral consciousness of our people. The fact that this consciousness, which originally resided to the same extent in all the people, later gained an independent organ in a specific lawyer class, should not be regarded as representing a change in the reasoning subject, but only as an internal breach and schism within the unitary consciousness whose content is our subject matter.

If the object of our task is easy to define, the question of how it is to be resolved is much more difficult. For the inner process by which concepts are produced cannot be directly observed. If it belongs to the past, it seems that every means by which it might be recognised has been lost, since no document announces the emergence or transformation of a legal concept. It seems that a given point from which secure knowledge could be gained seems to exist least of all if the question is formulated in terms of how a whole people has thought or is thinking in specific areas.

In fact, with questions whose substance is the development of mind [*das*

Werden des Geistes] it is not possible to talk of a resolution [sc. of the problems of research], only of an approximation [2] to the resolution. We cannot say whether the ability to add the mental sphere [*das Geistige*] to the subjects of exact science has been reserved for the distant future. Up to now, in any case, we have only just started, by empirical means on the one hand, and speculation on the other, to embark on the course by which we might approach an exact knowledge of the mind [*vom Geist*]. Above all, up to now we have lacked any secure basis for knowledge of the historical development of mental life in human collectivities. For, either our knowledge is based on the empirical observation of actual events, or it results from bold speculation fleeing towards a goal it has intuitively perceived, without thought of the yawning abyss below. If the latter lacks any certainty that its goal represents the truth and is not just an illusory fantasy, empirical reasoning is able to give meaning to the piles of historical material sifted by research, but cannot, with any certainty, come even one step nearer to the essence of mental development.

However, the path along which progress seems possible has already been prepared and is being followed. It is the replacement of purely rational observation [*verständige Betrachtung*] by the method of inductive inference, so as to complement and complete speculative deduction. Where the results of deduction are proved by inductive means, and conversely where findings gained by inductive inference are confirmed by speculative reasoning, then we can achieve the greatest degree of certainty possible. For in this way inductive thought overcomes the danger of false generalisation which, though lessened by the scope of the documentary material, can never otherwise be completely overcome; while deductive reasoning is assured that its point of departure is real and its abstractions meaningful. Of course this certainty extends only to the correctness of the path we are pursuing: however, it is enough to be certain that we *are moving* towards the goal of truth, even if this itself remains unattainable.

This method is the only possible one for the investigations at hand. On the one hand, we cannot do without deductive insights from ready-made, existing concepts. On the other hand, we must begin by ignoring the idea we are seeking, by collecting a number of concrete phenomena in which a related spirit seems to be at work and, in a manner of speaking, rediscover the idea by means of comparison and abstraction. In the first instance, for example, the spirit of the German people is assumed to be a historical entity; along with this spirit we presuppose a legal consciousness which evolves sufficiently to conform with the developmental stages of the folk spirit; finally, we deduce from the general content of this legal consciousness in each age, how it must have regarded the idea of a legal subjectivity over and above individual persons.[1] Then, conversely, we adopt the inductive procedure: initially [3] we assume that the people's spirit, legal consciousness and concept of corporation simply did not exist. Facts relating to the relationship between unity and plurality in a collectivity of persons are assembled for one specific time and one specific institution; from this, gradual inferences are made as to the existence and nature of a common philosophy. The concept arrived at in this way is evaluated, finally, as a symptom of a general mental development.

The facts which lend themselves to this kind of inference can be divided into two groups: first, those external products of legal consciousness which come to light in statutes; second, the direct expression of legal ideas. With the latter, however, the difficulty arises of separating individual opinions from generally current ideas. For the earlier period, in which the people created and declared its law for itself, we come across hardly any conflict in the legal convictions which generated the monuments of the law. However, from the time when the nation gained its own organ for the protection and development of law in the form of a body of lawyers, a division emerged between popular legal consciousness and that of the lawyers;[2] and within the latter individual opinions came to predominate. For this period, therefore, we prefer to give a history of the theory of corporation. Yet in so doing we must remember that a people, so long as it wants to be a people, cannot fully rid itself of its legal and moral consciousness; and that in fact the German people has never been entirely without a national legal consciousness, nor without influence on juristic dogma. The more, therefore, that juristic theories separate into different branches and culminate in hair-splitting and over-refinement, the more certain it is that, in order to be able to distinguish individual mistakes from historically accredited trends of thought, we will have to return to the ultimate source of all Right – the legal consciousness of the people. And the more powerful the pulsation of the newly awoken life of national Right, the more urgent it is that we meet the challenge of representing, above all, the broad characteristics of popular legal–moral ideas in all their clarity, and of testing whether they make credible the juristic political theory, which should clarify and refine them but not pervert and remodel them.

The difficulties of this investigation are to be found not only in the imperfection of method, but also in a degree of incongruity between our reasoning and the real world as such. Above all, we must accept the relationship between ideas and reality as being an unsolved riddle.

Whether, in the final analysis, ideas produce forms of life or are simply their product – who would like to say? For us, the relationship presents itself as one of *two-sided causality*† [*gegenseitige Kausalität*]. We see ideas as being conditioned and determined by factual circumstances and, [4] conversely, we regard them as reacting with the circumstances that motivate and shape them. Just as, in historical research, we are bound to end with contradictions and the ensuing constant clashes between freedom and necessity . . . without denying the philosophical postulate of a higher unity in which these contradictions are resolved; so too here we must posit *both* the free intellectual creation of ideas *and* conditions of life dominated by necessity, as independent factors in historical development, each of which equally presupposes the other and retroactively produces it.[3] In our case, therefore, we are obliged to regard the concept of corporation as both producer and product of certain transformations in the external form of the associations. For example, we believe we are only saying the same thing from different points of view, if we contend that the idea of the civic common life led to the concentration of town government in the hands of the council, and, conversely, if we say that the concentration of town government in the hands of the council produced the idea of the civic common life.

But the law of *reciprocal action* [*Wechselwirkung*],[4] which can be recognised here, dominates all historical development. It is for precisely this reason that life as it manifests itself is never completely incorporated in our reasoning. For the logic of our reasoning demands a secure and unshakable relationship between cause and effect in the chain of real connections between each of the simultaneous phenomena. Of these, according to our point of view, one or the other appears to be the causal link; while each is at once both cause and effect, both mover and moved [*Treibendes und Getriebenes*]. Who, for example, would care to measure or weigh to what extent the development of the civic common life is the basis of the upsurge in trade and commerce, and of the emancipation of these from land-ownership; and how far it is the result of these things: to what extent civic freedom furthered the rise in material prosperity in the towns, or how far, conversely, the latter was a determining factor in achieving civic freedom? Any attempt at a logical analysis of its nature is always left with an irreducible residue; or else we refer the question of ultimate causality from the realm of history to that of philosophy.

A similar situation pertains with the law of *transition*, which dominates

---

† Editor's italics.

historical development. Our thought processes, helpless without logic and system, demand the adoption of separate categories, divided by immovable barriers, so that jumping is the only way from one to another. In real life there are no separating partitions between things. The firm system of rational order exists only within us: outside, everything is interdependent in a living state of flux. Outside ourselves, there are no epochal divisions, no areas of the life of the people divided into separate pigeonholes; even states of being and [5] non-existence merge imperceptibly into each other. All the endless variety of single functions are tied into the unity of life by a thousand inextricable threads; contradictions which in our system seem irreconcilable are joined by a bridge.

Concepts of law too, so long as they have evolved and not been made, do not constitute an exception to this universal rule of historical growth. They do not come into being in the same form in which they are finally fixed by system and codification as logical categories, but as historical products. For this reason they are not, in the first instance, merely legal concepts, or juristic abstractions for specific ends; rather, their juristic content is inextricably entwined with the content of ideas which often encompass all other spheres of life. Furthermore, unlike logical categories, they do not exist in a ready-made and immutable form, but are caught up in a ceaseless process of development, of constant transition from one state of being into another. Lastly, in relation to other legal concepts, they are not divided into the fixed categories prepared for them, as in a system; but they come into contact with one another and merge into one another to such an extent that the artificial evaluation of our reasoning intellect is required to distinguish where one concept still predominates and where another has already superseded it.

Finally, knowledge of a mental process which already belongs to the past is also made more difficult by *subjective* factors. For, since we never think with the thoughts of other people but always with our own, as soon as we make the thinking of others the object of our own thoughts, we are always in danger of transferring our own thought processes on to the others. In order to understand an age which thinks differently, it is essential to operate only with its own concepts. As soon as a question of the genesis and the nature of old legal concepts arises, therefore, we must somehow try to put aside our own, more fully formed concepts [6], and measure the old concepts (at most) retrospectively by the standard of the new, revealing the germ of the latter at the centre of the former. Even in this way we will scarcely be able to renew the positive content of a vanished consciousness within ourselves. But we will at least attain an indirect reflection of it.

Incomplete as the solution to the task we have set ourselves must be, the result will, none the less, not be out of proportion to the not inconsiderable effort required for even a partial solution. It cannot easily be doubted that this is the only way to find a key to an understanding of our present-day corporation law, and of the dominant trend in this area; and the only way to gain the correct stand-point from which to judge present and future legislation, and from which to judge widely differing views. If, in spite of this, the investigation of the development of a single legal concept does not seem worth the space devoted to it, let me remind you that each particular moral and legal concept is closely connected with all the other contents of moral and legal consciousness; and that the concept of corporation seems above all suitable to be regarded as the pivot of the most important fundamental ideas. How one conceives the legal essence of a unity made up of a plurality determines the concept of the state itself; and the idea of the state is decisive for the whole conception of Right in its innermost depths. If the interest of the history of our concept is, in the first instance, purely juristic, a detailed study such as this deserves perhaps also to be credited with more general value for intellectual history, by virtue of the ground it has opened up and the relative certainty of its findings. For our knowledge of the mental process which is accomplished in the history of peoples is still not sufficiently advanced for it to be possible for more than single blocks to be brought together for a future building . . .

Chapter I

The concept of fellowship [35]

[865] Ever since the introduction of the concept of corporation into German life, the concept of fellowship in the legal sense has had to be defined differently and more narrowly than before, in two respects. First, the question, up to now left open, of whether it is in itself a specific legal entity, or simply a legal relationship between a number of persons, is being resolved for each fellowship-based group. Only in the first sense may one now talk of a 'fellowship' in the technical sense; in the second case it is at best a comradely common link. The old kind of fellowship can therefore now be divided into the new sort of (corporate) fellowship and purely comradely legal communities (see chapter 36). Secondly, state and commune [*Gemeinde*] are now gradually dissolving their links with the remaining fellowship-based groups. They too, in their corporate form, are basically fellowships, [866] but at the same time they are *more* than fellowships. They manifest themselves, therefore, as particular kinds of corporation and the *remaining* corporations are all that is left for the concept of fellowship in the technical sense.

The concept of fellowship, then, is the generic term for those corporations based on German law which are neither state nor commune. In relation to the concept of corporation it is a specialised concept. First of all, it is the expression for the particular form given to the concept of corporation by German law as opposed to foreign law. Second, however, it is the only German-law concept of corporation *in so far as* there is no prospect of this concept being extended to the level of state or communal life. It should, however, be observed that, because a common life is only a heightened form of fellowship, it too contains the concept of fellowship in a more limited sense. In the civic common life, in particular, the corporate concept of fellowship already exists. It emerges as a positive legal concept with a specific content, simply by means of divesting the

241

concept of town of the features it had accumulated, by virtue of being both a state and a commune in nature...

[886] Subsection v: collective personality [sc. in the fellowship]

The real goal of all corporate organisations is to shape their association into a living *collective personality*. All the progress which has been made in the corporate fellowship, as opposed to the old fellowship, can be traced back to the fact that the unity within the fellowship was recognised as a person and acknowledged in law.

The collective personality of the fellowship in its innermost essence is wholly analogous with that of the town, analysed above [chapter 31]. The common will, shaped (to be sure) out of partial wills and formed into a single entity by the organisation, which is embodied in the fellowship and which inspires and permeates the body, is represented as the ruler of a [887] legal sphere subject to it and to it alone. In this way, the fellowship as such achieves its own legal identity, which exists independently of the separate personality of its members, and remains immutable and unbroken even when members change. The legal identity of the fellowship is a *collective* personality, because it exists within a collectivity of fellows, acts from and within this base, and without it is as incapable of existence as an individual without a body. It is not, however, a collectivity of persons in the old sense, which was at once unity and plurality, a whole and the aggregate of members; rather, it is simply the *unity* within the collectivity, conceived as a person. The collective personality is not merely a fictitious being but a real one [*eine reale Existenz*]; yet, since it emphasises only a specific aspect of the group of fellows (which is not perceptible to the senses as a separate entity) over against the physical manifestation of the group, it is an abstract concept. Because the legal sphere ruled by this single entity is independent, it remains possible for there to be an organic connection between the right of the unity and the separate rights of the plurality. But, within the secure boundaries of the communal sphere, the person of the fellowship as such is the sole and unitary legal subject...

[905] Subsection vi: relation of the collective personality to collective plurality

If the fellowship was a unitary person, it was nevertheless a collective personality dwelling within a plurality. [906] For this reason the *relationship between unity and plurality* in the German fellowship was by no means simply one of opposites: they were also intimately linked. From this result the idiosyncrasies which are usually regarded as characteristic features of the fellowship in German law, as opposed to the *universitas* [corporation] of Roman law.

It is clear that, if one takes the concept of the absolute person of Roman law as the basis, the nature of its substratum is irrelevant to the nature of the juristic person as it is perceived as a person. The German concept of the person, on the other hand, by emphasising that the will is from the outset morally bound in its relationship to other wills, encourages the determination of the collective personality by the collectivity of persons linked within it. From the viewpoint of German law, it is in the nature of the fellowship to be a single entity within a plurality, and consequently, as such a single entity, to lead an independent existence beyond its members; but at the same time to be organically linked to the plurality of independent separate beings existing within it. The personality of the fellowship as such is, therefore, placed above but not outside the collectivity of persons which currently forms its body; it is a unity immanent within the body, and would evaporate into thin air as an insubstantial abstraction as soon as one was prepared to forget its relationship to a plurality of independent persons. It is a unitary being but at the same time a joint one [*gemeines Wesen*]. For this reason the person of the fellowship, like any other person, sees its immediate purpose in itself, or alternatively in the higher organism arching above and around it; but at the same time it is a tool for the separate aims of the individuals who go to make it up. And in the same way the individuals within it, while as separate entities they find their purpose within themselves, are also the means by which a higher joint purpose becomes apparent. Unity and plurality exist for each other, and, by determining each other, both are at the same time means and end. If this is the case, however, then this organic link will also make its mark on the legal relationships existing between them. Because they have separate personalities, all the legal connections which are possible between persons not organically connected, will be found in the same way among these persons. But, because they do not simply exist alongside each other as do individuals who have no links, but rather a closer and more intimate connection exists between the person of the fellowship and the persons joined within it, it is possible for a different legal relationship to exist between them, one which is not found outside the law of fellowship and which is characteristic of it...

Chapter II

Corporation and institution [*Anstalt*] [37]

Subsection iii: The possibility of a combination of corporate and institutional elements in the same group

. . . [975] We have seen the German concept of corporation develop from the old system of fellowships, without the addition of any institutional features, as the pure concept of collective unity was raised to the level of person. From then until the reception of foreign [sc. Roman] law, the perfected concept of corporation had not only achieved complete purity, but held such a dominant position for the entire law relating to groups that it frequently inhibited the development of a concept of institution free from any corporate elements. The last centuries of the Middle Ages were the apogee of the system of fellowship as rejuvenated by the principle of union [*Einung*]. In secular law at this time, there was no fully defined concept of institution to rival the concept of corporation; that which did exist still often [976] relied heavily on corporate principles. In church law, the canonical concept of the institution did assert its decisive importance; but it was never again to be modified and influenced by the Germanic concept of fellowship as much as it was in that period.

The situation was quite different in the period of the sovereign-state idea and of the adoption of foreign law [1525–1806]. The concept of the institution itself, becoming more and more sharply delineated, now took over the lead in shaping human associations. The concept of the corporation was, conversely, increasingly transformed and influenced by the idea of the institution, until finally there was no longer any pure concept of corporation in the sense intended by German law. Certain features of the institution were now regarded as essential to the concept of corporation as such. The model of canon law played a supporting role in this process, in particular the concept of the endowed institution [*Stiftung*], which was

244

insinuating itself as a mediator into secular private law. Most helpful of all, however, was the theory of corporation developed by Roman-law jurisprudence. Thus the civil-law corporation emerged, diverging at many points from our national concept of corporation. It is the history of this theory which will have to be examined in more detail [in the succeeding volume], as an introduction to the description of the law of fellowship current today.

As regards the future, the attempt to establish a theory of current fellowship law which corresponds to modern German moral and legal consciousness and its positive expression in law, will give me the opportunity to prove, first, that today the concepts of institution and corporation exist wholly independently alongside each other, as the twin manifestations of a personality which towers above that of individuals; and secondly, that, while the modern German concept of the institution follows its own principle, in all essential respects the modern concept of the corporate body [*Körperschaft*] is not the Roman concept of corporation [*Korporation*], but the reborn and thereby rejuvenated German-law concept of corporate body.[1]

[End of volume 2]

THE GERMAN LAW OF
FELLOWSHIP

VOLUME 3: THE DOCTRINE OF STATE AND
CORPORATION [*KORPORATION*] IN THE ANCIENT
WORLD AND THE MIDDLE AGES, AND ITS
RECEPTION IN GERMANY

Introduction: the genesis of the academic theory of state and corporation

[1] From the basis established in *The Legal History of the German Fellowship*, we demonstrated in *The History of the German Concept of Corporation* [*Körperschaft*] the developmental process which led our people from its most innate and primordial idea to a system of abstract legal thought of its own making, relating to the legal nature of human associations. We immersed ourselves deeply in the conceptual arena of the ancient German legal consciousness, to which the abstraction of an immaterial unity from its material representatives was still alien; and we subjected to a rigorous analysis the legal concepts, which correspond to the old fellowships and the old lordship groups – concepts which were as brimming with content and life as they were imperfect and fluctuating in form. Then we eavesdropped at the source of the slow, creative intellectual effort by means of which our people pushed their way through to more abstract concepts; and, step by step, we followed the intellectual progress which came about, through tight reciprocal action [*Wechselwirkung*], with the external transformation of the association system. Lastly, we assembled the results of this development and identified the fully developed German concept of corporation, and also its structural type and its contradictions [or 'opposites (*Gegensätze*)'].

The investigation revealed that German law did in fact achieve, from its own resources, a characteristic philosophical form for the legal entity of joint existences [*Gemeinexistenzen*] towering above individual existence. It had distinguished the common from the individual aspects of human existence, and recognised the inner differences in kind between norms directed towards the order of a communal existence and norms directed towards the realisation of individual freedom. Accordingly, alongside the legal subjectivity of individuals isolated within their particularity, it established legal subjectivity for the community [*Gemeinwesen*] that grows

246

out of the organic linking of individuals; it thus elevated the immaterial unities of groups, as distinct from their material representatives, to the [2] status of persons. In accordance with the age-old contradiction between lordship and fellowship, this immaterial group personality took shape in a two-fold concept: first, in the concept of corporation the unity immanent *within the collectivity*[†] was made the substance of a particular legal entity; while, second, in the concept of institution the unity imposed on the group *from the outside*[†] was made that substance. Thus German law made possible the greatest variety of combinations of corporate and institutional principles. It developed the concept of corporation in a wealth of corporate fellowships, political communes and state commonwealths [*politische Gemeinden und staatliche Gemeinwesen*].[1] The concept of institution made its mark on endowed institutions, church institutions and state sovereignty: without any branch of unitary principle, these conformed to the firm but elastic fundamental concept of their particular task. From the basis of new points of view, law embarked on a course to split asunder all the endlessly varied forms of vibrant associative life into separate areas of communal individual life and independent communal life, so as to subject the former to the law pertaining in communities, and to imbue the latter with the principle of common personality.

These legal principles, established in their essentials during the Middle Ages, were an achievement of the German spirit which has never been lost. They have never entirely died out in the consciousness of the people. They will only be extinguished in the future if the German spirit itself is extinguished. Their substance, therefore, forms the foundation on which every theory of current German fellowship law must be based.

Yet the German legal spirit, although it did have ideas about corporations, never achieved any theory of corporations. Everywhere we found ourselves obliged to recognise the legal concepts that ruled life from their manifestations alone. There was a total lack of any explicit formulation of concepts. All progress towards abstraction had led only to the threshold of that higher sphere in which abstraction becomes reflection.

The transition to reflection is always achieved first by scientific learning. The beginnings of a national jurisprudence had emerged in Germany with much promise. But it atrophied before it had flourished sufficiently to incite theoretical considerations on the subtle question of the character of group personality [*Verbandssubjektivität*]. We search in vain in the German law books of the Middle Ages for any independent discussion on

---

[†] Editor's italics.

the legal nature of collectivities. What there is of this in Germany during the Middle Ages is identical to the academic jurisprudence which was beginning to establish itself. Academic jurisprudence, however, is not built on the foundation of national law [3], and its victory in Germany meant the victory of foreign law. The history of corporation theory in Germany is, therefore, part of the history of the reception of foreign law.

The entire further development of our system of groups was determined by the *academic theory of corporations* which had been adopted. It still predominates today in scholarship, legislation and practice. It is therefore essential for us to pursue the evolution of this theory in detail. It will emerge later that an exposition of the history of the *theory of the state* in its juristic core will also be achieved by this means.

The theory of the corporation is in origin Italian, but in the course of its development it spread all over Europe. Its beginnings and growth coincide with the beginnings and growth of modern jurisprudence. Like all things modern it was produced by the spirit of the Middle Ages bringing about the revival of classical civilisation. With classical civilisation having torn apart the closed medieval system of thought, the freed elements of the abolished philosophical system fused with elements of classical thought to form new intellectual structures. Corporation theory grew from contact between medieval and ancient principles. Their confrontation kindled reflection, aroused controversy, and again and again produced attempts to find a higher unity.

The medieval elements of corporation theory originate from the closed world of ideas of a German spirit ruled absolutely by Christianity. Perceptions of state and law were Germano-Christian, until the reawakening of classical civilisation in Italy and France as well as in Germany. But German law did not run everywhere and in all cases. Roman law existed alongside it and pushed its way directly into the new law which had been forming since the mingling of the nations. But, if we disregard the fact that the public-law institutions which are our prime concern remained Germanic, the overall mode of thought which emerged in relation to all currently valid law was Germanic in type. The primordial legal consciousness of the romance peoples was shaped at its core by the youthful common Germanic philosophy of law.

Thus, to begin with, the fundamental popular perceptions as to the nature of human groups in romance countries were identical with those modes of thought which we have ascertained, when we analysed the ancient fellowship and lordship structures, to be the starting-points of German developments. Popular legal consciousness in these lands, as has been demonstrated in the case of Germany, aspired to more abstract concepts – considerably earlier in Italy because it first flourished there – and, by observing [4] ecclesiastical institutions, it worked its way up towards a concept of institution and, in the flourishing municipal life, to a concept of corporation. Hence, whatever academic corporation theory, as it first emerged in Italy, took from the life and philosophies of its own age, it was of Germanic flesh and blood. It was indeed a rich Germanic inheritance which academic jurisprudence received for the development of its doctrine of the group!

But progress from abstraction to reflection, from forming concepts to thinking about them, was not achieved by the scientific observation of living law. Here, as in Germany, purely national legal literature raised itself not far short of a point at which theoretical discussions on the legal nature of groups would have been conceivable. But, even in the works of the Lombard school of law, however highly we may value its significance for the development of scientific jurisprudence, we seek in vain for such problems to be posed and answered.

Rather, this was the point at which the spirit of *antiquity*, newly awakened from the dust handed down by tradition, intervened to kindle the development of thought. At one fell swoop, as soon as the apparently dead treasures of antiquity became the object of scientific research, speculation entered into jurisprudence. And so it is on the traditional classical foundation that medieval theories of state and corporation are raised.

We will see [sc. in volumes 3 and 4] how (in the main) three intellectual forces, closely connected with each other, worked in extending this theory: Roman jurisprudence, canonical jurisprudence and the philosophies of state and law found in the teachings of constitutional lawyers. Correspondingly, classical ideas on the nature of groups flow mainly from three sources in medieval theory: from the *Corpus juris civilis*, from the classical elements contained in the writings of the Church Fathers and the *Corpus juris canonici*, and from the philosophical writings of the ancients. It is however, the *Corpus juris civilis* which, since it aroused the first theoretical debates on the relationship of collectivities to the individual, is the basis of all corporation theory.

NOTES

Editor's introduction

1. *Neue deutsche Biographie*, vol. 6 (Berlin: Duncker und Humblot, 1963), pp. 374–5; J.D. Lewis, *The Genossenschaft-theory of Otto von Gierke*, University of Wisconsin Studies in Social Sciences and History, 25 (Madison, 1935); A. Janssen, *Otto von Gierkes Methode der geistlichen Rechtswissenschaft: Studien zu den Wegen und Formen seines juristischen Denkens*, Göttingen Studien zur Rechtsgeschichte, 8 (Göttingen: Muster-Schmidt 1974), especially ch. 4; H. Spindler, *Von der Genossenschaft zur Betriebsgemeinschaft: kritische Darstellung der Sozialrechtslehre Otto von Gierkes*, Rechtshistorische Reihe, vol. 16 (Frankfurt-am-Main and Bern: Lang, 1981); Erik Wolf, *Grosse Rechtsdenker der deutschen Geistesgeschichte*, 4th edn (Tübingen: Mohr, 1963), ch. 16; R. Emerson, *State and Sovereignty in Modern Germany* (Yale University Press, 1928), ch. 4; F.W. Coker, *Organismic Theories of the State* (Columbia University Press, 1910), pp. 76–81; Otto Gerhard Oexle, 'Otto von Gierkes "Rechtsgeschichte der deutschen Genossenschaft": ein Versuch wissenschaftlicher Rekapitulation', in N. Hammerstein (ed.), *Deutsche Geschichtswissenschaft um 1900* (Stuttgart: Franz Steiner, 1988), pp. 193–217.

2. See F. Calasso, *Medio Evo del Diritto*, vol. 1: *Le Fonti* (Milan: Giuffré, 1954), pp. 127–30; P. Gillet, *La Personnalité juridique en droit ecclésiastique* (Malines: W. Godenne, 1927), pp. 64–7.

3. Perhaps the best summaries of Gierke on group personality are by Maitland in his introduction to his translation of *Das deutsche Genossenschaftsrecht* (= *DGR*), vol. 3, at pp. xxviii–xxxv; and by Barker in his introduction to his translation of *DGR*, vol. 4 at pp. lvii–lxxxvii.

4. Oexle, 'Otto von Gierkes', pp. 197–8, 200; Gerhard Dilcher, 'Genossenschaftstheorie und Sozialrecht: ein "Juristensozialismus" Otto v. Gierkes?' *Quaderni fiorentini per la storia del pensiero giuridico moderno*, 3–4 (1974–5), 319–65; Hans Werner Mundt, 'Sozialpolitische Wertungen als methodischer Ansatz in Gierkes privatrechtlichen Schriften' (Dissertatio juris Frankfurt a.M., 1976); Friedhelm Jobs, 'Otto von Gierke und das moderne Arbeitsrecht' (Dissertatio juris Frankfurt a.M., 1968); Uwe Wesel, *Juristische Weltkunde* (Frankfurt a.M.: Suhrkamp/KNO, 1984), pp. 94–5.

5. Cf. Alexis de Tocqueville, *Democracy in America*, vol. 2, book 2, ch. 5 and book 4, ch. 7; J.S. Mill, *Principles of Political Economy*, ed. J. Robson, *Collected Works of John Stuart Mill*, vols. 2–3 (Toronto University Press, 1977), vol. 3, p. 775, and *On Liberty*, ed. G. Himmelfarb (Harmondsworth: Penguin Books, 1974), ch. 5 at pp. 180–1. Gierke quotes de Tocqueville, *Democracy*, at p. 894, n. 34 (below, ch. XVI, n. 7).

6. Cf. Janssen, *Methode*, pp. 20–31.

7. Ed. Helmut Coing, *Handbuch der Quellen und Literatur der neueren europäischen Privatrechtsgeschichte*, vol. 3, part 1 (Munich: Beck'sche, 1982), pp. 1421ff., 1562ff.; Wolf, *Rechtsdenker*, pp. 692–701.

8. See the section of Gierke's *Johannes Althusius*, trans. E. Barker, in Gierke, *Natural Law* (*DGR* vol. 4), trans. Barker, pp. 224–6. This 'historical' approach may partly explain why *DGR* vol. 1 ends with a detailed analysis of recent legislation on corporate bodies. Compare Hayek's account of the 'common-law' approach: F.A. Hayek, *Law, Legislation and Liberty* (3 vols. in 1, London: Routledge and Kegan Paul, 1982), ch. 4, especially pp. 83–5. Cf. Barker's introd. to his translation of *DGR*, vol. 4 at pp. l–lvi.

9. This of course runs counter to the view, surely no more justifiable historically, that holism tends to serve the ends of tyranny and 'totalitarianism'.

10. Charles Taylor, *Hegel* (Cambridge University Press, 1975), pp. 21–2, 30, 41–2; Wolf, *Rechtsdenker*, pp. 684–9. For Gierke on Fichte, see *DGR*, vol. 4, trans. Barker, index.

11. Ulrich Stutz, 'Zur Erinnerung von Otto von Gierke, Gedächtnisrede', *Zeitschrift der Savigny-Stiftung für Rechtsgeschichte, Germanistische Abteilung*, 43 (1922), vii–lxiii at x and xxxi.

12. *Das Wesen der menschlichen Verbände* (= *Wesen*), trans. Lewis, p. 150; cf. Lewis, Genossenschaft-*theory*, pp. 145–7.

13. Mack Walker, *German Home Towns: Community, State and General Estate 1648–1871* (Cornell University Press, 1971); R.H. Bowen, *German Theories of the Corporative State with Special Reference to the Period 1870–1919* (New York: McGraw-Hill, 1947).

14. Cf. Wolf, *Rechtsdenker*, p. 618.

15. Rudolph Sohm, *Die deutsche Genossenschaft*, in *Festgabe der Leipziger Juristernfakultät für Dr. B. Windscheid* (Leipzig: Academia Lipsiensis juristische Fakultät, 1889); cf. Rudolf Hübner, *A History of Germanic Private Law*, trans. F.S. Philbrick (New York: Kelley, 1968), ch. 3: 'Juristic persons'.

16. H.M. Magid, *English Political Pluralism: the Problem of Freedom and Organisation* (Columbia University Press, 1941); Rodney Barker, *Political Ideas in Modern Britain* (London: Methuen, 1978), ch. 4.

17. Cf. Alan Cawson, *Corporation and Political Theory* (Oxford: Basil Blackwell, 1986).

18. Cf. Antony Black, *State, Community and Human Desire: a Group-centred Account of Political Values* (Hemel Hempstead: Wheatsheaf, 1988).

19. Clifford Geertz, *The Interpretation of Cultures* (London: Hutchinson, 1973); Robert Trivers, *Social Evolution* (Menho Park, Calif.: Benjamin Cummings, 1985).

20. *Wesen*, trans. Lewis, p. 150. For the circumstances of the Ems telegram, of which a version published by Bismarck that day had an electrifying effect on

German opinion and was among the events leading up to the Franco-Prussian war, see Barker's introduction to his translation of *DGR*, vol. 4, p. lxix and n.

21. See Gierke, 'Grundbegriffe', and Lewis, Genossenschaft-*theory*, p. 59; Spindler, *Betriebsgemeinschaft*; Wolf, *Rechtsdenker*, pp. 693–701.

22. Gierke, 'German Constitutional Law'.

23. Gierke, *Deutsches Privatrecht*, vol. 1, p. 623.

24. Stutz, 'Erinnerung', xxx, xlii–xlv.

25. Janssen, *Rechtswissenschaft*, pp. 2ff. Hans Krupa, *Otto von Gierke und die Probleme der Rechtsphilosophie,* Untersuchungen z. deutschen Staats- und Rechtsgeschichte, 150 (Breslau: G. Märtin, 1940) notes that Gierke did not go far towards connecting people and race (pp. 63–4). R. Höhn, *Otto von Gierke's Staatslehre und unserer Zeit* (Hamburg: Hanseatische Verlagsanstalt, 1936) ineptly attacked Gierke for his individualism and attachment to state rather than *Volk*. Cf. Walker, *Home Towns*, pp. 417, 427, 429 for Nazism and *Genossenschaft*; and Barker, introduction to his translation of *DGR* vol. 4 at pp. lxxxiv–lxxxvi.

26. Compare *DGR* vol. 1, p. 328, l.6–7 (below, p. 44) with 'Sie sind alle nur Teil eines gesamten Grösseren', Hitler speech, 1937, in Ute Maas (ed.), '*Als der Geist der Gemeinschaft eine Sprache fand*': Sprache im Nationalsozialismus (Opladen: Westdeutscher Verlag, 1984), pp. 55–90. See especially Oexle, 'Otto von Gierkes', pp. 198–9.

27. Oexle, 'Otto von Gierkes', p. 202.

28. Cf. ed. J.H. Burns, *The Cambridge History of Medieval Political Thought* (Cambridge University Press, 1988), pp. 4–6. For evidence of Gierke's influence, cf. B. Möller, *Imperial Cities and the Reformation*, trans. H. Middelfort and M. Edwards (Philadelphia: Fortress Press, 1972), pp. 73, 112; Walter Ullmann, *Principles of Politics and Government in the Middle Ages* (London: Methuen, 1961), pp. 215ff.

29. In the Acton library, Cambridge University Library (Acton c. 34, 737–9).

30. Cf. Antony Black, *Guilds and Civil Society in European Political Thought from the Twelfth Century to the Present* (London: Methuen, 1984), p. 217.

31. Oexle, 'Otto von Gierkes', pp. 210–13, and 'Ein politischer Historiker: Georg von Below (1858–1927)', in Hammerstein (ed.), *Deutsche Geschichtswissenschaft*, pp. 283–312; Georg von Below, *Der deutsche Staat des Mittelalters: eine Grundlegung der deutschen Verfassungsgeschichte*, 2nd edn. (Leipzig: Quelle und Meyer, 1925).

32. David McLellan, *Marx before Marxism* (Harmondsworth: Penguin Books, 1970), p. 73. For the common heritage, see Taylor, *Hegel*, chs. 1–2; ed. and trans. Hans Reiss, *The Political Thought of the German Romantics* (Oxford: Basil Blackwell, 1955); Walker, *Home Towns*, pp. 257–8, 351. Is Gierke referring anonymously to Marx at p. 146 below?

33. Immanuel Kant, 'Idea for a Universal History with a Cosmopolitan Purpose', ed. Hans Reiss, *Kant's Political Writings* (Cambridge University Press, 1970), pp. 41–53.

34. Georg Beseler, *Volksrecht und Juristenrecht* (Leipzig, 1843); Stutz, 'Erin-

nerung', x–xv. On Beseler, see below, p. 254, n. 4. Note especially Gierke's introductions to *DGR*, vols. 2 and 3.

35. Cf. Michael Mann, *The Sources of Social Power*, vol. 1: *A History of Power from the Beginning to A.D. 1760* (Cambridge University Press, 1986), pp. 28, 126–7, 153–6. 519. Cf. below, pp. 6f., 68, 98, 149.

36. Cf. ed. Burns, *Cambridge History of Medieval Political Thought*, pp. 147–52; Max Weber, 'Der Streit um den Charakter der alt-germanischen Sozialverfassung', *Jahrbuch für National Ökonomie und Statistik*, 83 (1904), 433–70; J.P. Dawson, *A History of Lay Judges* (Harvard University Press, 1960), p. 35. I am grateful to Dr Canning for clarifying this point.

37. Cf. F. Rörig, *The Medieval Town*, trans. D. Bryant (London: Batsford, 1967).

38. R. Feenstra, 'L'Histoire des fondations à propos de quelques études récentes', *Tijdschrift voor Rechtsgeschiedenis*, 24 (1956), 408.

39. P. Gillet, *La Personnalité Juridique*, Brian Tierney, *Foundations of the Conciliar Theory* (Cambridge University Press, 1955); J.P. Canning, *The Political Thought of Baldus* (Cambridge University Press, 1987), p. 190, 'The Corporation in the Political Thought of the Italian Jurists', *History of Political Thought*, 1 (1980), 15ff., and 'The Political Thought of Baldus' (unpublished Ph.D. dissertation, University of Cambridge), pp. 114–16; Black, *Guilds*, pp. 19, 21.

40. Cf. A. Black, 'The Individual and Society', in Burns (ed.), *Cambridge History of Medieval Political Thought*, p. 588; A. Brandt, *Geist und Politik in der lübeckischen Geschichte* (Lübeck: Verlag Max Schmidt-Römhild, 1954), pp. 55–8, 68; Black, *Guilds*, pp. 13, 26–9. For a critique of Gierke on the history of contract, see H. Höpfl and M.P. Thomson, 'The History of Contract as a Motif in Political Thought', *American Historical Review*, 84 (1979), 919–27.

41. Methuen, 1955.

42. Ullmann, *Principles*, pp. 19, 291. Cf. F. Oakley, 'Celestial Hierarchies Revisited: Walter Ullmann's Vision of Medieval Politics', *Past and Present*, 60 (1973), 3–48.

43. *Principles*, pp. 197, 219.

44. For example, J.G.A. Pocock, *The Machiavellian Moment* (Princeton University Press, 1975), pp. 29, 334.

45. Max Weber, 'The Meaning of "Ethical Neutrality" in Sociology and Economics' trans. and ed. Edward Shils and Henry Finch, *Max Weber: The Methodology of the Social Sciences* (New York: The Free Press, 1949), pp. 1–49 at p. 5.

46. Cf. Oexle, 'Otto von Gierkes', pp. 213–17.

Volume 1: *The Legal and Moral History of the German Fellowship*

Introduction

1. Gierke here refers to the division of Germany – from the Middle Ages, and especially from 1648 – into a heterogeneous diversity of small and large states.

2. In Gierke's view, Roman law was the principal means by which throughout Europe associations had been and still were wrongly subjected to state power; he especially blamed the 'Reception' of Roman law in sixteenth-century

Germany, and the continued support for Roman-law ideas in his own day by, among others, Savigny (E. Wolf, *Grosse Rechtsdenker der deutschen Geistesgeschichte*, 4th edn. (Tübingen: Mohr 1963), ch. 12).

3. Rudolf Hübner, *A History of Germanic Private Law*, trans. F.S. Philbrick (New York: Kelley, 1968), pp. 156–9.

4. Hübner *Germanic Private Law*, pp. 156–9; *Neue deutsche Biographie*, vol. 2 (Berlin: Duncker and Humblot, 1953), pp. 174–5; Rudolf Hübner, *Georg Beseler* (Leipzig: Duncker and Humblot, 1901. A copy presented by the author to Lord Acton is in the Cambridge University Library). Beseler's *System des gemeinen deutschen Privatrecht* was published in three volumes, Leipzig-Berlin, 1847–55 (4th edn, 1885).

Chapter II. Up to AD 800, the feudal system, 800–1200 [2, 19]

1. Cf. Marc Bloch, *Feudal Society*, trans. L.A. Manyon (London: Routledge & Kegan Paul, 1961), pp. 408ff.; and below, ch. 3, n. 5.

2. See R. Hübner, *A History of Germanic Private Law*, trans. F.S. Philbrock (New York: Kelly, 1968), p. 116.

3. See Bloch, *Feudal Society*, esp. pp. 190ff.

Chapter III. Free union: gilds and craft gilds [26, 27]

1. Cf. Walter Ullmann, *Principles of Politics and Government in the Middle Ages* (London: Methuen, 1961), pp. 216ff.

2. Gierke's note: 'See especially [Karl F.] Eichhorn, [Deutsche Staats- und] R[echts]G[eschichte, 4th edn, 4 vols. (Göttingen, 1834–36) § 346; W. Wilda, *Das Gildenwesen im Mittelalter* [Halle, 1831]; J.M. Kemble, [*The*] *Saxons* [*in England* (London, 1849)], i, pp. 239–40 . . . [H.C.L. von] Sybel, *Entstehung des* [*deutschen*] *Königthums* [Frankfurt-a.M., 1844], pp. 19–20; . . . [F.C.C.H.] Münter, *Kirchengeschichte* [*von Dänemark und Norwegen*, 3 vols. (Leipzig, 1823–33)], i, pp. 181–2; Winzer, *Die deutschen Brüderschaften des Mittelalters* (Giessen, 1859); Hartwig, 'Untersuchungen über die ersten Anfänge des Gildewesens', *Forschungen zur deutschen Geschichte*, i, pp. 136–63; [L.] Ennen, *Geschichte der Stadt Köln* [Köln und Neuss, 1863] i, pp. 176–7, 404–5, 531–2, 714–15; ii, pp. 457–8. [Due to its contemporary interest, the study of gilds was well advanced: W. Wilda, *Gildenwesen* (repr. Aalen: *Scientia Verlag*, 1964) and the works of L. Ennen are still of value. See also now E. Coornaert, 'Les Ghildes médiévales (Ve–XIVe siècles): définition – évolution', *Revue Historique*, 199 (1947), 208–43; P. Michaud-Quantin, *Universitas: expressions du mouvement communautaire dans le moyen âge latin* (Paris: J. Vrin, 1970), pp. 180ff; O.G. Oexle, 'Die mittelalterliche Zunft als Forschungsproblem': *Blätter für deutsche Landesgeschichte*, 118 (1981), 1–44.]

3. Gierke proceeds to attempt to synthesise current interpretations into a coherently 'Germanic' account.

4. That is, 'peace' in the sense of truce, mutual forbearance and forgiveness (as opposed to vendetta), backed up by an attempt to impose 'law and order': cf. Wilda, *Gildenwesen*, pp. 124–9, 136–7; Coornaert, *Les Ghildes médiévales*, p. 34.

5. In addition to sources quoted by Gierke (*DGR*, vol. 1, p. 225, n.), cf. Wilda, *Gildenwesen*, pp. 39–40; Michaud-Quantin, *Universitas*, pp. 229–30.

6. Cf. Wilda, *Gildenwesen*, pp. 29ff.; G. Le Bras, 'Les Confréries chrétiennes: problèmes et propositions': *Revue Historique du Droit Français et Étranger*, series IV, 19–20 (1940–1), pp. 310–63, especially 316n., 324.

7. Compare the historically hypothetical argument of Robert Nozick: *Anarchy, State and Utopia* (Oxford: Basil Blackwell, 1974), pp. 1off.

8. See *DGR*, vol. 1, p. 236, n. 57; and Wilda, *Gildenwesen*, pp. 39–40; Michaud-Quantin, *Universitas*, pp. 229–30.

9. Gierke's note: [L.] Ennen and [G.] Eckertz, *Quellen [zur Geschichte der Stadt Köln* (Cologne, 1863–79)], i, pp. 148–9; . . .

10. On craft-gild origins, see now G. Mickwitz, *Die Kartellfunktionen der Zünfte und ihre Bedeutung bei der Entstehung des Zunftwesens: ein Studie im spätantike und mittelalterliche Wirtschaftsgeschichte* (Societas scientiarum Fennica: commentationes humanarum litterarum 8/3 (Helsinki, 1936), especially pp. 166–235; S. Thrupp, 'The gilds', in *Cambridge Economic History*, vol. 3 (Cambridge University Press, 1963), pp. 230–80.

11. Gierke's reference: T.J. Lacomblet, *Urkundenbuch für die Geschichte des Niederrheins*, i (Düsseldorf, 1840, repr. Aalen: Scientia Verlag, 1966), p. 251. [In Gierke's text, he or the typesetter made what was (for either of them) an extremely rare mistake in repeating 'linen-weavers' at the end of this sentence instead of 'blanket-weavers'.]

12. This view of Gierke's was criticised by Below, who argued that the *Zunft* was instituted by civic authority: O.G. Oexle, 'Ein politischer Historiker: Georg von Below (1858–1927)', in N. Hammerstein (ed.), *Deutsche Geschichtswissenschaft um 1900* (Steiner, 1988).

Chapter IV. The medieval cities, 1200–1525 [28, 33, 34, 35]

1. See now H. von Werveke, 'The Rise of the Towns', *Cambridge Economic History*, eds. M. Postan and others (Cambridge University Press, 1963), vol. 3, pp. 3–41. Georg von Below strongly criticised Gierke, arguing that cities originated not in free union and the gild movement but in exemptions granted by the feudal territorial powers: Oexle, 'Ein Politische Historiker: Georg von Below (1858–1927)', in M. Hammerstein (ed.), *Deutsches Geschichtswissenschaft um 1900* (Stuttgart: Franz Steiner, 1988), p. 295.

2. Cf. now Planitz, *Die deutsche Stadt im Mittelalter* (Cologne–Graz: Böhlau Verlag, 1954); F. Rörig, *The Medieval Town; La Ville*, Recueils de la société Jean Bodin, 6 (Brussels: Editions de la Libraire encyclopédique, 1954).

3. Cf. H. Planitz, *Die deutsche Stadt im Mittelalter*, especially pp. 116–19; and for parallel developments in Italy (largely ignored by Gierke), D. Waley, *The Italian City-Republics* (London: Weidenfeld and Nicolson, 1969), pp. 32, 39, 61–2.

4. Cf. Planitz, *Die deutsche Stadt*, pp. 297–9, 310–12; Waley, *Italian City-Republics*, pp. 62–5.

5. Cf. Mack Walker, *German Home Towns: Community, State and General Estate 1648–1871* (Cornell University Press, 1971), pp. 311, 347ff., 393ff.

6. *Schutzgenossen* ('denizens'), i.e. those with legal but not political rights – a distinction which Gierke understates by also calling them 'citizens'.
7. Cf. J. Heers, *Family Clans in the Middle Ages: a Study of Political and Social Structures in Urban Areas*, trans. B. Herbert (Amsterdam: North-Holland Publishing Company, 1977).
8. See Gierke, *DGR*, vol. 1, p. 323, n. 45.
9. Below, pp. 58–61.

Chapter V. The golden age of the craft gilds [38]

1. Cf. P. Michaud-Quantin, *Universitas, expressions du mouvement communautaire dans le moyen âge latin* (Paris: J. Vrin, 1970), pp. 149, 165; H. Planitz, *Die deutsche Stadt im Mittelalter* (Cologne–Graz: Böhlau Verlag, 1954), pp. 294–5.
2. For later revisions of this somewhat rosy view of craft gilds, see J. Heers, *L'Occident aux XIVe et XVe siècles: aspects économiques et sociaux*, Nouvelle Clio 23 (Paris: Presses Universitaires de France, 1973), pp. 225–6; and also, in general, Antony Black, *Guilds and Civil Society in European Political Thought from the Twelfth Century to the Present* (Methuen, 1984), pp. 6–11.
3. See below, pp. 221–5, where Gierke argues that producers' co-operatives in his own day could, if the same individuals both worked and owned the capital, realise personality.
4. See below, pp. 211–13 and ch. 19.
5. Gierke consistently emphasises the *genossenschaftlich* or 'democratic' aspects of gilds.
6. Cf. John Harvey, *The Gothic World 1100–1600* (London: Batsford, 1950), pp. 19–24; E. Coornaert, *Les Compagnonnages en France du Moyen Age à nos jours* (Paris, 1966).

Chapter VI. Political unions, city leagues, the Hansa [44, 45]

1. A clear example of Gierke's attempt to show the existence of a German practice of real group personality as a historical reality.

Chapter VII. The Empire as union [48]

1. That is, presumably, princes too were involved in federal movements among themselves, the logic of which could have been closer union within the Empire.
2. Cf. F. Hartung, 'Imperial Reform, 1435–1495', and K.S. Bader, 'Approaches to Imperial Reform at the End of the Fifteenth Century', in G. Strauss (ed.), *Pre-Reformation Germany* (London: Macmillan, 1972), pp. 73–135 and 136–62.

Chapter VIII. Rural communes and federations: Switzerland and North Germany [49, 50]

1. Apart from the case of the *Confederatio Helvetica*, it is difficult to see what basis there is for this statement.

2. Cf. William Martin, *Switzerland from Roman Times to the Present*, trans. J. Innes (London: Elek, 1971), pp. 19–45.

Chapter IX. The estates, representation and the territorial state [51]

1. Approx. 'freehold': see Marc Bloch, *Feudal Society*, trans. L.A. Manyon (London: Routledge and Kegan Paul, 1961), pp. 171–2, 268.
2. Cf. Bloch, *Feudal Society*, pp. 268, 372.
3. Gierke proceeds here to consider parliamentary estates as a manifestation of the 'union-movement'. Cf. Antonio Marongiu, *Medieval Parliaments: a Comparative Study*, trans. S.J. Woolf, (Studies presented to the International Commission for the History of Representative Parliamentary Institutions, 32) (London: Eyre and Spottiswoode, 1968).
4. Cf. above, pp. 36ff.

Chapter X. The peasantry and rural fellowships [52, 53]

1. Cf. K.S. Bader, *Studien zur Rechtsgeschichte des mittelalterlichen Dorfes*, part 2: *Dorfgenossenschaft und Dorfgemeinde* (Cologne–Graz: Böhlau Verlag, 1962); P. Blickle, 'Les Communautés villageoises en Europe occidentale du moyen âge aux temps modernes': *Flaran*, 4 (1982), 129–42; J. Heers, *L'Occident aux XIVe et XVe siècles: aspects économiques et sociaux*, Nouvelle Clio 23 (Paris: Presses Universitaires de France, 1973), pp. 322ff.
2. *Twelve Articles of the Peasants' Revolt*, trans. B.J. Kidd (Oxford University Press, 1911, repr. 1967), pp. 174–9.

Chapter XI. Corporations and the sovereign state, 1525–1806; the modern association movement, 1806 onwards: introduction [54]

1. On craft gilds and towns, see Mack Walker, *German Home Towns: Community, State and General Estate 1648–1871* (Cornell University Press, 1971); on gilds and 'the handicraft system', see T.S. Hamerow, *Restoration, Revolution, Reaction: Economics and Politics in Germany 1815–1871* (Princeton University Press, 1958), pp. 21–37, 150–5.
2. This passage is clearly influenced, however indirectly, by J.J. Rousseau, *Du Contrat Social*, I. 6 (London: Dent, 1973); and in turn influenced Ullmann, who was fond of drawing a categorical distinction between 'subject' and 'citizen' (e.g. *Principles of Politics and Government in the Middle Ages* (London: Methuen, 1961), pp. 49, 234.
3. 'What was then called "police" covered every kind of regulation considered necessary for the health, prosperity and moral welfare of the subject . . . [including] any control of industry and trade that was attempted' (W.E. Bruford, *Germany in the Eighteenth Century*, 2nd edn (Cambridge University Press, 1965), p. 17). 'The first *Polizeistaat* [under Frederick William of Prussia, 1620–1688] was, therefore, dedicated to . . . the protection of the population, the welfare of the state and its citizens, and the improvement of society . . . [it built up] an administrative system to provide the infrastructure of a strong,

centralized and hierarchically organized state. Its role was to establish what we would now call a mobilization system, and it developed strict rules for the proper management of the economy, for the internal security and provisioning of the population': B. Chapman, *The Police State* (London: Pall Mall Press, 1970), pp. 16–19, at pp. 16–17. Cf. M. Raeff, *The Well-Ordered Police State: Social and Institutional Change through the Law in the Germanies and Russia, 1600–1800* (Yale University Press, 1983); ed. M. Fleischmann, *Wörterbuch des deutschen Staats- und Verwaltungsrechts*, 3 vols. (Tübingen: J.B.C. Mohr, 1911–14), vol. 3, pp. 96ff.; Walker, *Home Towns*, p. 173.

4. Cf. Bertrand de Jouvenel, *Sovereignty* (Cambridge University Press, 1957), pp. 173ff., 192ff.; and F.A. Hayek, *Law, Legislation and Liberty* (London: Routledge & Kegan Paul, 1982), vol. 1, ch. 3.

5. With Gierke's interpretation of princely absolutism and benevolent despotism one should compare Michael Oakeshott, *On Human Conduct* (Oxford University Press, 1975), ch. 3, esp. pp. 267–78: Oakeshott characterises as *universitas* what Gierke here calls *Anstalt*, and as *societas* what Gierke later calls *Verfassungsstaat* or *Rechtsstaat*.

6. Cf. *DGR*, vol. 3, trans. F.W. Maitland as *Political Theories of the Middle Age* (Cambridge University Press, 1900), p. 100.

7. A similar view is expressed by Alexis de Tocqueville, *Democracy in America*, vol. 1, author's introduction; and *The Ancien Régime and the French Revolution*, part 2, ch. 8.

8. Cf. G. Strauss, *Law, Resistance and the State: the Opposition to Roman Law in Reformation Germany* (Princeton University Press, 1986).

9. For a thorough analysis of this question, see P.W. Duff, *Personality in Roman Private Law* (Cambridge University Press, 1938).

10. As opposed, that is, to the 'Germanic' idea of the corporate body with a 'real' personality which law and state have to acknowledge.

11. Cf. Walker, *Home Towns*, ch. 5, esp. pp. 161ff.

12. Cf. de Tocqueville, *Democracy*, vol. ii, book 2, ch. 5.

Chapter XII. Rural communities, 1525–1806 [55]

1. For a different recent interpretation, see Peter Blickle, *Deutsche Untertanen: ein Widerspruch* (Munich: Beck, C.H., 1981), pp. 23, 113–14: *Gemeindereformation* (Munich: Oldenbourg R/VM 1985), pp. 165ff.: 'Kommunalismus, Parliamentarismus, Republikanismus', *Historische Zeitschrift*, 242 (1986), 529–56 at 530ff.

Chapter XIII. Towns and cities from 1525 to the present [56, 57]

1. For a different view see Mack Walker, *German Home Towns: Community, State and General Estate 1648–1871* (Cornell University Press, 1971).

2. See Walker, *Home Towns*, p. 101.

3. Gierke here discusses aspects of the local-community/state relationship that were of particular importance in Germany at the time: Walker, *Home Towns*, pp. 311, 347ff., 393ff.

4. From Gierke's text: 'In this case it must be strictly borne in mind that this does not represent a transfer of part of the state's supervision but a division between the state's natural right to exercise supervision in the *Land* [*Landespolizei*] and the local community's natural right to exercise supervision in the locality [*Ortspolizei*]'.

5. It is not clear to whom Gierke refers here; it is possible that he was referring to Marxism.

Chapter XIV. Parliamentary representation and the development of the modern state [60, 61]

1. Cf. F.L. Carsten, *Princes and Parliaments in Germany from the Fifteenth to the Eighteenth Centuries* (Oxford University Press, 1959).

2. Gierke's note: [J.J.] Moser, [*Neues teutsches Staats-Recht*, vol. 13: *Von der teutschen Reichs-Ständen Landen* (Frankfurt-a.M., 1769)], p. 1012 . . .

3. 'Funeral pomp.' Gierke's note: Moser [as in n. 2], pp. 840, 1178.

4. Mack Walker, *Johann Jakob Moser and the Holy Roman Empire of the German Nation* (University of North Carolina Press, 1981).

5. On Pütter, see Mack Walker, *German Home Towns: Community, State and General Estate 1648–1871* (Cornell University Press, 1971), pp. 17–18; on Friedrich Karl Moser see Walker, *Johann Jakob Moser*, pp. 266–8; on Justus Möser, author of the famous *Patriotische Phantasien*, see Walker, *Home Towns*, pp. 174–84, and Jonathan B. Knudsen, *Justus Möser and the German Enlightenment* (Cambridge University Press, 1986); on David Georg Strube (1694–1776), see *Allgemeine deutsche Biographie*, ed. Historische Commission bei der königlichen Akademie der Wissenschaften, vol, 33 (Leipzig, 1893), pp. 635–9; on Karl Friedrich Häberlin (1756–?) see *Allgemeine deutsche Biographie*, vol. 10 (Leipzig, 1879), pp. 278–9.

6. Gierke here unconsciously echoes the view of Edmund Burke, expressed in his *Speech to the Electors of Bristol* (3 November 1774).

7. An evocation of St Paul, 1 Cor. 15: 10.

8. Cf. Pierre d'Ailly and Jean Gerson, in 1416–17, on the different ways 'fullness of power' is ascribable to pope, council and church: Antony Black, *Council and Commune* (London: Burns and Oates, 1979), p. 23.

9. Otto Bähr, *Der Rechtsstaat: eine publicistische Skizze* (Cassel and Göttingen, 1864); translated into Italian in 1891.

Chapter XV. The Empire, 1525–1806 [62]

1. Established in 1834, this created '"general, free, unrestricted commerce" among most of the German lands': T.S. Hamerow, *Restoration, Revolution, Reaction: Economics and Politics in Germany 1815–1871* (Princeton University Press, 1958), pp. 10–16 at p. 11.

Chapter XVI. Fellowships under benevolent despotism, 1525–1806; modern free associations, 1806 onwards [64, 65]

1. Cf. above, p. 60.

2. For a recent study following, unconsciously, Gierkean lines, see Thomas Nipperdey, *Verein als soziale Struktur in Deutschland im späten 18. und frühen 19. Jahrhundert* (Vandenhoek and Ruprecht, 1972), reprinted in *Gesellschaft, Kultur, Theorie*, Kritische Studien zur Geschichtswissenschaft, 18, pp. 174–205.
3. Cf. Hegel, *The Philosophy of Right*, trans. T.M. Knox (Oxford University Press, 1942), pp. 192, 200–2, 290; and Alexis de Tocqueville, *Democracy*, vol. 2, ch. 5.
4. I.e. Roman-law.
5. Gierke's note: Code pénal art. 291–294 . . .
6. Cf. Helmut Coing (ed.), *Handbuch der Quellen und Literatur der neueren europäischen Privatrechtsgeschichte*, vol. 3, part 1 (Munich: Beck'sche, 1982), pp. 1757–60.
7. Gierke's note refers to passages from a German translation of Thomas Erskine May, *The Constitutional History of England . . . 1760–1860*, 2 vols. (London, 1861), for example on 'societies sympathetic to the French Revolution such as democratic associations, the revolution society . . . the society of the friends of the people . . .', and on 'groups supporting Catholic emancipation and the opposing fanatical Orange-lodges . . . Of the strength of the political association, de Tocqueville says (*Démocratie en Amérique*, 277): "l'association possède plus de puissance que la presse".'
8. Gierke's note: On the founding, activity and organisation of such an association in Berlin, see the paper by J. Hirsch b. Eras: *Jahrbuch für Volkswirthschaft*, 1 (Leipzig, 1868), pp. 69–79.
9. See Gierke, *DGR*, vol. 1, p. 901, n. 48.
10. Cf. Mack Walker, *German Home Towns. Community, State and General Estate 1648–1871* (Cornell University Press, 1971), pp. 336ff.; and Gierke, *DGR*, vol. 1, p. 902, n. 50.

Chapter XVII. Free fellowships for economic purposes from 1525 to the present
[66, 67, 68]

1. *Genossenschaft* (see glossary) has as one principal modern meaning 'economic company' or 'co-operative', providing Gierke with a connection between the subject of the remaining chapters and fellowship in other senses.
2. From Gierke's text: In Brunswick these even have to be approved and inspected by the supervisory authorities of the *Land*.
3. For a different view see Mack Walker, *German Home Towns: Community, State and General Estate 1648–1871* (Cornell University Press, 1971) esp. ch. 3.
4. Walker, *Home Towns*, pp. 248ff.; T.S. Hamerow, *Restoration, Revolution, Reaction: Economics and Politics in Germany 1815–1871* (Princeton University Press, 1958) pp. 21ff.

Chapter XVIII. Economic fellowships based on property: the joint-stock company
[Aktienverein] and domination by capital [69, 70]

1. On joint-stock companies in nineteenth-century Germany, see *Cambridge*

Economic History vol 7, eds P. Mathias and M. Postan (Cambridge University Press, 1978), pp. 538–41, 567–8 and 724 nn. 163–4; W. Sombart, *Der moderne Kapitalismus*, 3 vols. (Munich and Leipzig: Duncker und Humblot, 1916–27), vol. 3, pp. 735–9. Cf. Maitland's introduction to his translation of *DGR*, vol. 3, at p. xxi.

2. From Gierke's text: This can be seen partly in the provision for penalties in company articles, partly in the disposition of the courts of arbitration.
3. 'Law', 'Right', 'sphere of justice' here are all attempts to render *Recht* (see glossary).
4. Gierke's note: Schäffle in *Staatswörterbuch* (iv), pp. 252, 256. [On Albert Schäffle (1831–1903), a leading corporatist thinker, see R.H. Bowen, *German Theories of the Corporative State* (1947), pp. 124–37.]
5. On German economic associations, cf. W. Wagner, 'Gesellschaftsrecht', in Coing (ed.), *Handbuch der Quellen und Literatur der neueren europäischen Privatrechtsgeschichte*, vol. 3, part 3, (Munich: Beck'sche, 1986), pp. 2969–3041; this includes a section on *Genossenschaften* (pp. 3025–8).
6. Cf. Theodor Cassau, *The Consumers' Cooperative Movement in Germany*, trans. J.F. Mills (London: T. Fisher Unwin, and Manchester: The Cooperative Union, 1925).
7. Cf. F. Baader, *Über das dermalige Missverhältniss der Vermögenlosen oder Proletairs zu den Vermögen besitzenden Classen der Societät* (Munich: Georg Franz, 1835; repr. in his *Sämmtliche Werke*, vol. 6 (Leipzig, 1854)); on Baader, cf. R.H. Bowen, *German Theories of the Corporative State with Special Reference to the Period 1870–1919* (New York: McGraw-Hill, 1947), pp. 46–57.
8. Cf. Karl Marx, *The Communist Manifesto* (1848), cited in T.B. Bottomore and M. Rubel (eds.), *Karl Marx, Selected Writings in Sociology and Social Philosophy* (Harmondsworth: Penguin Books, 1963), pp. 195–6.

*Chapter XIX. Economic fellowships based on personality: the producers' co-operative [*Produktivgenossenschaft*] [70 cont.]*

1. Gierks's note: see especially F.H. Schulze-Delitsch, *Associationsbuch für deutsche Handwerker und Arbeiter* (Leipzig, 1853), *Die arbeitenden Klassen und das Associationswesen in Deutschland* (Leipzig, 2nd edn, 1863), *Vorschutz- und Kreditvereine als Volksbanken* (Leipzig, 4th edn, 1867) . . . [On Schultze-Delitsch and the co-operative movement in Germany from 1846 onwards, see J.H. Clapham, *The Economic Development of France and Germany*, 4th edn. (Cambridge University Press, 1948), pp. 326–7; H. Grebing, *The History of the German Labour Movement*, trans. E. Körner (London: Wolff, 1969), pp. 42–3.]
2. The contrast intended appears to be between 'association' through fellowships and the 'mere' collectivisation of society as a whole.
3. Gierke's note: See especially Ferdinand J.G. Lassalle, *Herr Bastiat Schulze von Delitsch: der ökonomische Julian oder Kapital und Arbeit*. [This was reprinted in Berlin in 1893.]
4. Gierke's note: See V.A. Huber, *Staatswörterbuch*, 'Association', p. 466; Engel, 'Die Sparkassen in Preussen als Glieder in der Kette der auf Selbsthilfe aufgebauten Anstalten': *Zeitschrift der königl. preuss. statist. Büreau's* (1861),

pp. 117–18 . . .; [J.M.] Ludlow and [L.] Jones, [*Progress of the Working Class, 1832–1867* (London 1867)], pp. 138–89.

5. *DGR* vol. 1, p. 1043, n. 4 gives Gierke's sources for the co-operative movement in Britain ('England'): 'Since 1860 there has appeared in Manchester a monthly called "The Cooperator", which serves as an organ of the [co-operative] movement. See for English works, Henry Fawcett, *The Economic Position of the British Labourer* (London, 1865) [Gierke gives the title inaccurately as *The condition of the english* (*sic*) *labourer*]; Ludlow and Jones, *Die arbeitenden Klassen Englands*, trans. J. v. Holtzendorff (Berlin, 1868).'

6. In addition to the material cited in Gierke's n. 11, cf. Clapham, *Economic Development*, pp. 221ff.

7. Cf. de Tocqueville, *Democracy*, vol. 2, book 2, ch. 5.

8. Gierke's note: See on the English productive associations ('co-operative companies'), of which most modelled themselves on the Rochdale pioneers (the cotton mill and weaving mill founded in 1855), and are set up in individual plants, Huber, *Reisebriefe* [*aus Belgien, Frankreich und England* (Hamburg, 1855)] . . . , Konkordia, vols. 7 and 8 . . . On the French productive associations, which have been successful in small industrial plants of the same kind (tailors, piano-makers, tinsmiths . . . joiners . . .) see Huber, [*Reisebriefe*] . . .

9. Gierke's note: Unanimity is required by standard regulation (*Normalstatut*), section 45. See statute 4 of the Berlin bakery *Genossenschaft* . . .

10. Gierke's note: The Rochdale mill at first divided things up in this way, here following other societies . . . The Manufacturing Society at Manchester, however . . . divides the profit half and half between capital and labour . . .

11. Gierke's note: See the statute of the Berlin bakery *Genossenschaft*, sections 13–27. The German *Normalstatut*, because it is dealing with small co-operatives, lays down, between the management board (sections 5–30) and the general meeting (sections 33–44) only an auditor (sections 31–32) . . .

12. Gierke's note: See the paper of Engel, 'Der Arbeitsvertrag und die Arbeitsgesellschaft': *Arbeiterfreund* (1867), pp. 129–53.

13. Gierke's note: 'An act for the incorporation, regulation and winding up of trading companies and other associations' of 7 August 1862.

14. See H. Coing (ed.), *Handbuch der Quellen und Literatur der neueren europäischen Privatrechtsgeschichte*, vol. 3, part 3 (Munich: Beck'sche, 1986), p. 3036.

15. The only reference given by Gierke is: '. . . the Prussian ministerial instructions of 2 May, 10 August, 25 September and 26 October 1867 are collected by (Ludolf) Parisius, pp. 147–68' (*DGR*, vol. 1, p. 1106, n. 206).

Volume 2 *The History of the German Concept of Corporation* [Körperschaft]

Preface

1. In the event, volume 3 and the unfinished volume 4 were devoted mainly to non-German theories of state and corporation. Gierke seems never to have fulfilled his promise of a full-scale treatment of 'the current law of fellowship'; he deals with it partially in several works, notably those of 1874, 1887, 1889 and 1902.

Introduction

1. Sc. the idea of a moral and legal group person (see above, pp. xvi–xix).
2. Cf. Georg Beseler, *Volksrecht und Juristenrecht* (Leipzig, 1843).
3. Friedrich Engels referred to 'eine Wechselwirkung aller dieser Momente' (sc. of the superstructure), while maintaining that 'in the last instance' production etc. determine history; again, ideological factors, while ultimately produced by the economy, may in turn 'in sehr bedeutender Weise wirken . . . zurück auf die Ökonomie' (letters of 21–22 September and of 27 October 1890 respectively – I am grateful to Terrell Carver for the former reference: Karl Marx, Friedrich Engels, *Werke*, vol. 37 (Berlin: Dietz Verlag, 1967), pp. 463–492).
4. See preceding note.

Chapter II

1. See above, volume 2, Preface, n. 1.

Volume 3: *The Doctrine of State and Corporation [Korporation] in the Ancient World and the Middle Ages, and its Reception in Germany*

1. I.e. local communities which retained a degree of self-government, and states which had something of a communal or consensual character.

INDEX

265

UNIVERSITY OF LANCASTER

LIBRARY

Due for retu...
end of service on date below (or
earlier if recalled)

17. JAN. 1992	-9. JUN. 1994
	22. JUN. 1999
20. JAN. 1993	27. JAN. 1999
1. 5. JUN. 1995	
13. MAY. 1996	19 MAR 2003
12. JUL. 1996	CANCELLED
20. JUN. 1996	0'3 OCT 2006